D0344405

Advance Praise for
KOREA: WHERE THE AMERICAN CENTURY BEGAN

'Started to read and just could not stop. This richly informed study amply establishes that American global militarism has its origin in the Korean conflict. The incisive review of the historical record reveals how judicious statesmanship and even a dose of good common sense could have spared the people of Korea the horrors they have endured since the end of World War II and the constant threat of even worse. The lessons are all too pertinent in today's toxic political climate, with Korea once again a centerpiece and victim.'

Noam Chomsky

'This is a very important book, an eye-opening one, and a wise one. I read it in one go – fascinated, educated, appalled, amazed and gripped. I came away from reading the book in equal parts full of admiration for the book itself, and appalled by the story it tells. It lifts the lid on so many things.'

A. C. Grayling

'North Korea is an impossible country to understand, unless you start by reading a book like this. It movingly describes the inhumanity of US military policy – three years of carpet bombing, the use of napalm, calls for nuclear evisceration and biological warfare. No book could be more timely or with warnings more necessary to heed, if history is not to be repeated.'

Geoffrey Robertson QC, author of *Crimes Against Humanity*

'Michael Pembroke's *Korea* is a brilliant book, meticulously researched, comprehensive and extremely timely. It opens a new dimension of America's continuing war against anything different and esoteric and explains why, after seven decades...the Korean drama remains unsolved.'

Dr Leonid Petrov, Australian National University

'Compulsory material for anyone who wonders how the situation on the Korean peninsula deteriorated to the point it has today.'

Richard Broinowski, former Australian Ambassador to South Korea

Also by Michael Pembroke

Trees of History & Romance
Arthur Phillip: Sailor, Mercenary, Governor, Spy

KOREA:
WHERE THE AMERICAN CENTURY BEGAN

MICHAEL PEMBROKE

ONEWORLD

A Oneworld Book

First published in the United States and Canada
by Oneworld Publications, 2018

Copyright © Michael Pembroke 2018

The moral right of Michael Pembroke to be identified as the Author
of this work has been asserted by him in accordance with the
Copyright, Designs, and Patents Act 1988

All rights reserved
Copyright under Berne Convention
Library of Congress CIP data is available

ISBN 978-1-78607-473-7
eISBN 978-1-78607-474-4

Printed and bound in Great Britain by Clays Ltd, Elcograf S.p.A.

Oneworld Publications
10 Bloomsbury Street
London WC1B 3SR
England

Stay up to date with the latest books,
special offers, and exclusive content from
Oneworld with our newsletter

Sign up on our website
oneworld-publications.com

MIX
Paper from
responsible sources
FSC
www.fsc.org   FSC® C018072

For my father (1928–),
who was there.

*'I am opposed to having the eagle put
its talons on any other land.'*

Mark Twain, *New York Herald*, 15 October 1900

*'In Korea, Americans revealed all the arrogance,
the paternalism, the insensitivity in handling
of local people—and the local army—which
later revealed themselves in Vietnam.'*

Sir Max Hastings, *The Korean War*, 1987

*'In Korea, China convinced the whole world
that she was a force to be reckoned with, after
centuries in which she had been dismissed as an
ineffectual society of mandarins and warlords.'*

Sir Max Hastings, *The Korean War*, 1987

*'That men do not learn very much from the lessons of
history is the most important of all the lessons of history.'*

Aldous Huxley, *Collected Essays*, 1958

On War

Of all the enemies of liberty, war is, perhaps, the most to be dreaded, because it comprises and develops the germ of every other. War is the parent of armies; from these proceed debts and taxes; and armies, and debts, and taxes are the known instruments for bringing the many under the domination of the few. In war too, the discretionary power of the Executive is extended; its influence in dealing out offices, honours and emoluments is multiplied; and all the means of seducing the minds, are added to those of subduing the force, of the people. The same malignant aspect in republicanism may be traced in the inequality of fortunes, and the opportunities of fraud, growing out of the state of war, and in the degeneracy of manner and of morals, engendered in both. No nation can preserve its freedom in the midst of continual warfare...War is in fact the true nurse of executive aggrandizement... The strongest passions and most dangerous weaknesses of the human breast; ambition, avarice, vanity, the honourable or venal love of fame, are all in conspiracy against the desire and duty of peace.

James Madison
'Political Observations', 20 April 1795

Contents

Preface

Korea's shadow loomed over my boyhood. It was apparent to me that my father's experience was deep in his psyche and that it was impossible to conceal. I guessed that the irredeemable had happened; that violent and unmentionable things had occurred; things that were too painful to recall, or inappropriate to recount. I rarely asked and we spoke only cautiously. In a vague way, through that unfathomable process of intuition that a sensitive child possesses, I absorbed my father's experiences so that their darkest elements became a small part of my own subconscious. I knew they had been grim and frightening. I knew there had been fear and confrontation, desperation and death. Gradually I learned that the outcome of war is rarely good; that its most aggressive proponents are usually those who have never fought with butt and bayonet; who have never heard the moaning of the wounded or the anguished cries of innocent civilians; who have never been required to kill and maim in the name of their country.

I have waited a long time to tell this story. But there is more to it than my own insights, informed by one man's experience in a corner of a foreign field where blood was spilled in a desperate military conflict. It is a wider account, a cautionary tale, an explanation of the modern era. It is a story of politics and militarism, hubris and overreach.

Princeton, New Jersey
November 2017

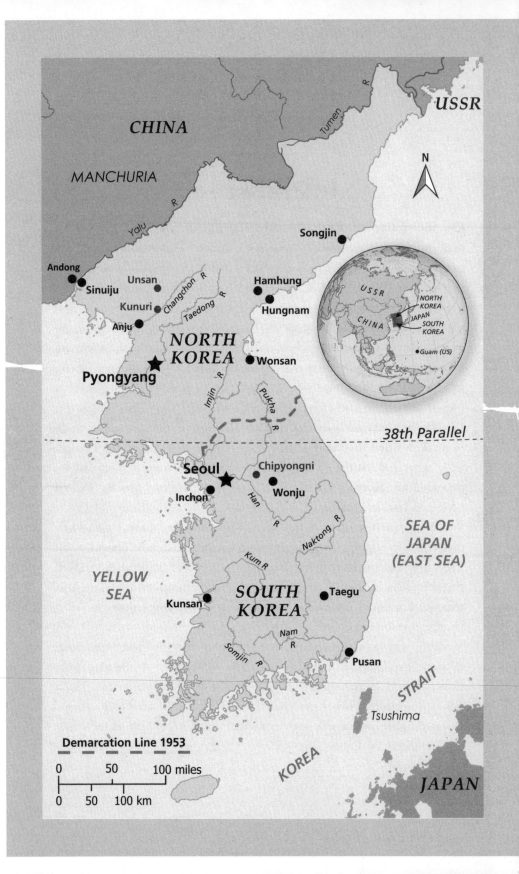

Introduction

For millennia the Korean peninsula was a place of continuous civilisation like no other; a world defined by virtue, nature and superstition; a society built on hierarchical respect; and a culture that was neither Chinese nor Japanese. By the seventh century it had been mostly unified. By the tenth century the kingdom of Koryŏ had more or less established the boundaries that continued into the modern era. In subsequent centuries the peninsula endured its share of invasion and conquest from the Mongols, the Japanese and the Manchus. But for most of the population, most of the time, the prevalent condition was one of prolonged and extensive stability, if not necessarily prosperity.

In the nineteenth century the historic rhythm of Korean life began to weaken when the missionaries, traders and gunboats of the Western powers arrived. At the end of the century, a rampant Japan returned—assassinating Korea's Queen Min and subjecting the peninsula to a savage period of colonial rule until 1945. In the final days of World War II, it was the turn of the Americans, who proposed an arbitrary division to suit their own perceived strategic interests. The partition was an invitation to conflict and made a war for the reunification of the peninsula inevitable, creating a source of discord and international tension that continues today. When war arrived, fewer than five years later, it became the first of America's failed modern wars—its first modern war against China—opening the door to ever-increasing military expenditure, marking the true beginning of the American Century, and launching the long era of expanding American global force projection. This is the story of how that war came to pass; how it was fought; how it was needlessly extended; how so much of it was characterised by hubris and overreach; and why its lessons have not been learned.

The war finished more or less where it began—along the 38th parallel. It started as a United Nations 'police action' to repel the North Korean invasion and restore peace at the border. After three months, Kim Il-sung's ambitious attempt to reunify the peninsula with Soviet tanks had been defeated, the mandate of the United Nations Security Council achieved, and the North Korean forces pushed back to the 38th parallel. But as has happened so often since, Washington's ideological and military enthusiasm ensured a wider and more substantial conflagration—continuing the war for nearly three more years. Civilian deaths are estimated to have been over three million, but we will never know. And the daily death rate for American servicemen over three years (1950–53) was more than four times the daily rate suffered in Vietnam over fourteen years (1961–75).

After repelling the invasion, the American-led crusade to cross the 38th parallel, to invade North Korea, to impose regime change and to threaten the Chinese border on the Yalu River, was an unmitigated disaster. The following words are as apt for Korea, as they were for Vietnam, and for so many subsequent American interventions: 'In attempting to snuff out a small war they produced instead a massive conflagration. Determined to demonstrate the efficacy of force employed on a limited scale, they created a fiasco over which they were incapable of exercising any control whatsoever.'

China reacted by entering the conflict in force—with great bravery and using exceptional infantry tactics. The resulting retreat by the Eighth Army was not merely the longest in American military history, it was 'the most disgraceful', 'the most infamous' and 'one of the worst military disasters in history'. In reality it was a rout and President Harry S. Truman declared a state of emergency. Legitimate questions about the wisdom, morality and legality of taking offensive action north of the 38th parallel were lost under a wave of moral righteousness and misplaced confidence. Doubters were sidelined, sceptics labelled as appeasers and allies were either 'with us or against us'. Washington wrapped itself in an armour of certitude.

In a pattern that has been repeated, the quest for UN authority to cross the 38th parallel was mired in unconvincing rationalisation, transparent ambiguity and diplomatic and legal machinations reminiscent of the wrangling over the invasion of Iraq in 2003. The British government agonised. Canada was troubled. India opposed, and Australia dared not disagree. Washington would not be deterred. A conflict that started with noble intentions as a United Nations police action, transformed itself into an unnecessary war in which the principal antagonists became China and the United States. But it did not have to be. And it only made things worse.

After the battle line settled around the 38th parallel, the profligate bombing campaign north of the border and the widespread use of napalm, flattened, burned and destroyed North Korea and instilled in its people a level of distrust and resentment that has shaped the country's continuing hostility toward the United States. In the re-built streets of Pyongyang, the legacy of bombing is bitterness. Not for the first time, American forces forfeited the moral high ground. It was in Korea, not in Vietnam, that the term 'gook' first became widespread. When hostilities ceased, the United States emerged diminished, its performance flawed; while China, the celestial empire, was morally rejuvenated after more than a century of humiliation. Popular patriotic rhetoric proclaimed, prophetically but a touch prematurely, that China had resumed 'her rightful place among the nations—the first place'.

Henry Kissinger said that if President Truman had been prepared to accept the status quo at the 38th parallel:

> he could say he had rebuffed communism in Asia…He could have shown a face of power to the world while teaching Americans the wisdom of constraint in using such power. He could have escaped terrible battlefield defeats, the panic and gloom that followed, and other grave difficulties.

Kissinger's US-centric analysis is important but it is only part of the story. The consequences to the Korean people were far more tragic; the effect on the long-term stability of the peninsula far more serious; and the prospect for ongoing conflict in Northeast Asia more worrying. The failed war in Korea established the pattern for the next sixty years, and we are reaping the consequences. The wisdom of constraint remains elusive. It has resulted in a 'strange new world' where Americans 'are finding it harder than ever to impose their will on anyone, anywhere'. As the bestselling writer, Alistair Horne, observed so wisely, 'How different world history would have been if MacArthur had had the good sense to stop on the 38th Parallel.'

Prelude

'Tyger, tyger burning bright, In the forests of the night'

The war has not ended. China's army has long since withdrawn but that of the United States has not. There has been no peace treaty between states, merely an armistice between military commanders. Its stated objective is to ensure a cessation of hostilities 'until a final peaceful settlement is achieved'. This has not occurred. Instead, over a million members of the armed forces of South Korea, North Korea and the United States of America remain on alert—stationed at or near the most dangerous and heavily fortified border in the world. Bill Clinton called it the 'scariest place on Earth'.

Paradoxically, the armistice has been the unintended cause of a unique ecological experiment in human exclusion. The terms of the agreement stipulated a military demarcation line commencing in the Han River estuary and extending for a little over 250 kilometres across the Korean peninsula from the Yellow Sea in the west to the Sea of Japan in the east. The opposing sides were required to withdraw from either side of the line to establish a 4-kilometre wide buffer zone—somewhat hopefully described as the demilitarised zone. Seen from space, especially in the west, it is a thin, verdant ribbon that separates the grey concrete sprawl of the Seoul conurbation from the brown and deforested wasteland around Kaesong. In the east, it merges in the green Taebaek-san mountain range before descending precipitously to the beaches of the east coast. The military demarcation line is now a recognised international border, which does not, as some believe, adhere faithfully or with cartographic precision to the 38th parallel. Its route is sinuous and complicated, starting slightly to the south and ending generously to the north of the parallel. It is, after all, a battle line.

In an ironic twist, the 1000 square kilometres that constitute the demilitarised zone have become an accidental wildlife refuge—a place where birds sing in greater numbers than at any other time in the history of the peninsula and where rare and endangered plants and animals, including some that were thought to be extinct, now flourish. Sandwiched between the armed forces of three military powers, bounded by a concrete wall on much of the southern side and formidable, multi-layered, barbed-wire fences on the northern side, overlooked by observation posts, beneath the intended trajectories of missiles and below the firing lines of the soldiers, the vegetation has been allowed to run riot. For over sixty years, with the exception of a small area near Kaesong, the tangled and impenetrable growth—especially in the mountainous east—has had no significant human intrusion, no cultivation, no pruning, no harvesting, no herbicide and no restraint on biological expansion other than the vicissitudes of nature and the everyday cycle of plant life.

This incongruous wilderness is home to thriving populations of birds, mammals, fish, amphibians, reptiles and insects. Zoologists have a special interest in the mammals, many of which are threatened or endangered. They include the Amur leopard, the Eurasian lynx, the Asian black bear and the long-tailed goral—a curious blend of goat and antelope. Even the legendary Siberian tiger from the Russian Far East, the Amur tiger, part of Korea's creation myth, is thought to be a denizen, although the more sceptical believe that its presence is confined to the rugged mountain fastness of Mt Paekdu in the remote north. It is as much a sacred symbol for Koreans as the bald eagle is to Americans.

The most visible inhabitants are the birds. Ornithologists have a field day on the periphery of the demilitarised zone—peering through high-powered lenses at the species that arrive with regular impunity on their seasonal migratory paths. These avian visitors are oblivious of the firepower surrounding them or the landmines beneath them. At least 150 species of cranes, buntings, shrikes, swans, geese, kittiwakes, goosanders, eagles and other birds have been recorded passing through or living within its boundaries. A special visitor is the 1.5 metre tall, red-crowned crane, the most elegant and highly regarded member of the crane family. It has been an Oriental symbol of fidelity and longevity for at least the last millennium. Half the world's population of this rare and endangered bird is estimated to visit the demilitarised zone. The white-naped crane, almost as rare, is another visitor. So too is the endangered black-faced spoonbill, of which the world population is only about 2000. And the Eurasian black vulture, which is only slightly smaller than the Andean condor, is yet another notable inhabitant. Its presence invariably indicates territory that is undisturbed, remote and devoid of human disturbance.

The armistice has given the demilitarised zone and its wildlife an opportunity that neither previously enjoyed. For centuries the land was heavily settled and farmed, then it was fought over and ravaged. In the mid-twentieth century it was the location of some of the most intense and hellish battles. The land that war protected is now a nature sanctuary; a testament to the folly of man and the tragedy of war; a triumphal demonstration that if given a chance, nature heals itself.

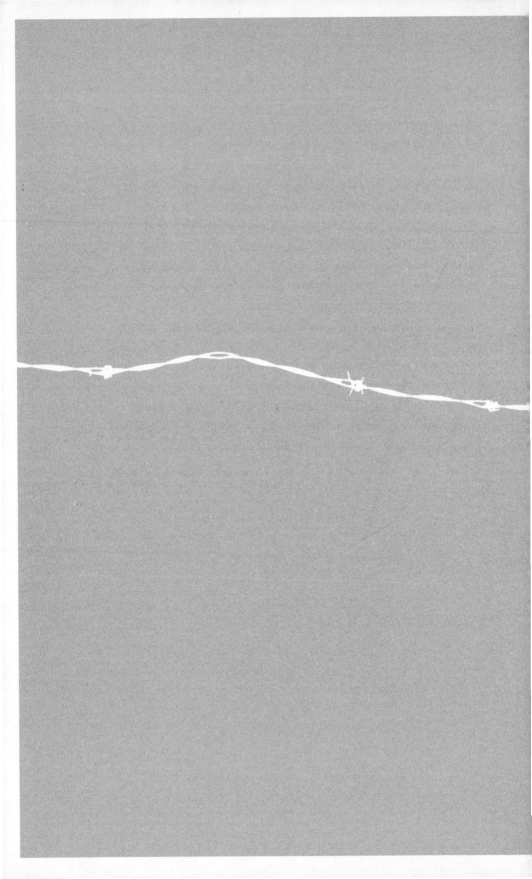

PART 1

Geography and History

CHAPTER 1

This Accursed Land

'Therefore a curse consumes the earth'

Korea's abiding problem is its geography. Its location and topography have together ensured its vulnerability. The peninsula is small, mostly physically inhospitable and predominately mountainous. Generally speaking, it is a harsh place where the living has never been easy. Its location between the ancient kingdoms of China and Japan is an age-old source of trouble and anxiety; its topography adds immeasurably to its difficulties; and its terrain and exposure to cold Siberian airflows during winter months are a recurring source of suffering and hardship. At similar latitudes, there is no place in the world that experiences winters as cold as those of Korea. This conundrum is not explained by Korea's distance from the equator. The approximate mid-point on the Korean peninsula is a mere 38°N, which is positively benign compared to London (51°N), Berlin (53°N) and Moscow (56°N). In other parts of the world the 38th parallel is a barometer of mild and temperate conditions. Spain and Portugal, for example, and California, the Azores, Athens and much of the Mediterranean Sea, all embrace the 38th parallel.

Siberian Cold

The source of Korea's uniquely harsh winter climate is the Siberian High, a high-pressure system that is the world's greatest cold air source. As it rotates in a clockwise direction, drawing in polar air, it produces an unparalleled mass of cold, dry air with regular surges during the winter months. The cold surges, which can produce continental minimum temperatures as low as minus 30 degrees to minus 50 degrees Celsius, occur on average three times a month in December, five times a month in January and three times a month in February. The minimum temperatures can exceed those inside the Arctic Circle. This pressure system, sometimes known as the Siberian anticyclone, affects much of the Northeast Asian landmass but is centred on a point at approximately 100°E and 50°N near Lake Huwsgul in remote northern Mongolia. It dominates Korean winters, especially as its effect is often accentuated by north-westerly winds that sweep silently and unheralded out of cold, clear blue skies.

In contrast, Japanese winters are not nearly so severe, as the bitter Siberian airflow is partially blocked by the mountainous spine of the Korean peninsula, modulated and warmed over the Sea of Japan and then further diffused by Japan's own coastal mountain topography. This phenomenon was observed by the first European visitor to Korea, a Spanish Jesuit priest named Father Gregorio de Cespedes, who had the misfortune to arrive during the winter of 1593–94 as chaplain to the Catholic troops among the occupying Japanese army. In a letter sent from the peninsula, he complained that the cold in Korea was 'very severe and without comparison with that of Japan'. Foreign troops of the twentieth century would learn this bitter lesson for themselves. They might also have done well to heed another of the earliest written European accounts, this time in 1666 by a Dutch sailor, Hendrick Hamel, who together with his crew, was shipwrecked on the island of Cheju off the southwest Korean coast and held in captivity on the mainland for over ten years. Somewhat understandably in the circumstances, he wrote in his journal: 'The Kingdom is very dangerous and difficult for strangers.' It was a salutary warning.

Foreign Invasions

Strangers have certainly come to Korea over the centuries, and the peninsula has long been a field of alien ambitions. But beyond a certain point, it is not possible to discern what really happened. According to one writer, Korea's ancient past is so opaque that it resembles 'a white stallion galloping through a snow-clad forest—briefly visible but mostly lost from sight'. Equally romantic is James Scarth Gale, the Canadian scholar, missionary and historian of Korea, who wrote: 'Korea takes its beginnings in the misty ages of the past that elude all attempts at close investigation, ages that lie somewhere between that of man and those of the angels and spirit beings, joining heaven on the one hand and earth on the other.'

We do know that in the seventh century some Korean tribes allied with armies of the Chinese Tang dynasty and engaged in a protracted struggle for supremacy on the peninsula. In the year 668, a unified Korean kingdom known as Silla emerged. It featured Chinese statecraft, Confucian philosophy, the Chinese written language and produced some of the world's greatest ceramics. In the tenth century Silla was succeeded and expanded by the kingdom of Koryŏ, whose ancient name, meaning 'high mountains and sparkling waters', indicates the linguistic provenance of the modern name 'Korea'.

In the thirteenth century the Mongols invaded China, eventually resulting in Kublai Khan's establishment of the Yuan dynasty in China in 1271. He waged six separate campaigns on the Korean peninsula between 1231 and 1259, devastating the kingdom of Koryŏ, which capitulated and became a Yuan vassal state. Mongol rule in China and on the Korean peninsula was surprisingly short lived, although quite long enough for the scholarly bloodlines of the Korean nobility to be fortified by inter-marriage with Mongol khans, princes and aristocrats. Even the Korean Crown Prince married one of Kublai Khan's daughters, who subsequently came to Korea in 1274 to sit on the throne beside her husband.

By 1368, the Mongols had been expelled from China although it took a few more decades to drive them off the Korean peninsula. Once they were gone, the Ming dynasty (1368–1644) emerged in China from the ashes of the Yuan; and the Chosŏn dynasty (1392–1897) rose in Korea in place of the Koryŏ. The arrival in Korea of the Chosŏn dynasty (the House of Yi) marked the beginning of the modern history of Korea. Its members remained continuously in power for over 500 years—until Japanese usurpation in the early twentieth century.

From the beginning, Chinese Ming and Korean Chosŏn had much in common. Both represented the overthrow of a Mongol yoke. And their mutual adherence to the same Confucian cultural norms of loyalty and hierarchy, not to mention their respective desire for peace, meant that their relationship was brotherly but separate. Throughout China's several centuries of Ming reign, the kingdoms of China and Korea enjoyed a harmonious trading and diplomatic association. The Korean minnow was, however, prepared to act independently on some issues. In 1446 it even chose to reject Chinese characters as a form of written language for ordinary people and proclaimed its own unique phonetic alphabet of twenty-four letters, known as Hangul. Its letters are composed of a mix of lines and circles that combine to form over 12,000 phonemes, and its three main vowels represent the sky, the earth and man.

Despite its grammatical independence, Korea continued to acknowledge the superior status of the Chinese emperor as the 'Son of Heaven' and behaved as a model tributary state, engaging in cultural and economic exchange and undertaking frequent tribute missions to Beijing. In return it received security, autonomy, imperial legitimation and support. China regarded Korea as a loyal family member that posed no threat and supported its regional security objectives. In Confucian terms, Korea's acceptance of a subservient role meant that the rules of reciprocity guaranteed the vital interests of both. From China's perspective, those interests naturally included the Korean peninsula, which it saw as a shield protecting its eastern flank and sometimes as a dangerous land bridge for foreign invaders. For Japan, across the sea, the Korean peninsula was the road to China.

Toyotomi Hideyoshi

No one at the Chosŏn court quite foresaw the furious onslaught that Toyotomi Hideyoshi, the Japanese regent and supreme military commander, would unleash in May 1592. For the previous two centuries, under the protective suzerainty of Ming China, the peninsula had known no war other than insignificant border raids and pirate attacks from the north. Seoul had become the capital of the Chosŏn dynasty and King Sŏnjo ruled over a stable, mostly agrarian and generally peaceful society, of which the dominant class was a type of scholar official known as *yangban*, and a third of the population were slaves. Confucianism, although not quite a religion, was the official ethical system.

In contrast, Japan was a warrior society dominated by the culture of the samurai. Unlike its neighbour, it had known almost continuous conflict for five centuries. Hideyoshi's goal was the conquest of China by way of the Korean peninsula. His military campaign was marked by shock and awe but it failed ignominiously. Pinned down in Korea and unable to reach or invade China, the Japanese troops departed after seven devastating years, leaving the Korean people and their countryside deeply damaged and battle scarred. One historian observed that the 'untold amount of misery and suffering served no purpose except to seal Korea hermetically against Japan and other nations for nearly three centuries'. What happened to Hideyoshi's failed campaign should have been a sobering lesson for future architects of a military offensive on the peninsula.

Hideyoshi's troops, like the Americans in 1950, landed at Pusan in the southeast corner of the peninsula, and proceeded along what would become a well-travelled invasion corridor on the less mountainous western side of the peninsula—to Taegu, Seoul and Kaesong, then to Pyongyang and onward to the Yalu River, Manchuria and China. At Kaesong, near the 38th parallel, Hideyoshi fatefully divided his army between his generals Konishi and Kato, choosing not to advance further with a unified force. Konishi commanded the western force, which continued northward through relatively open terrain to Pyongyang and beyond to the Yalu River. Kato led the eastern force, which advanced into the mountainous and wild northeast region, toward the Tumen River at the eastern extremity of the Manchurian border. The two commanders were at odds and their armies, which were separated by the Taebaek mountain range, operated without coordination. While Kato was sidetracked in the wilderness of the northeast, the strength of Konishi's thrust in the west was diminished and weakened.

With winter approaching and the Japanese forces at their weakest, Ming China chose the moment to come to the support of its little brother, sending 43,000 imperial troops across the Yalu. This unanticipated Chinese intervention turned the tide of the conflict. The Japanese, like the American troops in the twentieth century, were pushed back from the Manchurian border all the way to Seoul, where the front stabilised, a stalemate ensued and peace talks followed for four years. The precedent for the celestial army coming to the assistance of Korea had been established.

CHAPTER 2

Missionaries and Gunboats

'Our inheritance is turned over to strangers'

After the failed Japanese invasion in the 1590s, and during most of the long rule of the Qing dynasty in China, Korea basked in the relatively peaceful external relations that its brotherly relationship with China ensured. It was Beijing's most faithful tributary—'as close as lips and teeth' to use an old Chinese aphorism. But in the late eighteenth century, the winds of change began to blow, propelled by European merchants and traders and stimulated by the religious and scientific writings of intrepid missionaries. And in the late nineteenth century, Korea became an object of international rivalry; and Japan returned.

Winds of Change

Missionaries, led by the legendary Jesuit Francis Xavier, travelled first to Japan, then to China and eventually to Korea. By 1790, there were said to be 4000 Korean Catholics in Korea. This flowering of unorthodox devotion met much official resistance. The Korean king maintained, with considerable justification, that the converts subverted the established Confucian order and that they were 'stifling all feelings of filial piety, abolishing sacrifice to ancestors and burning memorial tablets'. Persecutions became rife and executions followed. By 1801 the remnant infant Catholic Church in Korea had gone underground.

In 1837 the Paris Foreign Missions Society secretly despatched a vanguard of priests across the Manchurian border into Korea. They

9

were like lambs to the slaughter—all soon betrayed, captured and executed, although not before steadfastly resisting their torturers and bravely refusing to reveal the names of their converts. The price of their faith was beheading; their reward was martyrdom. A few years later, the Society undertook a renewed push, successfully smuggling in a bishop, two priests and eleven converted Christians. But matters soon came to a head. The missionaries were seen as the forerunners of Western imperialism and the priests 'as pilots of the gunboat'. Korean foreign policy at the time was simple: no Christians, no trade, no treaties, no West and no Japan. Christianity was disparaged as Sŏhak or 'Western learning'.

In 1866 the reigning regent, known as the Taewongun—the father of the juvenile King Kojong—issued an anti-foreign edict, which was fixed on a tablet and placed in the centre of Seoul for the people to see and enforce for themselves. A violent anti-Christian storm broke out. The bishop and all but three of his missionaries were seized, imprisoned, tortured and beheaded and a nationwide search for converts was undertaken. There is no accurate estimate of the number of martyrs of the Korean persecution that commenced in 1866 but the dragnet caught many thousands over the next few years—reputedly 8000—most of whom were beheaded on the banks of the Han River. To expedite the process, a guillotine was developed that could remove twenty-four heads in one fell swoop.

International Rivalry

The persecution of the Catholics was not the only reason why 1866 was an eventful year in Korea. The drumbeats of Western power were sounding ever nearer and distinctly louder. In 1854 Japan had succumbed to the fearful intimidation of Commodore Perry's US Navy squadron. And China had been humiliated in 1860 by its disastrous defeat at the hands of British and French forces in the Second Opium War—an event that was accompanied by the ruthless sacking of the Old Summer Palace in Beijing by 3500 British troops. In Seoul, the news of these intrusions was received with apprehension, further stiffening resistance to the West. James Scarth Gale wrote that 1866 was the happy year of the young king's marriage 'yet it was a terrible year for Korea. Russians, French, British, Americans, Germans were all waiting just outside the barrier, intent on forcing an entrance'.

The problems started at the beginning of the year. In January, Russian ships appeared on the east coast, demanding trading and residency rights. In March, the executions of the French missionaries commenced, soon to be followed by those of their Korean converts. And in July, an event occurred that has achieved legendary status. The *General Sherman*, an armed, American-owned merchant steamship, entered the Taedong River in an attempt to reach Pyongyang. The ship's appearance excited the wrath of the Koreans, which was further inflamed by the aggressive and undiplomatic behaviour of the ship's captain and his officers. When the ship ran aground upstream, helpless on Yanggak Island, four days of fighting ensued. Distressed and affronted Koreans attacked and burned the ship and killed all on board. The monument erected on the site states, somewhat implausibly, that Kim Il-sung's great grandfather led the attack.

Matters only became worse in the next few years. In 1868, the unscrupulous Hamburg merchant, Ernst Oppert, accompanied by an American consular representative and a French priest who had been one of the last to escape during the 1866 massacres, concocted an eccentric plan. Their objective was to raid the tomb of the Taewongun's father, seize the remains and hold them until Korea agreed to open its ports to trade. Not surprisingly, when this sacrilege and attempted ransom were foiled, an international scandal ensued. A Hamburg court even declared that Oppert's ends—opening Korea to trade and Christianity—did not justify his means. And the American consular representative was indicted by the US chargé d'affaires in Beijing with assisting an expedition for the purpose of 'illegally and clandestinely exhuming and removing the remains of a deceased sovereign of Corea'. He was acquitted but in a trial that was said to be a 'perfect burlesque'.

By 1871 the Americans had decided that a considerable show of force was necessary to 'open' Korea. And President Ulysses S. Grant and his Secretary of State duly obliged. A disingenuous diplomatic cable to Beijing declared that a proposed American expedition to Korea was entirely peaceful, but this was a mere pretext. The arrival at the mouth of the Han River of five ships armed with eighty-five guns and 1230 sailors and marines, conveyed a different impression. When shots were fired from one of the Korean forts on Kanghwa Island, the American commander demanded an apology and issued an ultimatum. When silence followed, he launched a military assault against the forts.

Many more Koreans than Americans were killed but the old Taewongun remained undaunted and there was no negotiation, no treaty and no Western trade. On 3 July the American ships steamed away, leaving the Koreans more distrustful of foreigners than ever. The *New York Herald* reflected the chauvinism of the age by describing the incident as the 'Little War with the Heathen', but monuments were erected throughout the land commemorating the Korean 'victory' and praising the dead and wounded as national heroes.

Finally, and inexorably, in 1873 cracks began to appear in Korea's wall of isolation as King Kojong, now twenty-one years old, emerged as an independent monarch. One of his earliest of many unwise decisions was to adopt a policy of reconciliation with Japan, against the inclination of his steely consort Queen Min and leading members of the Chosŏn court. Japanese envoys soon came to Korea seeking the opening of Korean ports to trade. Nothing better reflected the cultural gap between the two countries at that time than the Western suits of the Japanese envoys. To the astonished Koreans, their strange clothing was an incomprehensible case of sartorial dementia. When no agreement was reached and mediation failed, Japan adopted military intimidation to open the ports—replicating the bullying methods of the Western powers.

In 1875 the Japanese warship *Unyokan* approached Kanghwa Island at the mouth of the Han River. Warning shots were fired from the shore battery and a gunfight ensued. Japanese troops were landed, many Korean soldiers were killed, villages were looted and weapons were captured. In February the following year, the Chosŏn court grudgingly accepted an unequal commercial treaty with Japan. It was Korea's first modern treaty with another country and provided Japan with preferential trading rights without equivalent Korean privileges.

In Beijing, the Qing court regarded Japan's treaty with Korea as a threat to its security. And as a means of deflecting Japan's manifest ambition it adopted a policy of introducing Western powers to Korea through trade treaties. Korea's treaty with the United States was the first of these Western power treaties. It was called a 'Treaty of Peace, Amity, Commerce and Navigation' and was signed in May 1882. Identical British and German treaties were signed in 1883. Further treaties using the same template followed with Russia and Italy in 1884 and France in 1886. China's determination to protect itself from foreign intrusion on the Korean peninsula was so great that it permitted the Chosŏn court only a minor role in the diplomatic process of treaty negotiation.

The Korean treaty with the United States was negotiated in China, drafted in the Chinese language and handed on a plate to Commodore Shufeldt of the US Navy with little Korean involvement. Shufeldt described with pride his accomplishment in having brought 'the last of the exclusive countries within the pale of Western Civilization'. But his bluff and swagger, not to mention his high-flown and insensitive language, indicate the real essence of what had occurred. He wrote that the Pacific is now 'the ocean bride of America' while China, Japan and Korea were 'the bridesmaids' and California 'the nuptial couch, the bridal chamber, where all the wealth of the Orient will be brought to celebrate the wedding'.

The Coming of the Japanese

The trade treaties were the beginning of a great power charge for Korea. In 1878 Japan opened a branch of the Dai-Ichi Bank and the British trading house of Jardine Matheson came shortly afterwards, as did several American commercial interests. By the 1890s, steamships, railroads, electricity, the telegraph, even journalism, began to appear; as did Christianity, which was now tolerated despite the Catholic massacres of 1866. This form of Christianity was the Protestant variety, mostly Methodist and Presbyterian from the United States and Canada, riding on the coat tails of American commerce. It spread rapidly, disseminated by the Church's followers, especially in schools that they established and sponsored.

China remained the dominant cultural influence but some young Korean idealists and reformers began to look further afield. They established an 'enlightenment' party in the 1880s, an 'independence club' in the 1890s and many other organisations with similar aspirations and goals. Their motivations were an attachment to Korean nationalism but not its traditional culture; a desire to free the country from Chinese domination; and a faith in Western education, science and technology. There were few limits to the enthusiasm and ambitions of these early crusaders and reformers, who no longer wanted to live in a hermit kingdom but sought to open the gates to Western commerce and end the *yangban* monopoly of power. This ferment constituted the cauldron from which Japan's eventual takeover of Korea would bubble forth.

The first serious discord occurred in 1884 when the government held a banquet for Korean officials and foreign diplomats to inaugurate a post office. Rather than a celebration, the banquet became the occasion for an attempted coup. On the night, seven officials were murdered, including senior members of the family of the anti-Japanese Queen Min. Suggestions of a conspiracy directed from Tokyo were inflamed by the fact that Takezoe, the Japanese Minister to Seoul, had privately urged Koreans to stand up for their independence from China. During the mêlée, under orders from Takezoe, guards from the Japanese legation mysteriously appeared, supported the uprising and took the king and queen into custody.

After three days, General Yuan, the head of China's military garrison in Seoul, moved 1500 Chinese troops into the royal palace, rescued King Kojong and Queen Min and forced the coup leaders and Japanese guards to seek refuge in the Japanese legation. Takezoe fled. The Japanese legation was burned down and most surviving conspirators escaped under Japanese protection to exile in Japan. The new post office, whose opening was intended to be an occasion for celebration, was a pile of rubble. The fracas temporarily reinforced Chinese dominion and raised the ire of Japan, which boldly demanded an apology from Korea and reparations for the damage to its legation. General Yuan was appointed as the Chinese Resident in Korea and directed its affairs for the next ten years. And China and Japan entered into the Treaty of Tianjin, which provided for a mutual troop withdrawal from Korea, subject to conditions allowing the return of troops in certain circumstances.

Japan was uneasy about the presence of a Chinese Resident on the Korean peninsula. At the same time, the 'Great Game' between the United Kingdom and Russia spread to northeast Asia and added a further complication. Each was worried that the stalemate between China and Japan over Korea would create a power vacuum on the peninsula. In a pre-emptive move in 1885, the Admiralty despatched three Royal Navy warships to an island off Korea's southeast coast. Russia responded by despatching to Seoul its senior diplomat in Tokyo, Alexis de Speyer, who melodramatically claimed to have instructions to 'annex ten Korean acres for every one that Britain claimed'. King Kojong even approved secret talks for a Russian protectorate of Korea— the first of many occasions when he would seek Russian assistance.

Eventually, anxiety about the looming Russian presence in the Far East, coupled with rising internal Japanese militarism and resentment at China's hold on Korea, crystallised Japan's intentions. It wanted its own bridgehead on the Korean peninsula before any great power annexation of it. The catalyst for change came in 1894 in the form of a rebellion in southwest Korea by a disparate peasant nationalist group known as the Tonghak. A nervous Kojong called on Beijing for military aid, which was duly reciprocated. It was an opportunity for which Japan was waiting, giving it a mutual right under the Treaty of Tianjin to send its own forces back to the peninsula. By early June both China and Japan had begun to pour troops into Korea. On 23 July the Japanese army occupied the royal palace, took control of Kojong and detained Queen Min and her children. And the elderly Taewongun, whose antipathy toward Queen Min could be counted on, was brought back as the representative of a Japanese puppet government.

As it had done in the past and would do in the future, China responded to the provocation on the Korean peninsula. A full-blown war soon erupted. It was known as the first Sino-Japanese War (1894–95) and this time resulted in humiliation for China. In short measure, Japan overran Korea, invaded southern Manchuria and northern China and commanded the sea approaches to Beijing. The outcome, including the massive reparations that Japan extracted from China, constituted a political disaster that was the beginning of the end for imperial China and heralded the fall of the Qing dynasty. China lost Taiwan, which was ceded to Japan; its political influence in Korea was negated; and Korea declared its independence. The British government even suggested that Korea become 'a protectorate of the international powers'.

Japan's military success brought the Korean peninsula increasingly under its influence. Reform after reform was introduced, eating away at almost every vestige of ancient Korean life. Many reforms were designed to destroy traditional Korean society or to serve Japan's strategic interests, although some could hardly be criticised, including the separation of the royal household from government and the introduction of a prime ministerial cabinet system. And most Koreans welcomed the requirement that the native Hangul script, rather than the Chinese written language, be used in school texts, government edicts and royal pronouncements.

The Japanese-inspired reforms provided the ancient kingdom of Korea with a foretaste of modernity, but Japan's mantle as an 'agent of providence' was short lived; its brutal self-interest was soon apparent; and its alienation of the Korean people was swift. In the autumn of 1895 General Miura, the new Japanese Minister in Korea, exceeded all reasonable bounds. He became enraged by Korean resistance to Japan's social and political reforms. The object of his rancour was Queen Min, who exercised the power behind the throne, remarkably like her Chinese contemporary, the Empress Dowager Cixi. Min was an obstacle to

Japanese ambitions but nothing justified her politically inspired murder at the royal palace on the night of 8 October. It ranks with Hideyoshi's invasion in the sixteenth century as one of the cornerstones of Korean antipathy toward Japan.

Miura and senior Japanese military and civilian officials plotted the murder, almost certainly with the knowledge and approval of the Japanese cabinet. Japanese rōnin assassins—unemployed samurai—were commissioned to do the work. They not only slashed and dismembered the Queen with their sabres and knives but dragged her into the garden where they incinerated her body to destroy the evidence. Japan brazenly denied any involvement but Russian and American advisors to the Korean court had witnessed the murder. To appease foreign outrage, Japan put fifty-six men on trial, including Miura, but no reliable witness was prepared to testify and all were acquitted due to lack of evidence.

Russian Duplicity

The Korean relationship with Japan now spiralled further downwards. The widowed Kojong was understandably afraid of the Japanese and increasingly sought Russian protection. And his behaviour became more erratic. In February 1896 he and the Crown Prince disguised themselves as court ladies and travelled incognito to the Russian legation, hiding in the royal women's cloistered sedan chairs—'crouched, pale and trembling'. Kojong stayed at the legation for almost exactly a year, afraid to return to his own palace. The business of government went on, however, and Kojong somehow managed to dismiss his pro-Japanese cabinet, promote pro-Russian ministers and despatch his wife's relative Prince Min as Korea's first envoy to Russia, to attend the coronation of Tsar Nicholas II in Moscow.

When Kojong eventually returned to the palace in February 1897, matters became stranger and stranger. He proclaimed that his country was now an 'empire' and that he was its 'emperor'—so as to put Korea on an equal constitutional footing with the empires of China and Japan. Then, after consulting the royal astrologers, he decreed that his inauguration would take place at the inconvenient time of three o'clock in the morning, on 12 October. A grand imperial procession to mark the king's elevation to emperor duly occurred in the pre-dawn darkness, witnessed by bemused, bleary, perplexed and kowtowing foreign diplomats. Some doubted his sanity let alone his credentials as a modern leader.

In the meantime, Korea's fragile overtures to Russia continued. But it was a dangerous ploy, for Russia had its own designs on the Korean peninsula. When Prince Min visited Moscow and St Petersburg in 1896 for the Tsar's coronation, he had no knowledge that Japan and Russia had entered into a secret agreement that stipulated that each enjoyed equal rights in Korea, including the right to station troops and place military and financial advisors in the country. Nor did he know that Japan had opened tentative discussions with Russia about the partition of Korea at the 38th parallel. But this novel and surprising idea was ahead of its time and Russia rejected it.

Soon, however, Korea had the feel of a tacit co-protectorate under both Russia and Japan. Russian military and financial advisors now appeared in greater numbers in Seoul; an influential British advisor to the Korean government was controversially replaced with one of Russia's own; and Russia's commercial interests on the peninsula expanded, as did military tension and diplomatic duplicity. Unknown to Japan, Russia entered into a secret Chinese alliance, giving it unrestricted access to Manchuria and a lease over the Liaodong peninsula in Korea's northwest. Both areas were strategic springboards to the Korean peninsula.

The hapless Kojong looked fruitlessly to Europe to bolster Korean independence. In 1897 he sent Prince Min to Queen Victoria's Diamond Jubilee celebrations in London. The mission appeared to achieve some modest success when the future Lord Curzon, then Under-Secretary for Foreign Affairs, told Parliament that 'the British government would maintain Korean independence, neither allowing it to be absorbed by any of its neighbours nor permitting it to be used by any other power for gaining control of the eastern seas'. But Curzon's words were hollow and he soon left the Foreign Office to become Viceroy of India. In truth, the United Kingdom was not committed to Korean independence. In 1902 it abandoned its policy of isolation and concluded the first Anglo-Japanese alliance, expressly recognising Japan's 'monopolistic privilege over the peninsula'.

The British treaty emboldened Japan. As the new century opened, storm clouds gathered over the Korean peninsula. In 1903 Japan demanded that Russia acknowledge its special interest in Korea in return for Japanese recognition of Russian interests in Manchuria. Moscow unwisely rejected the proposal but responded with a counteroffer to create a neutral zone in Korea north of the 39th parallel, which Japan in turn rejected. Negotiations stalled until the inevitable conflict unfurled. It became known as the Russo-Japanese War (1904–05). In February 1904 Japan launched a surprise attack on the Russian naval squadron at Port Arthur on the Liaodong peninsula. In March it landed its army in Korea and overran the country without serious opposition. In May, Japanese forces travelled further north and attacked the Russian army in southern Manchuria. The culmination came in May 1905 with the annihilation of the heart of the Imperial Russian Navy in the Tsushima Strait, the broad channel that connects the Sea of Japan with the East China Sea. Over two days, the Russian fleet was decimated, losing eight battleships and more than 5000 men.

Both the United Kingdom and the United States aided and abetted the Japanese war effort. Britain obstructed and delayed Russia's Baltic Fleet en route to the Far East, barring it from using the Suez Canal or any British port. And the United States provided financial support to Japan, partly because President Theodore Roosevelt regarded it as a paragon of Asian modernisation. In September 1905, at Portsmouth in Maine, Roosevelt brokered a peace treaty to end the war, for which he earned himself a Nobel Peace Prize. Under the treaty Russia agreed to recognise that Korea was part of the Japanese sphere of influence. It also agreed to remove its military and civilian personnel from Manchuria. The outcome was a humiliation for Imperial Russia that would not be forgotten.

Japanese Dominion

A few months after the peace treaty, Hirobumi, the former Japanese Prime Minister, was sent to Seoul to demand that Korea become a Japanese protectorate. Kojong was unwilling to cooperate and refused to apply his seal to the treaty document, but five members of his cabinet collaborated with the Japanese. The ensuing Japan-Korea Protectorate Treaty of November 1905 resulted in Korea forfeiting control of its foreign affairs and losing its domestic autonomy. The brief and comical Korean 'empire', which Kojong had proclaimed in 1897, was over. Prince Min unsuccessfully attempted to have the treaty annulled, and then suicided by cutting his throat with a dagger—'sacrificing his body to preserve his integrity'. Waves of righteous Koreans protested. But Japan had long planned to conquer Korea and with the confidence flowing from its defeat of Russia, nothing would stop it.

The history of Korea's next forty years is a tale of brutal suppression and Japanese rapacity. The protectorate was followed after only five years by formal annexation, resulting in the amalgamation of Korea into the Japanese empire. The ancient throne of the Chosŏn dynasty was surrendered and the kingdom came to an end. The Japanese army ensured a virtual police state. Most Korean political and social organisations were dissolved; freedom of speech, the press and assembly were curtailed; the Korean army was disbanded; and many tens of thousands of Korean people were jailed or beaten. For Japan, Korea was a producer of food and raw materials and a source of labour. It appropriated land, shipped rice to Japan and instituted large-scale industrial projects for Japanese military and commercial ends.

Industrialisation expanded in the 1930s to support the Japanese war effort in Manchuria and China. Korean labour was used to build more roads, longer railways and further electrical, chemical, hydro-electric, fertiliser and munitions plants. Hundreds of thousands, and later millions, of Koreans were forcibly mobilised and shunted to the wastelands of Manchuria, the mountains of northern Korea or the factories of Japan, to provide the labour that these enterprises necessitated. For many, it was a one-way trip. Their ultimate destiny was death in slave labour conditions. In 1937, on the eve of the Japanese invasion of China, there was a final indignity. Japan banned the Korean language in all schools and publications and at public meetings; ordered Koreans to adopt Japanese names; and dissolved all remaining Korean social, political and cultural organisations.

This was a dark age for the Korean people. And nationalists of one sort or another kept up a dangerous running battle with the Japanese. There were regular waves of protest and frequent brutal crackdowns. In 1919, when activists peacefully but provocatively proclaimed the independence of Korea and the liberty of the Korean people, Japanese reprisals are said to have left over 7000 dead, almost 16,000 wounded and approximately 46,000 arrested. Opposition to Japanese authoritarianism stoked the fire of the resistance. Nationalist groups coalesced on the right and left of the political spectrum. They were motivated by patriotism; their inspiration was nationalism; and their goal was independence.

On the right, the American-inspired Protestant missionaries and their followers were influential. They had flourished in the late nineteenth century in Korea and were tolerated by Japan to avoid international criticism. On the left, communism was particularly strong in the far south, but less so in the north. Everywhere there was a yearning for liberation from the Japanese yoke. At both ends of politics there were radicals and gradualists and, as always, there were collaborators. Eventually, in 1945, the nightmare of the Japanese occupation of Korea concluded with Japan's defeat at the end of World War II.

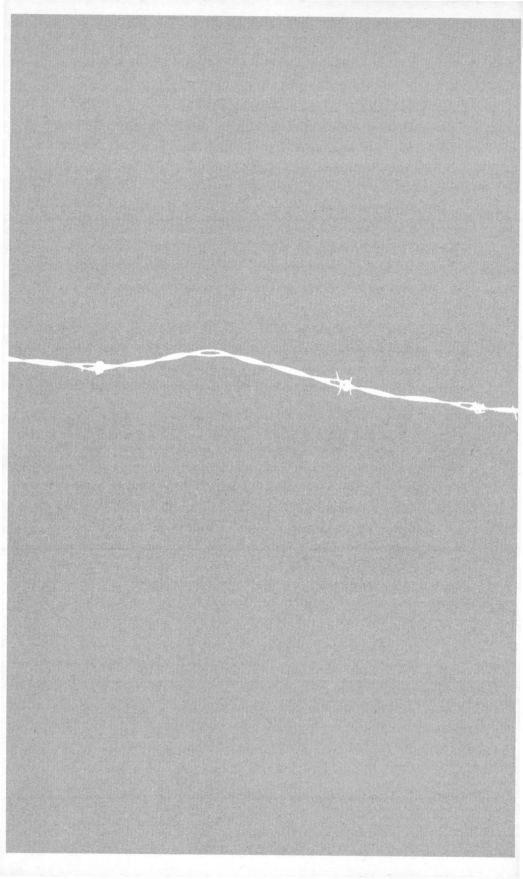

PART 2

Origins of Conflict

CHAPTER 3

A Fateful Division

'If hopes were dupes, fears may be liars'

When Imperial Japan formally surrendered aboard the USS *Missouri* in Tokyo Bay on 2 September 1945, one occupation of Korea followed the other. The Japanese occupation of the whole was succeeded by American and Russian occupations of separate parts. Each of them was repressive in one form or another. The fateful proposal that the Korean nation should be partitioned at the 38th parallel was an American initiative, made by a little-known wartime policy committee, the State-War-Navy Coordinating Committee—called 'Swink' after its acronym, SWNCC. It was a precursor to the National Security Council. The proposed dividing line was selected on 10 August 1945 by two young colonels from the State Department working late in the evening in the Pentagon. They were given half an hour for the task and a map of 'Asia and Adjacent Areas' from a 1942 *National Geographic* magazine. One of the colonels was Dean Rusk. A few days later President Truman confirmed the selection.

The Decision

The partition was a unilateral initiative. The United Kingdom was not consulted, nor was any other allied power. Korea was ignored. The decision was prompted by the entry of the Soviet army into Manchuria and came in the immediate aftermath of the detonation of atomic bombs on Hiroshima on 6 August and Nagasaki on 9 August. Stalin acquiesced, intriguingly, and without demur. The division of Korea was not entirely without precedent, as Imperial Russia and Japan had considered a partition in 1896 and again in 1903—although no member of SWNCC had any idea of those events.

The determining consideration had been Russia's intervention in the Pacific war. Stalin had agreed at the Yalta Conference to enter the war against Japan within three months of the end of the war in Europe. The German surrender took place on 8 May 1945 and precisely three months later, on the evening of 8 August, Soviet Foreign Minister Molotov informed the Japanese ambassador of his government's hostile intentions. That night around midnight, the Soviet army moved into Manchuria on a grand scale. Its front—consisting of three army groups, 1.5 million men and over 5000 tanks—extended more than 4600 kilometres from the Pacific coast to eastern Inner Mongolia. Its manifest ability to occupy the whole of the Korean peninsula before American forces could arrive was a source of consternation in the Pentagon. Within days, the first elements of the Russian 25th Army had entered northeast Korea. A fortnight later they had completed occupation as far south as Pyongyang. By 1 September they had effected occupation to the 38th parallel. So impressed was one American military historian that he named the Soviet invasion of Manchuria and the Korean peninsula 'Operation August Storm'.

A divided Korea was not what Franklin Delano Roosevelt had contemplated. But he died in April and President Truman was a more conservative man. Roosevelt had embraced a postwar world order that included a vision of a free and independent Korea, to be preceded by a period of international trusteeship to prepare it for self-rule. As early as March 1943, he raised the concept of a trusteeship of Korea with the British Foreign Secretary, Anthony Eden; and the principle was subsequently embodied in the Cairo Declaration in December that year. Shortly afterwards, he raised it with Stalin, who responded favourably, although he thought the period of trusteeship should be as short as possible. On 2 August 1945 the final proclamation at the

Potsdam Conference in Brandenburg reiterated that 'the terms of the Cairo declaration shall be carried out'.

But as the radioactive fallout from Hiroshima and Nagasaki settled over Japan, a not so subtle metamorphosis was occurring in Washington. Roosevelt's concept of an international trusteeship for Korea was buried by the pressing weight of expediency, apprehension of Russian intentions and Truman's implacable anti-communist resolve. The United States had invited and encouraged the Soviet army's movement into Manchuria and Korea and had urged Russia to declare war on Japan, but some in Washington were beginning to have reservations. There was a newfound perception of the strategic importance of denying a substantial part of Korea to Soviet Russia. One historian noted drily: 'The fate of the Korean peninsula suddenly became of interest to the Americans.'

The change of thinking by the Truman administration led to a change of direction that altered the course of history in the region. Russia's aspirations were entirely expected. It had long held a natural and understandable interest in Korea and Manchuria, where it had been humiliated in the Russo-Japanese War (1904–05). But the United States had not previously expressed any strategic interest or concern. It had even been advised internally that, in return for their assistance in the war against Japan, the Soviets 'would want all of Manchuria, Korea and possibly parts of North China'. This was the price to be paid. And the reason was clear. Until the atomic bomb made it unnecessary, the Americans expected heavy losses in their planned invasion of the Japanese mainland but believed that the casualties to be incurred by the Russians in invading Manchuria and Korea would be greater. A Joint Chiefs of Staff document stated unambiguously that 'our objective should be to get the Russians to deal with the Japs in Manchuria (and Korea if necessary)'. The quid pro quo for persuading the Russians to do the nasty work was the probability that they would appropriate Manchurian and Korean territory on their far eastern border.

But in August 1945, when the Soviet army entered the war, Truman and those advising him decided that they no longer wanted to pay the price, at least in Korea. The balance had shifted, as it so often seems to do, in favour of those who preferred confrontation, the establishment of clear territorial boundaries and the use of military force and occupation. America was not faced with 'an entirely new strategic situation in the Far East' but created its own. For ideological reasons, it wanted a defensive wall. And so it made a scramble for Korea. By late August, the journal of XXIV Corps, the intended US occupying army in Korea, stated: 'Truman anxious to have Korea occupied promptly.'

Thus only a week after Potsdam, one of America's most pressing political and military objectives suddenly became the perceived need to secure and cement an artificial division of Korea at the 38th parallel— and to occupy the country south of the proposed dividing line as soon as possible. It was a reactionary and strategic decision that marked the beginning of the most anomalous period in Korean history since 668 CE, when the kingdom was first substantially unified. Not only did the partition ignore the Korean people but its practical effect was to undermine Roosevelt's notion of trusteeship, with its correlative standard of international fiduciary behaviour 'higher than that trodden by the crowd'. For it was clear that once division and competing antagonistic occupations were embedded, future unification would be increasingly unlikely—as it surely proved to be.

One former US Foreign Service officer proffered this heartfelt and damning description:

> No division of a nation in the present world is so astonishing
> in its origin as the division of Korea; none is so unrelated to
> conditions or sentiment within the nation itself at the time
> the division was effected; none is to this day so unexplained;
> in none does blunder and planning oversight appear to
> have played so large a role...[and] there is no division for
> which the US government bears so heavy a share of the
> responsibility as it bears for the division of Korea.

Operation Blacklist Forty

What followed for the next three painful years until 1948, were separate foreign military governments in the north and the south. The melodramatic code name for the American occupation—Operation Blacklist Forty—suggested its heavy-handed nature. It was neither subtle nor peaceful and the Korean people's initial goodwill toward their American occupiers rapidly evaporated. The main body of troops disembarked at Inchon on 8 September from a convoy of twenty-one ships, which included five flanking destroyers. The Korean people, desperate for liberation from the tyranny of Japanese rule, clamoured for the Americans' attention and greeted their arrival with excitement. But their hopes and dreams were not the concern of General Hodge, the US Army commander, who rebuffed them repeatedly and contemptuously. He saw his first duty as establishing 'order'—not in the interests of the people of Korea but in the interests of the United States.

Hodge's homespun simplicity, insensitivity and bluntness were not surprising from someone of his background and experience. He was a man of his time and his type who reflected the attitudes of the era, the army and of many ordinary Americans. But his personal qualities did not equip him well for the position to which he was appointed in September 1945. Korea's history and circumstances called for more and its people deserved better. Hodge failed to sense or respect the extreme feelings of the Korean people for their newly liberated country. In a pattern that has become familiar, he set about the installation of an anti-communist government in the south, as a bulwark orientated toward American interests. But it was a short-term approach. The fact that any such government might be headed by a brutal ideologue, whose rigidity and antagonism made conflict with the north inevitable, did not seem to be his concern. Unwittingly, Hodge's administration in southern Korea ended up generating antagonism 'toward the Military Government, toward US objectives in Korea, and even toward the US itself'. Much worse, it brought about a situation that inhibited future political stability in Korea, contributed directly to continuing civil unrest and led to the war that subsequently ensued.

From the outset, Hodge misconceived the true nature of the American occupation. Korea was neither an enemy ally nor an enemy aggressor. It was simply a victim of Japanese colonialism. Yet Hodge briefed his officers to regard Korea 'as an enemy of the United States' that was subject to the terms of the Japanese surrender. Embarrassingly, he described Koreans as 'the same breed of cat as the Japs'. And his colleague, Major General Arnold, caused serious affront when he publicly referred to the earnest efforts of well-intentioned Koreans calling for an early national election as a 'puppet show'. Racism, condescension and cultural disdain permeated the relationship. Hodge's army did not set out to build trust. It set out to seize and control. Its role was negative and pre-emptive—to deny territory to Soviet Russia and repatriate the Japanese.

An underlying problem was that Hodge and his administration found it easier to deal with the Japanese. The Americans admired Japanese precision, orderliness and efficiency, appreciated their impeccable correctness, and shared a mutual respect and camaraderie through their common military experience. That is why, to the bewilderment and dismay of Koreans, Hodge initially confirmed Japanese colonial officials in their positions, retained Japanese as the principal language of communication and gave chief responsibility for maintaining law and order to Japanese soldiers and police. Korean resentment at American insensitivity was heart-felt. As one perceptive US naval officer later confessed, 'Our misunderstanding of local feelings about the Japanese, and our own close association with them, was one of the most expensive mistakes we ever made there.' When political pressure eventually forced Hodge to dispense with the aid of his newfound Japanese administrative allies, he replaced them with Koreans drawn from the hated well of Japanese collaborators—only compounding local antagonism and distrust.

The bone-hard politics of the American occupation was almost immediately evident. McCarthyism was not yet born, but in the minds of some military leaders and Washington policymakers, incipient communism loomed as a greater evil than the Japanese imperialism they had just defeated. Truman's antipathy toward Soviet Russia was well known. And Hodge's entrenched personal political views infused his every decision during the occupation. There was little discrimination—he treated a farrago of vague leftists, nationalists, opponents of colonialism, radicals and advocates of land reform as 'communists', and effectively declared war on them all. And worse, he promptly shunned, and later outlawed, the centrist Korean People's Republic, a genuine nationalist coalition of widely differing factions united by a common desire to unify the country and committed to major social and labour reforms. Its policy called for 'the establishment of close relations with the United States, USSR, England and China', but Hodge would have none of it.

It is true that a divergent range of nationalist groups and people's committees proliferated in response to the iron fist of Japanese rule and the disappointment of American occupation. And it was obvious that the mushrooming of these organisations presented law and order issues. They split broadly between capitalist evangelical nationalists at one extreme and communist nationalists at the other, with many in intermediate positions. The far southern provinces in particular, including the island of Cheju, were and had been since Japanese times a hotbed of Marxist radicalism and resistance to authority. But the excitable, unruly and even obstreperous Koreans who flocked to the nationalist groups were not all communists, let alone committed ones. And the paramount concern of most was not ideology but the establishment of an independent Korean state. The task was difficult but Hodge's administration was so heavy handed, so focussed on America's perceived security interests and so unable (or unwilling) to deal fairly with the genuine concerns of the Korean people that the Americans soon found themselves to be 'a common reference point of opposition for all parties and shades of political opinion'.

Syngman Rhee

In the search for a local political leader with whom he could be comfortable, Hodge actively sought out conservative candidates, whose one virtue in most cases was simply a reflexive anti-communism. Early in the occupation his head of military intelligence reported with evident satisfaction that he had found several hundred conservatives who might make good leaders. But the several hundred were tainted by collaboration with Japanese imperialism and Hodge wanted a patriotic right-wing figurehead who stood apart from Japan, exemplifying 'the American propensity to go for the man rather than the movement', or as another historian put it 'the US preference for charismatic individuals (who spoke fluent English) over mass political movements'. In this task, the Office of Strategic Services (OSS) excelled. It was the wartime predecessor of the Central Intelligence Agency (CIA) and a place where, according to some, 'every eccentric schemer with a harebrained plan for secret operations would find a sympathetic ear'. Between the OSS, MacArthur and Chiang Kai-shek, the fervent anti-communist Chinese nationalist leader in Taiwan, they came up with the name of Syngman Rhee.

Rhee had been known to US intelligence officers for a long time. He was a seventy-year-old Korean expatriate firebrand with a history of mendacious activity, who had been an anti-Japanese campaigner for decades and more recently a fanatical anti-communist. As a young man Rhee had been imprisoned or arrested in Korea several times— once for his role in a plot to remove King Kojong and a second time in connection with an attempt to assassinate the Japanese Governor-General. In 1925 he was impeached and removed from office as president of the exiled and self-appointed Provisional Government of Korea in Shanghai. In one guise or another, Rhee had managed throughout his life to continue agitating for the independence of Korea and his own personal aggrandisement. During the war against Japan, his many activities included assisting the OSS with anti-Japanese strategies. By 1945 US intelligence well knew Rhee's weaknesses. He is said to have 'haunted and irritated Foggy Bottom [State Department] for years'. A declassified CIA report stated that he was 'essentially [a] demagogue bent on autocratic rule' and that 'his intellect is a shallow one and his behaviour is often irrational'.

None of that deterred MacArthur, Hodge's commanding officer in Tokyo, who was bent on parachuting Rhee into Korea, regardless of the State Department's well-founded opposition. MacArthur was assisted in this murky venture by a mysterious figure called M. Preston Goodfellow, who was a deputy director of the OSS and became Rhee's sponsor and later his arms buyer and fundraiser. During the war Goodfellow interceded on Rhee's behalf to obtain limited liaison status for him with the War Department. In August 1945 he interceded again, this time with the State Department, to approve Rhee's credentials for travel to Japan. This was a mere ruse— as Rhee's intended destination was Korea not Japan, and Goodfellow knew that the State Department would not approve Rhee's entry into Korea.

When Rhee reached Tokyo on 12 October he was the guest of MacArthur, who sent a cable to the War Department confirming his arrival. By coincidence or design, Hodge was also in Tokyo and met Rhee in secret. MacArthur joined them. They agreed not to announce Rhee's presence in Seoul when he arrived but to wait until the timing was propitious. On 15 October Rhee flew in MacArthur's private aircraft to Seoul, where he was put up in a suite at the Chosŏn Hotel, then the preserve of the most senior American military officers. As one leading American historian has said: 'Let us be frank: Hodge, MacArthur, Goodfellow and Rhee conspired against established State Department policy [to return Rhee to Korea].' Sir Max Hastings was less direct but equally damning: 'There appears to have been at least a measure of corruption in the [murky] transaction.' It is evident that there were sound reasons for the State Department's opposition to Rhee, for he proved to be a living powder keg.

For the next five years, until the powder keg exploded in 1950, Rhee waged a brutal and vitriolic campaign. The result soon was, as the CIA reported, that 'extreme Rightists control the overt political structure in the US zone'. Their power was enforced mainly through the agency of the Japanese-built Korean National Police, which was ruthlessly brutal in suppressing disorder. It became a bastion for the ugly authoritarian side of southern Korean politics. The police violence was often extreme, gratuitous and visceral. Many tens of thousands of southern Koreans were imprisoned, tortured or killed. A good number was condemned on little more than vague suspicion or black malice. Order was maintained only through a police state machinery of espionage, censorship, propaganda and repression. By December 1947, there were more political prisoners in southern Korea under the American occupation than there had been under Japanese rule.

The shameful collaboration between the right-wing extremists and the American military government in southern Korea was a matter of concern to Patrick Shaw, then head of the Australian diplomatic mission in Tokyo, later Chairman of the United Nations Commission on Korea and later still, as Sir Patrick Shaw, Australian Ambassador to the United States. In November 1947 he reported that 'Real Power is apparently in the hands of the ruthless police force which works at the direction of the G-2 Section of the American GHQ and Syngman Rhee...Korean prisons are now fuller of political prisoners than under Japanese rule.' He added disquietingly: 'The torture and murder of the political enemies of the extreme Right is apparently an accepted and commonplace thing.' The two outstanding South Korean nationalist leaders who were opponents of Rhee, Yŏ Un-hyŏng and Kim Koo, were both murdered. Yŏ had struggled since 1945 to build a broad, unified nationalist front. The price of his attempt to reach accommodation with the north was an assassin's bullet. The same fate befell Kim, a staunch nationalist who opposed the division of Korea and was dogged by charges of being soft on communism. It is no wonder that inside the British Consulate, Rhee was regarded as 'a dangerous fascist, or lunatic'; and no wonder that the US State Department opposed his entry into Korea in 1945.

Rhee was, however, MacArthur's man. And there was nothing even-handed about the United States' occupation of southern Korea. By its single-minded pursuit of its own strategic and ideological objectives, it facilitated the conditions that allowed Rhee's brand of right-wing extremism to prosper. The determination of Hodge and the stubbornness of Rhee led to personal differences between them, but Hodge ensured that he achieved what he had come to Korea to do, regardless of the longer-term consequences. And in 1948, when Rhee was made president of the newly founded southern state known as the Republic of Korea, Hodge and MacArthur stood proudly beside him on the platform—as if it were mission accomplished. In truth a fundamentally corrupt and authoritarian society had been created. Out of expedience and self-interest, the Americans had transferred power to a conservative faction led by men who, to use Hastings' words again, were 'willing tools of a tyranny that a world war had just been fought to destroy'. By June 1949 the last of Hodge's XXIV Corps had departed, leaving the Korean tinderbox to ignite at the least spark. Peace was not in prospect; polarisation had merely sharpened.

Northern Korea

In northern Korea, the Soviet military occupation did not encounter the same difficulties or the degree of hostility and turmoil that the American administration endured in the south. To start with, the opposition was weaker and the Russians were better prepared. Russia's immediate strategic concern in northern Korea was to exclude Japan from its border, but its occupation was also built on a deeply felt historical foundation. Stalin had a longstanding desire to control territory that had been contested in the Russo-Japanese War (1904–05). The old wounds were apparent in his speech on the occasion of Japan's formal surrender, when he declaimed that:

> The defeat of Russian troops in the period of the Russo-
> Japanese War left grave memories in the minds of our
> people. It fell as a dark stain on our country. Our people
> trusted and awaited the day when Japan would be routed
> and the stain wiped out. For forty years we, the men of the
> older generation, have waited for this day. And now this day
> has come.

In occupation, the Russians behaved as they had in Eastern Europe, seizing industrial centres, mines, hydro-electric plants and transportation assets, most of which were in the mountainous regions of northern Korea where eighty per cent of the country's heavy industries and mineral resources were located. A feast of reparations was shipped back to industrial centres in the Maritime Province and Siberia—whole factories, machine tools, coal, minerals and lumber, even telegraph poles.

A singular aspect of the Russian occupation of the north—one of many features distinguishing it from the American occupation of the south—was the presence with the Soviet army of a special political detachment from Headquarters, 1st Far Eastern Front. Its task was to organise political development within the occupation zone. In carrying out its objective, it was assisted by the mobilisation and return to northern Korea of large numbers of ethnic Koreans who had been forcibly re-settled in the Soviet interior, particularly in Uzbekistan and Kazakhstan, following Japan's invasion of China in 1937. This pool of Soviet Koreans was a valuable human resource whose members were already Soviet citizens, usually committed communists and generally spoke both Korean and Russian. One former official called them 'the translators' and said they were 'powerful ambassadors of Soviet Army Headquarters'.

Another factor that made the northern occupation easier was the departure of hundreds of thousands of potential opponents of Soviet rule who fled south—Christians, Japanese collaborators, landowners and other political and economic refugees. In July 1947 the *New York Times* put the figure, somewhat excitedly, at 'nearly two million'. A more reliable estimate is probably 700,000 to 800,000 between August 1945 and September 1948. It is impossible to know, but whatever the correct number, there was undoubtedly a convenient exodus of a substantial number of opponents of the regime, which the Russian occupying force naturally welcomed.

While General Hodge's administration in the south was unable to communicate in the Korean language; declined to use or recognise any existing Korean parties or politicians; rebuffed the people's committees;

and outlawed the Korean People's Republic; the Russians were inclusive, at least initially, only excluding from political life those who had actively collaborated with the Japanese. They turned the all-party Korean councils, local governing groups and people's committees 'into core institutions of the pro-Soviet regime'. And although the Russian troops behaved badly on arrival, as was their habit, Stalin moved to stop the rape and pillage. He ordered the commander of the Soviet occupation force to 'give instructions to the troops in northern Korea to strictly observe discipline, not offend the population, and conduct themselves properly'. To ensure compliance, the military police were given orders to shoot on sight 'any Russian soldier caught raping a Korean'. Allegedly there was a marked improvement in discipline. In the result, Korean resistance to the Russian occupation was remarkably short-lived—despite the extensive requisitioning of rice and food supplies and the divestment of property that was placed under the protection of the Soviet military power.

Kim Il-sung

As the Americans had done in the south, so the Soviet authorities did in the north. They brought in an expatriate political leader. Several candidates were considered, including Cho Man-sik, a devout Christian and nationalist who commanded great respect among the people and was known as the 'Korean Ghandi'. The ultimate winner, however, was the Manchurian candidate, Kim Il-sung. Stalin had some involvement in the selection—certainly he disapproved of some candidates and endorsed Kim, who was not the grey-haired veteran that the public expected. Their initial reaction when Kim appeared at a rally in Pyongyang in October 1945 was not favourable. But the Soviet authorities remained firm and, according to one account, afterwards 'placed enormous emphasis on improving Kim's image through propaganda activities'.

The truth about Kim's birth and antecedents is now obscured beneath a smokescreen of legend, hagiography and propaganda. Much of it is recent invention or enthusiastic romanticisation. Some facts are tolerably clear. He was born in 1912 near Pyongyang and spent the first thirty-three years of his life under Japanese colonial rule. From the age of thirteen, he chose a life of exile in Manchuria. By the early 1930s he was thoroughly radicalised, living a difficult and dangerous life as a guerrilla in the Kapsan mountains of Manchuria, where his band supported the Chinese in their struggle against the Japanese. By 1936 he had effectively become the leader of the Korean communists in eastern Manchuria. And for a brief time in 1940, he was the most wanted guerrilla in the region, with a price of 200,000 yen on his head. By 1942 he had been inducted into the Soviet army and was a captain in the Soviet 88th Brigade based at Khabarovsk, 800 kilometres north of Vladivostok, where his unit carried out clandestine reconnaissance and infiltration operations into Japanese-controlled areas.

By the time of the Japanese surrender, Kim was a Korean nationalist and a Soviet loyalist, steeled by conflict and struggle. When he arrived in northern Korea in late September 1945 he did not come down out of the hills, but disembarked with about sixty of his band of brothers from the Russian ship the *Pugachev* at Wonsan harbour on Korea's east coast. He was greeted personally by General Chistiakov, the commander of the Soviet occupation army. This was enough to excite attention but a few weeks later there were other indications of his destiny. At Kim's first public appearance in October, he was introduced by the venerable Cho Man-sik and appeared on the podium with a parade of the most senior officers in the Soviet occupation army. Chistiakov championed Kim and soon tired of Cho, whose protection of Christianity, civil liberties and property rights made him an unlikely candidate for Soviet preferment. In February 1946 Cho was sent to jail, where he remained, and Chistiakov installed Kim as head of the first centralised administration in northern Korea, the Interim People's Committee.

Under Kim's leadership, and Chistiakov's supervision, the Committee quickly went to work—nationalising banks and Japanese-owned industries and publishing a reform plan that involved the confiscation and re-distribution of land, the forgiveness of debt and the lowering of taxes. Things moved so rapidly that within a year, allowing for those who had fled south, 'almost every adult northern Korean had found a place in the all-embracing socialist system, as party members or belonging to party auxiliary associations'. Kim was now firmly in power in a society that was tightly controlled and where the contours of the future North Korean regime had already begun to take shape. And like his counterpart in southern Korea, he harboured a conviction to unify the country by whatever means necessary.

CHAPTER 4

Two States Emerge

'The agony of separation is the human agony'

Once in place, the partition along the 38th parallel rapidly became intractable. Military severance transformed itself into political division, which hardened and embedded opposing antipathies, ensuring that there would be no going back on the peninsula. Roosevelt's trusteeship principle was an early casualty. It was nominally revived in Moscow in December 1945 at a meeting of foreign ministers of the United States, the United Kingdom and the Soviet Union. But although the meeting produced the high-sounding 'Moscow declaration' in favour of the international trusteeship of Korea, it was a vastly different story on the ground. The Soviet and American occupation commands encouraged the consolidation of their own client governments, ensuring that the implementation of the principle of trusteeship and unified national government would be impractical. It never really had a chance.

Trusteeship Abandoned

The Moscow declaration proposed a joint commission of Soviet and American occupation representatives to formulate recommendations for establishing a single national interim government. It would be overseen by an international trustee group for a period of up to five years. The suggested trustees included the Soviet Union, the United Kingdom and the United States. Molotov, the Russian Foreign Minister, conducted the meeting at the Spirodonovka Palace in Moscow in a manner that was said to be 'keen, ruthless and incisive', but he probably knew that the proposal was a pipe dream. The United Kingdom agreed but would have preferred not to be involved and gave notice that it might wish to substitute Australia. The United States also agreed but the proposal was doomed, in part because it never enjoyed the support of General Hodge and his US occupation command in Korea, let alone of the War Office. Hodge's political advisor in Korea even wrote to the Secretary of State saying, 'I am unable to fit trusteeship to the actual conditions here or to be persuaded of its sustainability from moral and practical standpoints and therefore believe we should drop it.' It is clear that, whatever was meant by 'moral standpoints', the American military in Korea did not want the complication or the uncertainty of trusteeship, let alone the practical risk of a left-leaning government of the country as a whole. The only remedy that Hodge wanted was an independent, right-wing government in southern Korea.

The initial reaction of Koreans on all sides was to greet the Moscow declaration with loud, unanimous and horrified protests. They regarded it as delaying independence and amounting to political tutelage. But there was a Machiavellian twist in early January 1946 when the Soviet leadership in northern Korea unexpectedly decided to support the Moscow declaration. Like Hodge, they could no doubt see where interim national government and trusteeship might lead. The issue became highly charged—support for the Moscow declaration became a matter of party loyalty for those on the left; and opposition became an article of faith for moderates and those on the right. General Hodge knew trusteeship would undermine his objective, and he even 'stepped out of bounds of his authority' by openly siding with the right in its opposition to the Moscow declaration.

It is no surprise that the Joint Commission meetings dissolved into unrepentant discord. At a general level, there was some force in the Soviet denunciation of the American position as not being in accordance with the aims and spirit of the Moscow declaration. But General Shtykov, Stalin's newly appointed mastermind in northern Korea, overplayed his hand when he insisted that there should be no consultation with groups that opposed the Moscow declaration. He knew that this would exclude all right-wing and moderate groups in the south. Hodge also went too far on other issues but the reality was that the American delegation had little interest in reaching agreement on an interim national government.

When the first meeting of the Joint Commission reached gridlock in March 1946, the process of negotiation was suspended and the path to permanent division appeared more certain than ever. Hodge and his occupation command held firmly to the view, contrary to the State Department, that the Moscow declaration was unworkable. They were convinced that only the establishment of a separate state of 'South Korea' would give Koreans 'the independence they wanted while shielding [them] from the ruthless political machinery of the north'. This stance, part ideological and part pragmatic, was the first clear step toward the later reality of separate states. From Hodge's perspective, a separate state in southern Korea would serve American interests and strategic objectives, while a unified independent government of the whole of the country, with or without trustees, would be impossible to control and ran the risk of being aligned with Russian interests.

In the autumn of 1946 the political stalemate over the future of Korea led to a mushrooming of violence, recrimination and industrial discord in the south, directed against the American military government and those who worked for it. It was known as the Autumn Rebellion. Hodge believed that communists had instigated the troubles. He declared martial law and many thousands of alleged leftists were arrested. When order was restored 'policemen and their rightist allies exacted revenge'. Syngman Rhee now contended that reconciliation with the north was impossible. He actively petitioned for a separate government in Seoul; publicly repudiated the Moscow declaration; described the administration in northern Korea as 'smallpox'; and stated emphatically that he would not unite with the 'Reds'. Although the State Department still clung to the principle of trusteeship with the objective of achieving unified national government, it was becoming increasingly obvious there was force in Hodge's view that this goal was untenable. In December Hodge created a Korean Interim Legislative Assembly, whose laws were to apply only in the American zone. But it achieved nothing other than to reinforce the separateness of the south.

In 1947 the Joint Commission met again, only to repeat the process of ineluctable disputation. At its third and final meeting in September, Shtykov made a surprising proposal. He said the Korean people should be given the opportunity of forming their own government, and that Russian troops would be withdrawn from the north if US troops were withdrawn from the south. This seemingly reasonable decision was unpalatable to Washington for the unstated but fundamental reason that it provided no guarantee that the outcome would be a Korean regime supportive of the strategic objectives of the United States. Indeed, there was a reasonable likelihood that such a regime would not be supportive, at least initially, and that it might well be aligned with Soviet Russia. But America's dilemma was based on self-interest, not the natural desire of the people of Korea for their own independence.

The UN Election

In October 1947, the United States decided to transfer responsibility for the Korean issue to the General Assembly of the United Nations. It blamed Soviet duplicity but both were at fault. On 14 November the General Assembly resolved to establish a United Nations Temporary Commission on Korea to facilitate, expedite and observe the election of representatives to a national assembly, which would then convene and form a 'National Government' of Korea. Paragraph 5 of the resolution made clear that its object was 'the attainment of the national independence of Korea' and the 'withdrawal of occupying forces'. The proposal seemed anodyne and it was not difficult to obtain general support for it despite Soviet opposition. But in reality it was a hopeless cause and Washington appears to have known it, regardless of its ritual incantations about the establishment of a united and independent Korea. The opportunity for a unified, independent Korea had already been lost and American support for the resolution was not what it seemed.

When the delegates of the Commission arrived in Seoul in January 1948, they were denied permission to enter the north. Tellingly, President Truman had anticipated this outcome and expected that the work of the delegates would 'be confined to Southern Korea'. He had said so to the Canadian Prime Minister on 5 January. His true objective, and the only thing he knew the Commission could practically achieve, was the validation of a separate state in southern Korea that would be supportive of the United States.

As the Commission was unable to travel, observe and consult throughout Korea, as it was required to do, it concluded that it could not achieve its mandate to facilitate a 'national Korean government'. The chairman of the Commission was K.P.S. Menon, an Oxford-educated Indian diplomat and India's first Foreign Secretary. He was the antithesis of General Hodge and did not share his US-centric bias, at least in relation to the Korean situation. And he was unaware of Truman's pessimistic expectations and could not have known of his guile. Menon developed a deep attachment to Korea, writing with feeling in his autobiography some years later that:

> If the Koreans were tenacious of independence, they
> were equally tenacious of their unity. Nothing was more
> remarkable than the homogeneity of the Korean nation.
> They belonged to the same race, spoke the same language
> and were proud of the same traditions...until recently
> the terms 'North Korea' and 'South Korea' were simply
> unknown. Providence meant Korea to be one. The North
> could not live without the South, nor could the South
> without the North...Korea was thus indivisible, whether
> one looked at the problem from an economic, political or
> historical point of view.

In his report to the Interim Committee of the General Assembly, Menon pointed out with considerable justification that 'the formation of a separate government in south Korea will not facilitate the twin objectives laid down in paragraph 5 of the resolution, namely the attainment of the national independence of Korea and the withdrawal of the occupying troops'. He added that 'it [would] be unrealistic to treat any scheme of election in south Korea, even though that scheme may apply theoretically to all Korea, as national'.

This was correct but it was not what Washington wanted to hear. It ignored Menon's considered opinion and the near unanimous concerns of his colleagues and haughtily dismissed Menon as leftist or untrustworthy for no sound reason other than that his views were unpalatable. Its response was to invest much back-room effort in an attempt to influence the Interim Committee to compel the Commission to proceed, regardless of the practical impossibility of conducting or observing elections in the north. Its self-interested object was to keep alive the contemplated process of supervised elections in the south, even though national elections for the whole of Korea were not feasible. By this means, it hoped to validate the right-wing regime that it had put in place in southern Korea. The pressure on the Interim Committee, which was orchestrated by the Republican consultant to the State Department, John Foster Dulles, succeeded. Menon said that soon after he submitted his report, the United States 'introduced a resolution leading to the establishment of a separate sovereign state in South Korea' and 'brought considerable pressure to bear on the members of the UN'. It was, he said painfully, the 'first formal step towards the division of Korea'.

On 26 February 1948 the Interim Committee ordered the Commission to implement the program for the supervision and observation of elections 'in such parts of Korea as are accessible to the Commission'. All knew that this meant only southern Korea. Menon was right. It was another step toward cementing the division of Korea, as Truman appears to have foreseen, Hodge always wanted and Dulles well knew. But there was resistance from an unexpected quarter. On 11 March the members of the Commission voted on whether they would comply with the directive of the Interim Committee. Despite 'sustained United States pressure', the Australian and Canadian representatives voted against implementation of the Interim Committee's directive.

Their principled stance was based on the contention that an election that only took place in the south would not advance the cause of Korean unification and would be boycotted by all but the extreme right. They were correct, of course. But Korean unification was not really the American objective, despite token acknowledgement. Hodge, Dulles and Truman had a different agenda. This was made pellucid when Hodge ludicrously denounced the Australian and Canadian representatives for 'general appeasement of Soviet Russia' and for 'not understanding the bitter cold war against communism'. But the Australians and Canadians were a minority on the Commission and their protest had no practical effect. Even the Chairman, K.P.S. Menon, felt obliged to accept the directive of the Interim Committee.

So a limited election was scheduled for May. Rhee supported it enthusiastically but it encountered broad-based opposition within Korea. Everyone could see what would happen. With the exception of Rhee, the most prominent leaders in southern Korea, including conservatives, wrote to Kim Il-sung to propose a political dialogue between north and south. A 'North–South Political Leaders Coalition Conference' was arranged for April. The Australian and Canadian representatives on the Commission supported it. So did 'a majority of the public, intellectuals (including 108 well-known writers and journalists) and newspapers'. General Hodge denounced the conference as a communist plot, as did Rhee. But the conference went ahead and hundreds of delegates from the north and south attended. Their joint declaration at the conclusion of the conference called for the formation of a united government and the withdrawal of all foreign troops; specifically rejected 'dictatorship and monopoly capitalism'; and stressed the conference's opposition to separate elections. It added one item that should have sounded a warning of things to come: 'separate elections in South Korea, if held, cannot express in any way the will of our nation, and will be regarded as a fraud.'

Despite rational objection and popular opposition, the United States would not be deterred. Its determination to proceed with separate elections in the south was forged by what Hastings decried as an American policy in postwar Korea that 'reflected not only a lack of understanding, but a lack of interest in the country and its people, beyond their potential as bricks in the wall against communist aggression'. At the election on 10 May, only candidates loyal to Rhee or his future deputy participated and they won 190 of the 198 seats. The poll was accompanied by what has been described as 'a campaign of officially sponsored violence and intimidation that saw 589 people killed'. Another historian wrote bluntly: 'Rhee's police goons used considerable brutality to rig the outcome of elections, which the opposition boycotted.' A significant proportion of the nationalist right, as well as those on the left, boycotted the election. They contended, with good reason, that the election would perpetuate the division of the nation. None of the Commission members regarded the outcome as having established a Korean national parliament. And the Australian government pronounced itself 'far from satisfied' with the election, a view that it communicated to the US Secretary of State.

For the next seven weeks until 25 June, argument and counter-argument took place about the validity, propriety and legitimacy of the election and whether it should be recognised and validated. Throughout the debate, and despite the reservations, there was 'continuing United States pressure' to approve the election result. Ultimately, but only in the absence of the Australian delegate who had been instructed to absent himself in protest, agreement was reached to declare the election 'a valid expression of the free will of the electorate in those parts of Korea which were accessible to the Commission'. This unsatisfactory compromise was an effective acknowledgement of the point made by the Australian government that 'the government as now constituted in Seoul cannot be regarded as the government envisaged in the resolution of the General Assembly of 14 November 1947'.

It was not a 'National Government' and would not further 'the national independence of Korea', as the General Assembly's resolution contemplated. The British Consul-General in Seoul was also troubled, writing of 'the difficulty of blessing as the government of Korea a body which manifestly has neither title to represent the people north of the

38th parallel, nor any authority over them'. And the Foreign Office in Whitehall thought that unqualified recognition would be 'both foolish and improper'. Humorously, in retrospect, Hodge complained of 'pettifogging obstruction where it was least expected, the British Empire'.

As far as Washington was concerned, the equivocal language was sufficient to achieve its ends and events now moved quickly. The elected representatives from the south were constituted as a national assembly, a constitution was drawn up and Rhee was elected as chairman. On 12 August the United States hurriedly recognised the new body in Seoul as the national assembly and national government, which had been envisaged in the 1947 United Nations resolution, even though it patently was not.

On 15 August the newly founded state known as the 'Republic of Korea' was proclaimed and Rhee was inaugurated as its president. Ominously, his first statement was bellicose and provocative— immediately announcing that his mission was to reunify the peninsula. And on 12 December the United Nations General Assembly agreed to a masterpiece of compromise and obfuscation. It acknowledged that the objectives of its November 1947 resolution had not been accomplished, namely that the 'national independence' of Korea had not been established, but it resolved to give the government in Seoul qualified recognition as 'having effective control and jurisdiction over that part of Korea where the Temporary Commission was able to observe and consult'.

Two Separate States

Almost simultaneously in northern Korea, a parallel state quietly came into existence, with significantly less discord but without the imprimatur of the United Nations. Its emergence provided a study in contrasts: 'a cohesive, peaceful, and highly disciplined North against the increasingly chaotic, violent, and unstable South'. The path to statehood in northern Korea started when the many local people's committees appointed a Convention of People's Committees that met in Pyongyang in 1947. The Convention set up a further body known as the Supreme People's Assembly, which approved a constitution based on that of the Soviet Union in April 1948. And on 25 August voting took place in what was said to be a national general election, and 212 members were elected to the Assembly. The figures lack independent verification but an election of some sort was undoubtedly held.

On 9 September the 'Democratic People's Republic of Korea' was proclaimed and Kim Il-sung was named as premier—a title that he held for many years until he became president under a new constitution. The North Korean army, known as the Korean People's Army, with many returned veterans who had fought in China's civil war, had been established earlier in the year. In December the Soviet occupation army withdrew and never returned, as did many, but not all, Soviet advisors. A contemporary report from the British Foreign Office remarked on North Korea's relative autonomy, stating that it had 'an apparent similarity to the more autonomous western Communist states such as Yugoslavia'.

After their establishment within weeks of each other, each of the southern and northern republics soon became a recognisable sovereign state. Each government exercised effective rule over its respective area, north or south of the 38th parallel, although both expectantly professed to exercise dominion over the territory of the other. The rule of each was treated by its respective population as being the sole source of civil and military authority in the area that it controlled. And both entered into diplomatic relations with other sovereign states. For some years, international recognition of both states was poisoned by the politics of the period—withheld or bestowed depending on cold war allegiances. But the existence of a state depends on the practical realities of control and jurisdiction over a defined area, not the political preferences of other nations. Nor does it depend on whether one election was sponsored by the United Nations and the other was not.

North Korea was therefore a sovereign state. It is now recognised as such by most countries. The United States and South Korea are notable exceptions. But the issue is one of fact not ideology. And America's continuing non-recognition is a testament to the parallel universe of its own domestic politics. Nor does it matter that such a state, whether recognised or not, may have territorial aspirations more extensive than the reality of its current domain. Only the realities are decisive. The King of England's claim to be ruler of France, for example, did not make the Battle of Agincourt part of a civil war.

A State of Warfare

The sad outcome was that three years after the military partition, the foreign policy of the United States, with Soviet concurrence, had succeeded in dividing the nation. The military partition became an effective international border and the former single state was cleaved into two rival republics. Before 1945, a Korean war was inconceivable. After 1945, it was inevitable. Both Kim Il-sung and Syngman Rhee were intent on unification by force. By 1948, a state of incipient warfare existed on the peninsula.

Hostilities started well before the formal invasion in June 1950. For much of the previous year, both sides had been feinting, thrusting and skirmishing in both directions across the parallel. And not all of them were mere raids. In May 1949, the south initiated a battle at Kaesong that lasted four days and took an official toll of 400 North Korean and twenty-two South Korean soldiers, as well as civilians. In late June, the north was responsible for heavy fighting on the Ongin peninsula. Only a fortnight earlier, the South Korean commander had told United Nations observers that 'the moment of major battles is rapidly approaching'. In early August 1949, more than 4000 North Korean border-guard soldiers attacked with artillery and mortar fire South Korean units that were occupying a small mountain north of the 38th parallel. The American ambassador Muccio said that the southern forces were 'completely routed'. And in late August, the south boldly sent several naval patrol boats up the Taedong River, 'sinking four North Korean ships in the 35 to 45-ton class'.

The British complained that the South Korean commanders' heads 'are full of ideas of recovering the North by conquest'. And the Americans were constantly warning the Rhee administration that a northward attack 'would result in the stoppage of American aid [and] the withdrawal of the

Military Mission'. As the 1949 border fighting died down, Syngman Rhee and Kim Il-sung looked to their big-power guarantors. Kim itched to invade and hoped for a clear southern provocation, while hotheads in the south hoped to provoke an 'unprovoked' assault in order to ensure American military assistance. It was a case of waiting to see who would move first. In January 1950, Kim finally twisted the arm of a cautious and reluctant Stalin. He decided to move first.

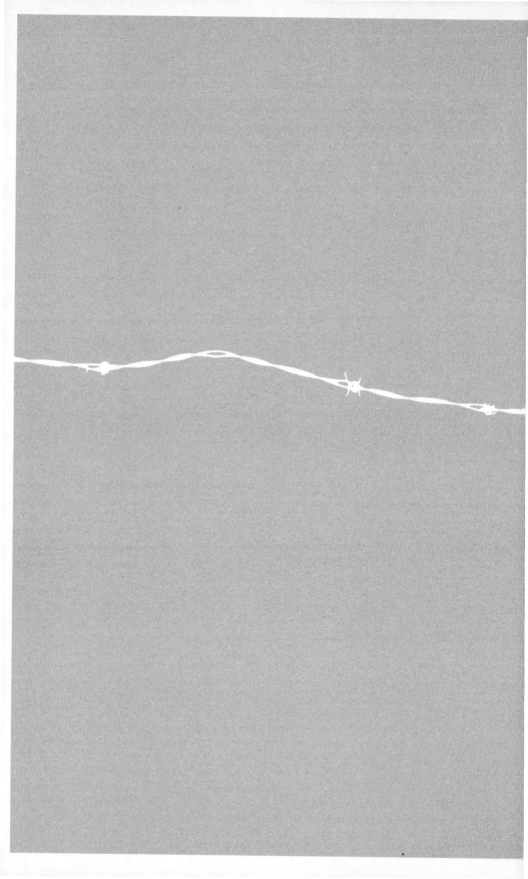

PART 3

China Goes to War

CHAPTER 5

Power Play

'And in their greed they will exploit you with false words'

Until January 1950 there was no hint of any Soviet interest in military expansion on the Korean peninsula. Quite the reverse. A Russian Foreign Ministry report in 1945 made clear that although Moscow did not want Korea to be in hostile hands, it did not seek annexation of the peninsula. Its sole aspiration then was that any government established in Korea have 'friendly and close relations' with Soviet Russia. The report stated that 'the independence of Korea must be effective enough to prevent Korea being turned into a staging ground for future aggression against the USSR, not only from Japan, but also from any other power'. This explains why Stalin accepted Roosevelt's proposal for trusteeship of Korea and subsequently agreed to the American proposal for partition, even though at the time the Soviet Army was well able to take control of the whole country without opposition.

Russian Enigma

Stalin's early conciliatory attitude to the American occupation was a source of frustration for Korean communists in the south, who were agitating in late 1945 for recognition of the Korean Communist Party in Seoul. Stalin would not permit any intervention on their behalf. Instead, the Soviet occupation command issued a punctilious instruction to the southern communists to cooperate with American authorities in their sector because 'The ideals of the United States, the leader of capitalism, and the Soviet Union, the fatherland of the proletariat, are to be expressed in Korea without contradiction'.

Stalin's conundrum was that while he had no desire to extend control into southern Korea, the fervently nationalistic northern Korean communists under Kim Il-sung were determined to reunify the country. From 1947 virtually every one of their communications to Moscow referred to Korea's eventual reunification—in language that was inevitably ardent and always imploring. Stalin was caught by his own rhetoric. The doublespeak of his support for trusteeship, with its implied commitment to unification and independence, was adopted by the leadership in Pyongyang to push for Russian support to achieve by force a goal that he did not really desire.

By late 1948, when separate Korean republics were inaugurated, the practical likelihood of peacefully establishing a unified government for the entire country had disappeared from sight. The United States and Soviet Russia had built, funded and armed compliant states. The oft-stated political objective of the complete independence and unity of Korea was no longer realistic. In March 1949, six months after the establishment of the Democratic People's Republic of Korea, Kim made his way to Moscow. Following a week of economic and trade negotiations, he addressed his primary goal—securing Stalin's approval and assistance for his planned military conquest to reunify the peninsula.

Stalin was less than enthusiastic. He feared military conflict with the United States and wished to avoid it at all costs. His interest had only ever been the strategic and economic significance of northern Korea as a security buffer and as a source of resources. He told Kim in no uncertain terms that he should not advance to the south, expressing a concern that the Americans might intervene, especially if 'the agreement on the 38th parallel is broken by our side'. He did give some hope to Kim though, telling him that if the adversary starts the aggression, a counter-attack 'will be understood and supported by everyone'. Stalin was not the only one to believe that Rhee's forces would be the first to attack. Certainly, the volatile Rhee constantly said he would do so. And in April, Stalin expressed concern to Shtykov, his ambassador in Pyongyang, that the purpose of the proposed American troop withdrawal in 1949 was 'to give freedom of action to the South Korean Army'.

Stalin's expectation was wrong but his interest in a possible confrontation with the south, so long as the involvement of the United States could be avoided, appears to have been piqued. Nevertheless, he remained cautious for the rest of 1949—refusing to approve a proposed limited pre-emptive campaign on the Ongjin peninsula on the west coast; not wishing to give the Americans 'cause for interference'; rebuking Shtykov for allowing Kim's army to launch dangerous border skirmish attacks; and expressing concern that any provocation might 'induce the adversary to launch a big war'.

Kim bombarded Stalin with no less than forty-eight telegrams appealing for a decision. Eventually, in response to yet another pleading request, the Soviet leader replied on 30 January 1950 saying that he was ready to help—as a facilitator, not an initiator—and that he would receive Kim in Moscow to discuss it. His change of heart coincided with a visit to Moscow by Mao Zedong, with whom Stalin had decided to conclude a new Sino-Soviet Treaty of Friendship. Mao departed in late February after a marathon visit and Kim followed him to Moscow on 30 March and stayed until 25 April. Kim was so excited that he said he had trouble sleeping. He presented what he called the 'Korean People's Army Pre-emptive Strike Plan'. It envisaged a swift surprise attack lasting only a few weeks. Stalin approved the plan and encouraged Kim's initiative, advising him of the need for thorough preparation and the necessity to form 'elite attack divisions'. He also counselled him on the importance of the North Korean army having 'more weapons, more mechanised means of movement and combat' and promised him that 'Your request in this respect will be fully satisfied.' He was referring among other things to the Russian T-34, the legendary tank that stunned the Wehrmacht during World War II.

Stalin now crucially believed that the United States was unlikely to intervene. And he thought the victory of Mao's communists in

China had improved the international environment because 'China is no longer busy with internal fighting and can devote its attention to the assistance of Korea'. He remained wary, however, even worried, about possible conflict with the United States and stated bluntly to Kim that there would be no direct Soviet participation. He told him that he should seek Mao's approval, adding coldly, 'If you should get kicked in the teeth, I shall not lift a finger.' Stalin's support for Kim, which was at first reluctant, was now cautious and qualified. He was opportunistic and mendacious but he did not intend to make it Moscow's war, let alone a war for all Asia.

American Anxiety

In contrast, when Truman received the news of the North Korean invasion at home in Missouri on a Saturday night, he had no doubt that it was Moscow's war. He concluded immediately and emphatically that Soviet Russia had passed beyond subversion and was now prepared to engage in armed invasion and war; that North Korea's war for reunification was the prelude to a general Soviet offensive in East Asia; and that 'If we let Korea down, the Soviet army will keep on going and swallow up one piece of Asia after another'. Russian experts in the State Department had their doubts about that, as did the Joint Chiefs, but when Truman gathered his senior advisors around him on the Sunday night in Washington, no one disagreed. George Kennan, the pre-eminent Soviet expert in the State Department and soon to be the ambassador in Moscow, was excluded from the decision-making process. As the American historian Clay Blair observed:

> All the prior policies set forth in various position papers, reached after years of careful study—that South Korea was of little strategic importance and should not be a casus belli—were summarily dismissed. On 24 June 1950, South Korea had suddenly become an area of vital importance, not strategically or militarily...but psychologically and symbolically.

58

This was not a case of sleepwalking into war; it was a case of embracing an opportunity for war with gusto. Not for the first or last time, the United States 'impulsively attributed earth-shattering significance to a development of middling importance'. The provenance of this overreaction lay in the progressive deterioration in relations with Soviet Russia that had occurred since the end of World War II. And it was fuelled by a pervasive anti-communist sentiment, akin to a faith-based movement, that permeated all levels of American society. By the time of Senator Joseph McCarthy's famously incendiary speech at Wheeling, West Virginia, in February 1950, Stalin, the wartime ally of Roosevelt, had become Truman's implacable enemy. Distrust rushed headlong into outright hostility. Apprehension of Soviet intentions, at all levels of society, became dangerously overwrought. But as Secretary of State Dean Acheson later ruefully conceded, 'We overreacted to Stalin, which in turn caused him to overreact.'

The spiral of deterioration in the once cooperative relationship had its origins in February 1946 at Moscow's Bolshoi Theatre. Amid continuous cries of 'Cheers for great Stalin', the Russian President gave a nationally broadcast election speech designed to mobilise the public for the Herculean effort of recovery and re-building after the loss and devastation of the war—the 'Great Patriotic War', as World War II in Europe was known. Russia had been almost ruined and famine threatened—'about half of the country had been destroyed by the Germans; everything: buildings, railways, highways, everything'. Stalin told his audience, somewhat improbably, that the Soviet victory refuted assertions of Western economic superiority and demonstrated that 'the Soviet social system has proved to be more viable and stable than the non-Soviet social system...a better form of organisation of society'. He did not rest with this extravagant contention, however, for Stalin knew that the people and the party required more 'than happy talk about the virtues of the Soviet system' to sustain their faith in his leadership. He needed the perception of a hostile world to legitimise his autocratic rule.

Stalin's method was to play on the traditional and instinctive Russian sense of insecurity. His rhetoric, sprinkled with references to capitalist encirclement, and predicated on a native fear of the outside world, was underlined by an attitude of total suspicion toward the motives of the West. Stalin emphasised that the capitalist development of the world economy made war inevitable; that Soviet Russia must prepare to defend the Motherland; and that the Russian people must gird themselves for more austerity. Alarmingly for Washington, he also signalled that he would not allow the United States to maintain its monopoly on the atomic bomb. Another speaker even declared improbably, 'All those who may think of organising new war against the Soviet Union should remember that it is already a mighty power.'

In reality, the Russians 'were in no position to fight a new war, nor did they want to'. Stalin's rhetoric was overblown. Despite his florid language, he was determined to avoid being drawn into conflict with the United States: 'Stalin [unlike Hitler] did not intend to conquer other parts of the world...his military activities were just defensive.' The core belief in Washington at the time, that the Soviet Union would resort to military conquest to impose its absolute authority over the rest of the world, was misplaced. George Kennan well understood this. He knew that at the 'bottom of the Kremlin's neurotic view of world affairs is the traditional sense of insecurity' and that Soviet Russia's territorial ambitions were limited and defensive, unlike those of Nazi Germany. He understood that Stalin's behaviour, like that of the tsars before him, reflected the 'fears, paranoia and isolation from neighbours that had been so much a part of the country's past' and that the vast Soviet army would not invade anyone. The foreign correspondent Henry Lieberman put it well in the *New York Times Magazine* on New Year's Day in 1950, explaining that Soviet foreign policy was essentially subversive and 'may be summarised as an effort to achieve without war, certain objectives of a kind traditionally achieved by war'.

Others in Washington saw it differently. For them, Stalin's speech was a 'delayed declaration of war on the United States'. Unwittingly, Kennan played into the hands of those in Washington who now regarded Russia as a dangerous adversary. His secret cable in February 1946, known to history as the 'Long Telegram', is possibly the most famous diplomatic cable of all time. Its length (over 5000 words) was part of the problem. Kennan relished the opportunity to state his position, but his prolixity and colourful turns of phrase caused misunderstanding. In melodramatic language, he described Soviet Russia as 'a political force committed fanatically to the belief that with the US there can be no permanent modus vivendi'. He recommended a policy of containment 'by the adroit and vigilant application of counter-force at a series of constantly shifting geographical and political points'. What Kennan did not make obvious was that he favoured containment by political and economic methods rather than by the use of military force; and that in his view Russia had no intention of attacking the United States.

Some saw in the cable what they wanted, not what was intended. When it was substantially re-published in 1947 in *Foreign Affairs* magazine, Kennan's voice carried and his reputation was made—for the wrong reasons. He lived till the age of 101 and was hailed as America's most famous diplomat but never ceased to regret how his words were seized upon by those who favoured a militarist and confrontational approach to Soviet Russia. Kennan mused, 'My thoughts about containment were of course distorted by people who understood and pursued it exclusively as a military concept.' He lamented repeatedly that 'it was absurd to suppose that [the Soviets] were going to turn around and attack the United States'. In his view, the basic error was to assume that Stalin was committed to global military conquest. He called it 'a very serious and inexcusable error of policy, of thinking, on the part of the people in our government'.

But Kennan was too elliptical, his thinking too subtle, for most Americans, who were inclined to treat pronouncements from Moscow literally. This was especially true of President Truman who hated communists and had a simpler, more robust view of the world. Kennan knew, but others in Washington could not comprehend, that 'Stalin saw anti-capitalist talk as essential to internal Soviet stability', and that for Russians 'the deepest of their convictions is that things are not what they are, but only what they seem'.

The inflammatory corollary to Stalin's speech was Truman's own nationally broadcast address to a joint sitting of Congress on 12 March 1947. It served to amplify antipathy toward Soviet Russia and added to a growing siege mentality in the United States. The context hardly seems to have justified Truman's alarmism. Greece had requested assistance in its civil war against what Truman called 'the terrorist activities of several thousand armed men led by communists'; and Turkey was locked in an ongoing dispute with Soviet Russia over shipping access through the Turkish Straits between the Black Sea and the Mediterranean. In language that was both 'apocalyptic' and 'grandiose and sweeping', Truman intimated that Western civilisation was imperilled. He coupled a request for Congressional funding of $400 million for Greece and Turkey with a breathtaking and open-ended promise 'to support free peoples who are resisting subjugation by armed minorities or by outside pressures'—wherever they were. This single sentence became the 'Truman Doctrine'. It rang in the cold war and marked the beginning of a dangerous foreign policy, fostering a climate of intolerance and encouraging a world view of undifferentiated communism.

Kennan was unhappy at Truman's broad and uncertain commitment and thought his speech unwise, excessive and unrealistic. But his own coldly rational assessment that the Soviet threat was chiefly political and subversive—not openly militaristic—was lost beneath an avalanche of fear and suspicion. Truman's uncomplicated view was that 'the Soviet Union was trying to take over the world' and that Soviet expansionism represented a global challenge for the West. For him, memories of the appeasement of Hitler at Munich seemed too compelling to ignore. But the analogy was unsound. And Acheson, who became Secretary of State in 1949, shared Truman's views and had been the principal drafter of his address to Congress. Truman and Acheson were both wrong, but by 1950 a number of troubling events had occurred in Europe that unsettled America's postwar sense of imperium. Not the least of these was the Soviet blockade of road, rail and canal access to the Western-controlled sectors of Berlin, which was followed by Russia's successful testing of its own nuclear weapon. When Mao Zedong proclaimed the People's Republic of China in October 1949, Acheson declaimed—erroneously and dramatically— that Mao's communists 'represented not independence for China but the establishment of imperial control by Moscow as part of its drive for worldwide dominance'.

NSC 68

A high point of American ideological antagonism toward Soviet Russia came in April 1950 with the first draft of the top secret National Security Council Report 68 (NSC 68). Its torrid language and startling overstatement suggest an almost boyish intoxication with melodrama. It was 'as much a work of advocacy as of analysis'. And its rhetoric conveniently served to galvanise those who, a few months later, would rush to conclude that the North Korean invasion was the prelude to a general Soviet offensive. The report announced portentously: 'The issues that face us are momentous, involving the fulfilment or destruction not only of this Republic but of civilisation itself.' Its equally foreboding conclusion was that the United States 'must organise and enlist the resources of the free world in a positive program to frustrate the Kremlin design for world domination'. The report envisioned permanent mobilisation for a clash of civilisations and a quadrupling of the defence budget. The war in Korea soon provided the impetus for the contemplated state of permanent militarism. And it has continued unabated ever since.

Conventional weapons, troops, ships and aircraft were to be multiplied; the nuclear arsenal substantially augmented; and the capacity of the United States to conduct covert operations, including economic, political and psychological warfare, enlarged. Acheson brusquely swept aside criticism that NSC 68 'inflated Moscow's capabilities while ignoring its limited intentions', but he later disturbingly justified it by saying that the report's purpose was to 'bludgeon the mass mind of top government' and that 'dramatization and magnification were necessary to push the people where they should go'. When approved by Truman in September, NSC 68 became a blueprint for the military-industrial complex that Eisenhower later so lamented. Kennan despaired. He predicted presciently that NSC 68 would 'militarise American foreign policy and bring a constant escalation of the arms race' between the United States and Soviet Russia, which of course it did.

China Syndrome

China, like Soviet Russia, was another wartime ally of the United States with whom the relationship deteriorated in the postwar period. The catalyst for the change of attitude was the rise of Mao Zedong's Chinese Communist Party in 1949 and the sudden and unexpected collapse of 'nationalist' China. American public and political opposition to communist China was led by the strange phenomenon known as the China Lobby—a loose alliance of China extremists with influence far beyond their numbers. They were principally Americans who had made a lifetime commitment to the advancement of Christianity in China and wealthy expatriate Chinese who were linked to the families of the nationalist leader Chiang Kai-shek and his wife. In truth, China Lobby supporters were as much interested in China's vast markets as they were in its hundreds of millions of potential converts to Christianity.

The lobby's influence was so pervasive, so penetrating, that it was regarded at the time as the most powerful that had ever operated for a foreign power in Washington. Known today as the Taiwan Lobby, it remains influential. In 1950, its avowed object was to obtain American military, financial and political support for Chiang Kai-shek's nationalist forces, who had been engaged since 1927 in a civil war with the communists for control of China. There had been a temporary truce when Japan invaded China in 1937 but after Japan surrendered in 1945, and an American mediation attempt failed in 1946, full-scale civil war resumed. The United States provided Chiang's forces with huge quantities of arms, ammunition and funding, but it was to no avail. General George C. Marshall, who was sent to China to lead the mediation attempt, complained bitterly that Chiang Kai-shek was 'the worst advised military commander in history' and that he was 'losing about 40 percent of his supplies to the enemy'. Mao even joked that Chiang was his 'supply officer'.

As Mao's army gradually achieved success across the mainland, Chiang and his followers retreated to Taiwan, a Chinese island 180 kilometres off the coast whose control had been returned by Japan at the end of World War II. There in late 1949, the nationalists set up an alternative government that remains to this day. It is the last remnant of the original 'Republic of China' that Sun Yat-sen founded in 1912 after the Qing dynasty collapsed. China Lobby supporters were not deterred by the retreat to Taiwan, and their campaign to support Chiang's nationalists and demonise Mao's communists only intensified. Lobby spokesmen in Washington promoted the nationalist cause with fantastic exaggeration and relentless over-statement, mercilessly targeting anyone, especially politicians, who proffered a different point of view. Their mendacious, sometimes risible, rhetoric included claims that America 'lost' China; that the State Department was controlled by communist sympathisers; and that the Chinese Communist Party wanted to enslave mankind. This mantra resonated with the prejudices and insecurities of many Americans and their politicians, few of whom were well informed about China.

No American did more to shape public opinion and advance the cause of the China Lobby, or was as blind to the weaknesses of Chiang, than the remarkable Henry R. Luce, founder of *Time* and *Life* magazines. His obsessive commitment was derived from an anti-communist Christian zeal and a childhood spent in China with missionary parents. He used his magazines as instruments of his will, shamelessly exercising editorial control to advance the lost cause of nationalist China. Nothing could dissuade Luce from the improbable idea that China wanted a destiny shaped by Christian America and led by the Methodist Chiang. He foresaw a church on every hill. By July 1950 Chiang had appeared on the cover of *Time* seven times, a record then equalled only by General Douglas MacArthur. Luce constantly lauded MacArthur, who shared his ambitions for Asia and the Chinese nationalists. His admiration knew no bounds. The copy for the 10 July

1950 edition of *Time* contained bizarre encomiums to MacArthur attributed to his senior staff officers, including adulatory descriptions such as 'God, the man is great', 'He's the greatest man alive' and 'He's the greatest man in history.'

The China Lobby's supporters secretly hoped for a reason to return Chiang's forces triumphantly to China under an American banner, to continue the fight against Mao's communists. Their rallying cry became—'Back to the mainland.' What they really wanted was 'something like a war between the United States and China'. Luce's sister, Elisabeth Moore, once revealingly said, 'Part of him wanted the Korean War to become an American war with China.' He was not alone. MacArthur harboured the same notions, wanting to overthrow 'Red China' and 'remove her as a further threat to Asia for generations to come'. Until his dismissal by Truman in 1951, MacArthur consistently sought to broaden the war in Korea and complained that he was not 'allowed to use my full military might' to do so. At a meeting with General Ridgway in August 1950, he discounted the prospect of Chinese intervention but added, 'I pray nightly that they will—would get down on my hands and knees [in order to have the opportunity to fight the Chinese communists]'.

Luce, MacArthur and the China Lobby helped poison the well of Sino-American relations for years to come. The United States' tentative rapprochement with China under President Nixon would not happen until 1972 and formal recognition of the People's Republic of China would not eventuate until 1979. The United Kingdom recognised the 'new' China in 1950, as did other countries. And most of the rest of the world had done so before the United States finally acted. John King Fairbank, Dean of China Studies at Harvard, said that 'The epitaph for America's China policy in the 1940s should begin by noting the Americans' profound ignorance of the Chinese situation' and their 'preoccupation with anti-communism'. Hastings' explanation was that the policy of the United States in the Far East was held back by 'the deep bitterness and frustration of the American people about the loss of China to the communists'.

Motivation of Mao

Mao Zedong's attitude to the looming conflict in Korea was different to that of Stalin. When he stood at the Gate of Heavenly Peace on 1 October 1949 to proclaim the People's Republic, he was supremely confident and proud but he was not looking for another war. Other than the completion of his campaigns against the nationalist forces on the islands of Hainan and Taiwan, his primary goals after two decades of conflict and revolution were national unity, reconstruction and political consolidation. Those goals were tempered, however, by an ever-present fear of American military intervention, something that was an abiding national anxiety. Whether justified or not, the Chinese leadership had long suspected that 'the US would militarily intervene in China to serve its expansionist aims in Asia'. There appeared to be reasons to be fearful. America had sent approximately 60,000 troops to China during World War II and landed 50,000 Marines at key ports and communication centres after the war. And it had openly taken the side of the nationalist army in the civil conflict. It made the US Air Force available to transport half a million nationalist troops to areas in China previously occupied by the Japanese; it airlifted nationalist armies to Beijing, Tianjin, Shanghai and Nanjing; and its naval forces aggressively challenged Chinese communist forces at the strategically sensitive port of Yantai in northeast China.

The roots of China's deep-seated suspicion of American motives lay in the nineteenth century, when Western aggression and invasion during the Opium Wars and the Boxer Rebellion so humiliated the Qing dynasty that it never recovered. Two millennia of imperial rule imploded with the collapse of the 'Great Qing' in 1912. And suspicion was exacerbated by General George Marshall's mission in 1946 to mediate between the nationalists and the communists. Zhou Enlai, Mao's astute principal negotiator at the mediation, justifiably complained that: 'The United States in reality [is supporting Chiang] through stationing troops [on China's coast] and providing Chiang with military and financial assistance.'

Truman had no intention of being impartial. He had given a confidential instruction to Marshall that even if the nationalist government refused to make any concessions to the Chinese communists, the mission should 'continue to support the [nationalists] and help it transport troops into North China and Manchuria'. And in June, in the middle of Marshall's negotiations between the communists and nationalists, the House Foreign Affairs Committee reported favourably on a military assistance bill that led Truman to immediately announce the provision of $51.7 million in aid to the nationalist government. Marshall was appalled and told Truman that it would be impossible for him to continue in his mediation role.

By 1948 the Central Committee of the Chinese Communist Party had adopted an explicit 'anti-American policy', of which a key principle was 'to prevent the US imperialists from colonizing China'. In September 1949 Mao announced that 'our national defence will be consolidated so that no imperialists will ever again be allowed to invade our land'. And in October he reassured the crowd at the inauguration of the new republic that 'Ours will no longer be a nation subject to insult and humiliation'. In the aftermath of a century of resistance to foreign invasions, the most powerful moral conviction in postwar China, 'spanning the spectrum of ideologies', was that 'the Chinese people must stand up to imperialism'.

It was no surprise, therefore, that in 1949 Mao set out to build an economic and military alliance with Soviet Russia or that Chinese news and propaganda vociferously promoted an anti-American ideological campaign. Mao believed that 'it would never be wrong to ally with an enemy's enemy'. In June a secret delegation travelled from Beijing to Moscow and held four preliminary meetings with Stalin, who showed unusual grace by conceding that he had erred in not offering as much help to the Chinese communists in their revolution as he should have. In December Mao journeyed to Moscow by train, in an armoured carriage, for face-to-face meetings with Stalin. It was an eventful and at times exasperating visit that lasted two months. Mao's pride and Stalin's paranoia made for an uncomfortable personal relationship.

Mao was ignored and left alone to stew for weeks on end. Eventually, on 14 February 1950, he came away with a package of economic and military assistance known as the 'Treaty of Friendship, Alliance and Mutual Assistance', but it was not generous and Mao would have a long memory for the way he had been treated. The Harvard political scientist and foremost Russian authority, Adam Ulam, wrote: 'It is no wonder that Mao conceived, if he had not nurtured it before, an abiding hatred of the Soviet Union.' But for the time being, he needed Russian assistance.

Kim Il-sung followed Mao to Moscow in April. After completing his lengthy consultations with Stalin, he travelled to Beijing to confer with Mao, as Stalin had urged him to do. The first round of discussions between Mao and Kim continued until after eleven o'clock on the night of 13 May. During the meeting Mao learned for the first time of Kim's military plan for the reunification of the Korean peninsula and that Stalin had approved it. Despite the late hour, Mao immediately sent Zhou Enlai to the Soviet embassy for clarification of Stalin's attitude. The Russian ambassador dutifully received him at half-past eleven and conveyed Mao's enquiry to Moscow. Stalin replied the next day saying that the 'final decision' should be made between Kim and Mao and that 'If the Chinese comrades do not agree', Kim's reunification plan should be changed.

When Mao and Kim resumed discussions on 15 May, Mao was faced with a fait accompli. Having just concluded an alliance with Soviet Russia that was essential for his country's economic development and national security, he was in no position to refuse the offer of assistance to Kim that Stalin was counting on. Stalin had 'manoeuvred Mao into a position in which it was virtually impossible to veto' Kim's planned attack. According to the rose-tinted account given to the Soviet ambassador by the grateful and enthusiastic North Koreans, which was then relayed by the ambassador to Stalin on 16 May, Mao promised that 'if Americans take part in combat activities, then China will help North Korea with its troops'. In fact, Mao was more cautious, more qualified and more self-interested than the ambassador's telegram implied. He thought it would be necessary 'to take precautions'. He suggested: 'China might deploy three armies along the Yalu River, and if the United States did not intervene, no damage would be done. If the United States intervened but decided not to cross the 38th parallel, Chinese troops would not cross the Yalu.'

China's engagement in the Korean conflict therefore hinged on whether the United States intervened and crossed the 38th parallel. If it happened at all, it would be an essentially reactive and defensive move. In any event, Kim had assured Mao that the reunification war would be short and there would be no time for American intervention and no need for Chinese troops. In the meantime, Mao was busy with his mopping-up campaigns against the remaining nationalist forces of Chiang Kai-shek. He had taken Hainan in May and was focussed on Taiwan in June.

Russia's opportunistic involvement was guaranteed but it was to be limited to arms, advisors and materiel. It was predicated on the assumption that American intervention was possible but unlikely. The supply of a substantial quantity of Russian armaments to the North Korean army, including the formidable T34 tank, was already well underway. Stalin replaced his senior military advisors in Pyongyang with veterans with extensive combat experience who worked closely with the North Koreans on Kim's invasion plan. The attack came in the pre-dawn light of Sunday 25 June 1950. It was Saturday afternoon in Washington. The South Korean army was no match for the Russian tanks and the invasion would have been wholly and rapidly successful had it not been for the prompt UN Security Council resolutions authorising the use of collective force and the hasty despatch of American troops from Japan.

Mao was neither consulted about nor informed of the proposed date for the North Korean attack and did not learn about it until Seoul was captured several days after the invasion. He had not made any decision for intervention, and would not do so until October, after much agonising, and only when it became clear that Washington was not content with the restoration of the status quo and had chosen instead to continue the conflict. As Selig Harrison wrote, when the decision for Chinese intervention came, it did not reflect cold war communist solidarity but 'China's bedrock national interest in drawing a line that would set the limits of American influence in Korea'. The disaster that followed was of Washington's own making.

CHAPTER 6

American Hubris

'Where there is strife, there is pride'

Three months after it started, the North Korean invasion had been repulsed and the mandate of the United Nations achieved. The war should have been over. The Security Council resolution of 25 June had called on the authorities in North Korea to 'withdraw their armed forces to the 38th parallel' and the resolution of 27 June had recommended that assistance be provided to South Korea 'to repel the armed attack and restore international peace and security in the area'. There was no ambiguity. The two resolutions pointed to the same objective and imposed the same limitation. Although the UN did not then recognise North Korea as a sovereign state, it did recognise the significance of the border at the 38th parallel. The sole purpose of its collective intervention was to rebuff the invasion by the Korean People's Army and to restore the integrity of the border. The appropriate legal and moral response, and the only one then authorised by the UN, was to meet the North Korean aggression, halt it and defeat it, but not to become an aggressor oneself. This meant nothing to Syngman Rhee. And it meant little to President Truman.

Respecting the Parallel

On 13 July Rhee pronounced that the North Korean attack had 'obliterated the 38th parallel and [that] no peace and order could be maintained in Korea as long as the division at the 38th parallel remained'. This self-serving declaration, from the man who sought overall control of the two countries, prompted an immediate denial from an American army spokesman, who stated that the United States had intervened 'solely to push the North Koreans back across the line'. Curiously, Truman did not close the issue down. A few days later he even requested recommendations from the National Security Council, which advised against crossing the 38th parallel. But others in Washington, including the Joint Chiefs, perceived a strategic opportunity—one that, they optimistically hoped, could be used to diminish the size of the worldwide communist bloc and displace part of the Soviet orbit. As with Iraq in the twenty-first century, so with North Korea in the mid-twentieth century. Enthusiasts for cold war belligerence demanded that American-led forces invade North Korea. They lost sight of the limitations implicit in the moral principle of repelling aggression.

One of the most fervent enthusiasts was John Allison, director of the State Department's Office of Northeast Affairs, who assumed overall charge of studies on future Korean policy on 22 July. He quickly became a self-appointed exponent of the American moral conscience, exemplifying a tendency toward moral absolutism; invoking that indeterminate and unreliable concept known as 'the decent opinions of mankind'; and advocating going north to the Manchurian border in strident language. He asked rhetorically, 'When all legal and moral right is on our side, why should we hesitate?' And he accused opponents of a crossing of the parallel of being guilty of 'appeasement' and of 'a surrender of moral principles'.

Allison was part of a trinity of hardliners within the State Department, the others being Dean Rusk and John Foster Dulles, who successfully pressured foreign policy staff to support a crossing. George Kennan alone consistently urged restraint. He thought going north would be a tragic mistake. He encouraged Acheson to abandon any idea of crossing the 38th parallel; to ignore those who were 'indulging themselves in emotional moralistic attitudes'; and to recognise the 'unease and humiliation Moscow [let alone Beijing] would feel if US forces moved north'. But Kennan had lost favour and was soon sidelined. He retreated to the towers and spires of Princeton, amid the half-forgotten dreams of dead statesmen, where he was isolated from the levers of influence. Acheson certainly did not heed his advice.

In Tokyo, MacArthur regarded the expansion of the war into North Korea as a foregone conclusion. He told Generals Collins and Vandenberg during their visit to his headquarters on 13 July that he intended to destroy the North Korean forces and compose and unite Korea, adding that it might be necessary to occupy the whole of the country. There was not a shadow of authority for what MacArthur proposed but the old man had acted throughout his life 'on the assumption that the rules made for lesser men had no relevance to himself'. He had been a commissioned officer for nearly half a century and a general for the last thirty years and was no longer the type to await or even follow orders if it did not suit him to do so. Anomalously, the United Nations had no power to exercise operational control over MacArthur. The Security Council vested command of the UN forces in the United States, which appointed MacArthur, who answered only to President Truman as his commander-in-chief. And on the issue of expanding the war, Truman's own public statements were becoming more aligned with those of MacArthur. The language of restoring the border at the 38th parallel was being quietly forgotten.

In a special message to Congress on 19 July, Truman abandoned the circumspection of the first days of the war and pointedly referred to the restoration of peace and security to 'Korea' and the 'effort to ensure the people of Korea an opportunity to choose their own form of government free from coercion'. Acheson, always in lock step with the President, wrote that MacArthur could not be 'expected to march up to a surveyor's line and just stop'. But the issue was downplayed for the rest of July and August as the war went badly and American troops were besieged and almost overrun in the southeast corner of the Korean peninsula at Pusan. In early September, as the supply lines of the North Korean army became stretched, the momentum for a larger war returned. Truman, who was under domestic political pressure to respond to Republican critics who accused him of being soft on communism, declared that the people of Korea had 'a right to be free, independent and united'. And shortly afterwards, the National Security Council produced a secret recommendation (NSC 81/1) that this time approved crossing the parallel but required MacArthur to consult Washington before doing so. Truman signed it on 11 September. For the time being, however, the issue remained hypothetical. Neither the public nor America's allies knew anything.

The Inchon Effect

The critical event, the one that turned caution and propriety on their heads, was the outstanding success of MacArthur's audacious amphibious landing of 70,000 Marines and soldiers behind enemy lines at the South Korean port of Inchon on 15 September. It reversed the fortunes of war, scattered the North Korean army and led to the liberation of Seoul. The ensuing euphoria resulted in galloping optimism that killed all sober analysis, unleashed a dangerous hubris and whetted an unseemly appetite in Washington for a larger war. As the enemy melted back across the border, MacArthur was hailed as a genius and applauded as a brilliant strategist; his judgement was vindicated; his determination to continue the drive into North Korea emboldened. On 26 September, even while the battle for the liberation of Seoul still raged, MacArthur instructed his staff officers to prepare an outline of a plan for a landing invasion on the northeast coast of North Korea. Authority from the Joint Chiefs of Staff was not wanting. Their confidential directive duly arrived the next day.

The Joint Chiefs' 27 September instructions to MacArthur, approved by the President, ignored the limitations contained in the UN Security Council resolutions of late June and stated starkly that MacArthur's military objective was 'to destroy the North Korean forces'. He was authorised to advance north of the 38th parallel and as far as the Yalu River, so long as only South Korean troops were used in the Chinese and Russian border areas. If 'major Soviet or Chinese communist forces' entered, or there was an announcement of their intended entry, he was required to consult with Washington.

Around the world there was anxious consideration of the sensitivity and significance of any incursion into the territory of North Korea. The former Australian Prime Minister, Ben Chifley, put the problem succinctly when he said in parliament, 'If those forces continue beyond the 38th parallel they will become aggressors.'

It is no credit to Acheson that on the direct question of whether the 38th parallel should be breached, he attempted to avoid debate in the United Nations in the hope of presenting the movement of armed forces into North Korea as a fait accompli. The transparency of this approach is no better illustrated than by the troubling cable from General Marshall to MacArthur on 29 September. It was marked 'For his eyes only' and informed MacArthur that 'We want you to feel unhampered tactically and strategically to proceed north of 38th parallel.' Marshall then explained that it was the 'evident desire...not to be confronted with necessity of a vote on passage of 38th parallel, rather to find you have found it militarily necessary to do so'. This was followed by an even more explicit and revealing message from the Joint Chiefs, who counselled MacArthur to proceed 'without any further explanation or announcement and let action determine the matter. Our government desires to avoid having to make an issue of the 38th parallel until we have accomplished our mission of defeating the Korean forces.' In the words of one historian, 'So the Truman administration decided to avoid the issue, to do what must be done without any public proclamation.' It was taking the matter into its own hands.

MacArthur needed no encouragement. The opportunity to impose regime change on North Korea was too exhilarating to resist. His reply to Marshall stated: 'I regard all of Korea open for our military operations.' On 30 September, South Korean troops under MacArthur's command crossed the 38th parallel. Two nights later in Beijing, Zhou Enlai, the Chinese Prime Minister, observed that 'the United Nations may find itself faced with a fait accompli dictated by MacArthur'. Zhou's expectation was percipient and the United States was being less than frank. While MacArthur was receiving secret communications authorising him to feel unhampered in taking UN forces across the 38th parallel, neither the United Nations nor America's allies were kept fully informed or asked for their approval. Acheson feared opposition from any major allied partner, especially from the United Kingdom. He preferred to 'let action determine the matter', while allowing a 'long running international minuet [to be] danced around the parallel crossing issue'.

As late as 3 October, the British Foreign Office was wholly unaware of the situation. Its cable on that day to Washington enquired: 'Have any instructions been issued to General MacArthur regarding this [authority for crossing] or are any contemplated?' The concern was prompted by an anxious report from Sir Alvary Gascoigne, the British representative in Japan, who was worried by a wild statement from MacArthur that if Chinese units entered Korea he would 'immediately unleash his air force against towns in Manchuria and North China including Peking'. Whitehall had not been told of any instruction to MacArthur about the crossing of the 38th parallel, let alone the bombing of cities in China including Beijing. By 5 October, British understanding of the true position had progressed from abject ignorance to tentative speculation. On that date a senior official of the Foreign Office wrote that 'it would appear, although the situation was somewhat confused, that the Americans had given General MacArthur authority to advance'.

Acheson well knew that senior British officials and military personnel, notably the Chief of Air Staff and the First Sea Lord, had grave reservations about crossing the 38th parallel. Lord Tedder, the ranking British military representative in the United States, even met with General Omar Bradley, Chairman of the Joint Chiefs, and informed him directly that the British military command and the Foreign Office questioned the wisdom of a crossing. Bradley ignored this unwelcome advice. And Acheson ducked the issue, absenting himself in New Haven and avoiding an anxious meeting on 6 October with the British ambassador, Sir Oliver Franks. On this most vital question of the Korean War—the issue that transformed a successful three-month

UN 'police action' against North Korea into a failed three-year war with China—comity between allies was undermined by American political ideology and military enthusiasm.

Trickery and Guile

At a time when the British were insisting on the need to obtain broad United Nations authority for any operations in North Korea, Truman had already approved an advance across the 38th parallel and MacArthur held clear but secret instructions to do so. Truman's agreement to the British proposal to obtain UN authority was guileful. Acheson recommended resort to the General Assembly in order to circumvent a probable Soviet veto in the Security Council. The General Assembly had a subsidiary power, albeit a limp one, to 'discuss and make recommendations' on matters within the scope of the UN Charter. It was better than nothing. A prolix and ambivalent draft resolution was duly drawn by the British delegation in consultation with the State Department and approved by Truman and Acheson. It was intended to be anodyne but it was deliberately deceptive. The primary proposal was that yet another 'commission' be established. The ancillary 'recommendations' included that 'all appropriate steps be taken to ensure conditions of stability throughout Korea' and that 'all constituent acts be taken...for the establishment of a unified, independent and democratic government in the sovereign state of Korea'.

The language of the resolution was 'wondrously loose'. And its opacity avoided the central questions. Clay Blair said it was 'ambiguous to an absurd degree'. There was no recommendation, let alone resolution, for invasion and regime change. There was no acknowledgement of the dilemma involved in the United Nations prosecuting a war of aggression in its own right, nor any recognition of the likelihood of Soviet or Chinese opposition or how it was to be dealt with. And the significance of the primary authority from the Security Council was ignored. The resolutions of 25 and 27 June did not contemplate offensive action north of the 38th parallel and had only called for North Korean forces to be repelled, not destroyed. Nonetheless, bolstered by the weight of uninformed popular and congressional opinion in favour of a crossing, Washington's warriors chose to seize the opportunity to 'roll back' communism. It was as if Korea was being re-opened for foreign reorganisation.

The warriors assumed that United Nations forces would simply advance into North Korea unopposed and conduct supervised elections for the purpose of achieving the reunification of Korea. But this naiveté was not necessarily shared. Alan Watt, Secretary of the Australian Department of External Affairs, warned that the draft resolution 'appears to be in such wide terms that it could be interpreted as authorising United Nations forces to operate north of the 38th parallel irrespective of the question whether Russian or Chinese communist forces are at that moment present in North Korea'. The form of the resolution was however pre-ordained and Truman had no interest in entertaining such criticisms. He approved it without any opportunity for amendment.

Tellingly, Acheson later acknowledged that the General Assembly would not have accepted such a broad resolution if it had thought that it was authorising military operations north of the 38th parallel against Russian or Chinese communist forces in North Korea. But this is exactly what it did do. In fact, Acheson weakly blamed MacArthur, saying that 'General MacArthur at once stripped from the resolution of 7 October its husk of ambivalence and gave it an interpretation that the enacting majority in the General Assembly would not have accepted.' But Acheson was being disingenuous. He and Truman were determined to impose regime change on North Korea and the United Nations was their chosen vehicle for prosecuting a political agenda conceived in Washington. And in those early days 'the state of the world guaranteed that it [the UN] was virtually an instrument of US power'. The criticism of the resolution by the British historian Paul Johnson was forceful. He said that it 'undermined the concept of the UN as a useful, but limited body, and set it on a course which transformed it into an instrument of ideological propaganda'.

So it happened that on 7 October, the pivotal resolution was passed in the General Assembly by forty-seven votes to five, with seven abstentions. There is little doubt that 'The passage of this resolution... transformed the nature of the Korean War, but few could see any danger signals at that time'. Matters were made worse on 9 October when, away from the gaze of the United Nations, President Truman and the Joint Chiefs quietly waived the principal restriction stipulated in the Joint Chiefs' confidential 27 September directive to MacArthur. They allowed him to proceed to the Yalu without consultation, regardless of Chinese or Russian opposition, provided that in his judgement 'action by forces under your control offers a reasonable chance of success'. MacArthur's forces had already commenced their crossing of the parallel. The British request for a 'gap' between the UN resolution and the advance, 'in order not to bring into question the good faith of many delegations voting in favour of the resolution', was largely ignored, as was the general opposition of the Indian government to any crossing of the 38th parallel.

The United Nations had moved from containment to pursuit. And Washington was encouraged by the scent of outright victory. MacArthur's biographer, William Manchester, wrote that the President, 'despite his press conference assurances, had acted without consulting America's allies'. And the historian Walter Millis observed: 'Perhaps the one most critical decision of the Korean War had been taken. But it had been taken in the worst way, for confused reasons, on deficient intelligence and with an inadequate appreciation of the risks.' With the benefit of considered reflection, it is obvious that the United Nations could not credibly act as both major protagonist and objective arbiter. Nor could it reasonably justify an invasion of the territory of North Korea—a state that had come into existence in 1948 as the natural consequence of the United States' postwar policy on the Korean peninsula. Not for the first or last time, military and ideological opportunism had become the engine for action, at the expense of discernment and discrimination. In the words of Robert O'Neill, the official Australian historian of the war, 'The wisdom and morality of

United Nations Command forces crossing the 38th parallel tended to be submerged in general condemnation of North Korea as an aggressor who launched a war.'

Diplomatic Warnings

The period preceding the 7 October resolution was a time of lost opportunity and of warnings ignored. There were numerous diplomatic cautions from China about the dangers of crossing the 38th parallel—signals that were neither oblique nor vague; messages that were straightforward statements of future intention intended to be taken seriously; warnings that should have been heeded. Washington neither understood nor respected the Chinese leadership and was unwilling to give the cautionary statements from Beijing the credibility they deserved. Acheson, 'a bold, even arrogant man', was unable to 'grasp what impact MacArthur's advance on well-blazed Japanese invasion routes had on the Chinese'. And Truman—a man with many limitations—would not take Mao Zedong seriously, referring to him disparagingly as 'Mousie Dung'. He, Acheson and the Joint Chiefs simply thought—mistakenly and imprudently—that China was engaging in a poker game; that it was bluffing; that it was weak; that it was 'barely a working state'. Their attitude, wrote respected American historian William Stueck, 'combined arrogance, condescension and naiveté'. He might have added racism.

The first warning salvo was fired on 22 September after the Inchon landing, when it was apparent that the tide of war had turned against the North Korean army. The Chinese Ministry of Foreign Affairs issued a statement declaring, 'China will always stand on the side of the Korean people.' A few days later a senior Chinese officer in overall charge of military planning dined with the Indian ambassador to Beijing, K.M. Panikkar, one of the highest ranking diplomats in Beijing and a conduit between China and the West. The purpose of the meeting was to convey to Washington that the Chinese government would not tolerate continuous American provocation; that they had no option but to resist America if it did not stop; and that China could no longer remain patient. On 26 September Panikkar reported his conversation to New Delhi and also passed on the assessment of the Polish ambassador in Beijing that 'China will consider American army on her Manchurian flank as a grave menace to her'. The following day, the Indian Prime Minister Nehru conveyed the information verbatim to the British Foreign Secretary, Bevin, and added the following ominous prediction: 'that any decision or even suggestion that United Nations forces will move beyond the 38th parallel is likely to precipitate what might be world catastrophe.'

On 30 September, on the eve of the crossing of the 38th parallel, the Chinese Prime Minister Zhou Enlai issued a public warning, saying, 'The Chinese people absolutely will not tolerate foreign aggression, nor will they supinely tolerate seeing their neighbours being savagely invaded by the imperialists.' Matters then took on a note of urgency. On 2 October, approaching midnight—some sources suggest one o'clock in the morning—Panikkar was summoned to a meeting with Zhou, who told him that he had received news that South Korean troops had crossed the 38th parallel. He then said to Panikkar, 'The US troops are going to cross the 38th parallel in an attempt to extend the war. If the US troops really do so, we cannot sit idly by and remain indifferent. We will intervene.' Panikkar promptly informed the British, who passed the information on to the Americans. Zhou could not have been clearer. And Panikkar had no doubts about China's resolve or America's mistake. In the early hours of the following morning, he wrote in his diary:

> So America has knowingly elected for war, with Britain
> following. It is indeed a tragic decision for the Americans
> and the British are well aware that a military settlement
> of the Korean issue will be resisted by the Chinese and
> that armies now concentrated on the Yalu will intervene
> decisively in the fight. Probably that is what the Americans,
> at least some of them, want. They probably feel that this is
> an opportunity to have a showdown with China. In any case,

> MacArthur's dream has come true. I only hope it does not
> turn out to be a nightmare.

Panikkar's intuition was correct in every respect. He was a serious historian of colonialism in Asia, a confidante of Nehru and, like Menon, an Oxford graduate. But influential forces in America, represented by men with a deeply conservative orientation and a fervent anti-communist ideology, brimming with the false confidence that the military success at Inchon had given them, wanted to strike a blow against communism. Panikkar was rationalised away; his reliability attacked; his character doubted. Although he felt that he understood the forces driving the Chinese revolution, Panikkar was not sympathetic to communism, for he hated the lack of respect that it gave the individual in society. Yet Acheson and the CIA labelled him as a leftist, a mere mouthpiece for Beijing, and ignored his message. Acheson even characterised his warnings condescendingly as 'the mere vaporings of a panicky Panikkar'. These were shallow excuses. The truth is that the administration in Washington could not bring itself to believe that China was prepared to take on the United Nations or to fight the Americans. It was blinded by disdain for an enemy it did not know or respect.

Enter the Dragon

Mao Zedong felt deeply about China's past century of foreign invasions and had profound reservations about the motive of the United States in entering the Korean conflict. He doubted that its involvement on the peninsula was merely to defend South Korea. And those doubts were only strengthened by Truman's perplexing and provocative decision at the outbreak of war to station the US Seventh Fleet in the Taiwan Strait, from where the bombing or invasion of mainland China could be mounted. Mao explained to his advisers early on that 'we have to prepare for an emergence of war mania; we have to prepare for [the possibility] that the United States might provoke a third world war, or carry it out for a protracted time, or even use atomic bombs'.

On 10 July he despatched a Chinese military intelligence group to Pyongyang to observe and report on 'any change of battleground'. And around the same time, a series of national security meetings resolved to establish a north-eastern border defence command at Shenyang in Manchuria and to deploy troops along the North Korean border. To implement this objective, Mao signed a Central Military Commission resolution on 13 July entitled 'Defending the Northeast Border Security'. It re-organised the command structure and established the Northeast Border Defence Force, principally comprising the 13th Army Group.

A formal decision for Chinese intervention in the war was still a long way off, but in anticipation that it would happen, the 13th Army Group undertook logistical preparation and weapons training. Within the military command there seemed little doubt that the American-led forces would cross the 38th parallel, and a general expectation that if and when they did so, China would retaliate and enter the war. The commander of the 13th Army Group reported to the Central Military Commission on 31 August that this would be expedient because 'Then the war will not only be politically justified but also militarily advantageous'.

Chinese military leaders believed firmly in Sun Tzu's dictum that 'if you know yourself and know your enemy, you can fight a hundred battles with no danger of defeat'. Their analysis and assessment of the American forces was ongoing and constantly under review. At their September command meeting, the field commanders who were poised on the Manchurian border appeared confident that they could defeat the American forces, if they needed to. They recognised that the United States military enjoyed absolute air and sea superiority and relative superiority in firepower, equipment and mobility, but felt that it suffered from four vital weaknesses.

According to the notes of the meeting, these weaknesses were said to be: (1) a lack of political motivation because 'they are invading other people's country, fighting an unjust war'; (2) inferiority in combat effectiveness because 'although they have excellent modern equipment, their officers and soldiers are not adept in night battles, close combat and bayonet charges'; (3) poor flexibility resulting in 'dull and mechanical' field tactics while Chinese soldiers were 'good at manoeuvring flexibility and mobility and, in particular, good at surrounding and attacking enemy flanks...as well as dispersing and concealing'; and (4) an inability to endure hardship because 'they are afraid of dying and merely rely on firepower' while Chinese soldiers 'are brave and willing to sacrifice life and blood and capable of bearing hardship and heavy burdens'. This assessment, which was unerringly close to the mark, led the Chinese field commanders to advocate 'penetration, circling and disintegration, close combat, night strikes and quick battles', all of which the Central Military Commission endorsed.

When intelligence reached Beijing on 1 October that the first troops had commenced to cross the 38th parallel, Mao spent a long night with colleagues in discussions about the Korean situation. He prepared but did not send a draft telegram informing Stalin that 'We have decided to send troops into Korea in the name of the People's Volunteer Army.' At the meeting of the Politburo secretariat the next day, most participants were opposed to sending troops to Korea. A full meeting of the Politburo was convened for 4 October. Mao flew his trusted military commander Peng Dehuai back from his command post in northwest China and brought in other military commanders to support him at the meeting.

Mao's opponents believed that their country was exhausted economically and could not afford another war. But Mao was persistent, telling his comrades that the American intention to occupy North Korea was part of a grand strategy to dominate the Far East; that with a foothold consolidated on the Korean peninsula the United States would be free to undertake further aggression in the Taiwan Strait, Indochina and the Philippines; and that unless China intervened, its electric power plants, iron and steel plants, coal-mining bases and heavy industries in the northeast would be threatened. And he assured the group that the Soviet Union would provide military assistance and air cover. Most of all, he stressed that China's domestic stability and economic reconstruction would be disrupted if American troops were allowed to establish a permanent presence along the Yalu River. That threat would be unacceptable because 'We would have to wait there year after year, unsure of when the enemy will attack us'.

The Politburo reconvened on 5 October. Mao and Peng had met privately before the meeting, when Peng expressed his support for intervention and learned that Mao wanted him to be overall commander of the Chinese forces in Korea. Peng then addressed the meeting, saying, 'If its troops be poised on the bank of the Yalu and [on] Taiwan, the United States will be able to find a pretext to invade us at any time.' There was a shift in the mood of the meeting in favour of intervention, predicated on Mao's assurance that Soviet air cover and military assistance would be available.

On 8 October, the day after the United Nations General Assembly resolution, China formally decided to enter the war. Mao directed that the Northeast Border Defence Force be re-named the 'Chinese People's Volunteers' and that it should be made ready immediately to move into North Korean territory. He cabled Kim Il-sung to inform him that 'we have decided to despatch the Volunteers into Korea to help you'. And he sent Zhou Enlai on an urgent mission to Russia to finalise and secure Stalin's agreement to provide military assistance and air support.

Stalin was not in Moscow. He and his inner circle, including Malenkov, Beria and Molotov, were at his summer dacha at Sochi in the foothills of the Caucasus Mountains near Georgia on the Black Sea coast. Zhou travelled over 8000 kilometres to Moscow and then made the further journey to Sochi. A weary Zhou eventually met Stalin on 10 October at a meeting that is said to have gone all night and into the early hours of the morning. The outcome was disappointing. Stalin promised to provide military hardware, including enough tanks and artillery to equip ten infantry divisions, and also said he would despatch elements of the Soviet air force to protect China's northern and eastern coasts. But within hours he was backing off from the commitment. Molotov was sent to inform Zhou that the air force was 'not yet ready to assist in the Chinese military action in Korea and could only set out in two-and-a-half months' and that the munitions, equipment and supplies would have to be paid for. Stalin apparently had had second thoughts on supporting Chinese intervention. He was concerned that Mao would eventually try to push him into a war with the United States, which was something he wanted to avoid.

Mao was surprised and distressed, probably fuming, but not necessarily deterred. On 12 October he postponed the deployment of troops and notified Peng in Manchuria that 'the decision on the 13th Army Group's entry into Korea is now called off and the troops should stay within our border'. In the same telegram he requested Peng and his second in command to return to Beijing for an emergency meeting. And he cancelled a previous order that the 9th Army Group move from Shandong to the northeast. The next day the Politburo hastily re-convened, chaired by Mao. The uneasy consensus of the meeting was that China should enter the war even if the Soviet military would not assist. Mao directed Zhou to remain in Russia to negotiate credit terms for the provision of military assistance and to confirm eventual Soviet air support. His telegram to Zhou stated that if the Soviet leadership guarantees air support, 'we won't be afraid of massive air raids; at worst, [our troops] would have to endure some losses in the event of air attack in the next two and a half months'. Jung Chang said that when Zhou read this, he 'buried his head in his hands'.

Stalin was surprised and 'deeply moved' by Mao's willingness to make such a sacrifice. He would not allow Russia to be drawn directly into the war but he did approve a loan of 5.6 billion roubles to enable China to fund the acquisition of a huge quantity of military supplies. And he relented somewhat on the provision of Soviet air cover, but only after Chinese forces entered North Korea. Mao now fixed 19 October for the movement of the main body of the People's Volunteers across the Yalu. In fact, some troops started a little earlier.

CHAPTER 7

China Crosses the Yalu

'The horsemen and the footmen are pouring in amain'

The Chinese People's Volunteers were not volunteers. The name was designed by Mao Zedong to avoid the appearance of a state of war between China and the United States of America, and because he hoped not to impair his quest for United Nations recognition of the newly founded People's Republic of China.

The People's Volunteers

The 'volunteer' troops were regular soldiers of the People's Liberation Army, which had come into existence in 1927 following the split between the nationalists and the communists. As a fighting force, it had demonstrated considerable resilience in its successful civil war against the nationalists, most famously during the Long March in 1934 and 1935 when Mao, Zhou Enlai, Peng Dehuai and others led an extraordinary tactical retreat to Shensi Province in northwest China, marching more than 9000 kilometres over eighteen mountain ranges, across twenty-four rivers and through twelve different provinces. According to one account, they 'averaged nearly 24 miles a day for the 235 days and 18 nights of actual travel'. Despite its success against the nationalists, the People's Liberation Army was almost devoid of artillery, possessed little or no air force and its weapons and equipment were a jumble—principally captured Japanese stock or American arms seized from the nationalists, with a hotchpotch of Russian,

Czech, British and Danish elements. The Pentagon did not consider it to be a formidable fighting force. American generals referred to it disparagingly as a 'peasant army'.

The major component of the People's Liberation Army in northeast China was known as the Fourth Field Army, of which the 13th Army Group in Manchuria formed part. At that time, the Chinese soldiers were among the hardiest in the world. A large number had known no other life; many had played a prominent role in wresting control of the mainland from the nationalists during the civil war; and most were enthused by a spirit of pride and revolution. Some elements had travelled from Manchuria to South China, where they had made a successful amphibious attack on Hainan in May 1950. In June they were preparing for a similar attack on Taiwan when war broke out on the Korean peninsula.

Over the following weeks, these men and others from elsewhere in China were returned by train to Manchuria, mainly to holding areas in the vicinity of the border town of Andong (now Dandong), near the mouth of the Yalu River. This was the major crossing point into North Korea. Andong was joined to Sinuiju on the Korean side by two mighty parallel iron bridges—one was the largest ever rail bridge built by the Japanese and the other was a road bridge built by the American Bridge Company in 1900. These bridges, over a kilometre long, were the main route from Korea to Manchuria, the puppet state that the Japanese once called 'Manchukuo'. Although there were seven other main crossing points across the Yalu River, and three across the Tumen River in the far east toward the Russian border, none rivalled the twin bridges at Andong in size and importance.

As the tide of war turned and the American-led troops crossed the 38th parallel in early October, then captured Pyongyang and continued heading north to the Yalu River, the civilian population in Manchuria and especially at Andong lived in dread of invasion from the 'barbarians' as they called them. The experience of Japan's recent occupation was still raw and publicity given to MacArthur's threatening statements heightened their apprehension. In October the sense of approaching war became palpable as US Mustang fighter-bombers attacked the airfield and factories at Sinuiju on the south bank of the river. Sometimes they appeared to make a determined effort to hit the bridges. Occasionally they overflew Chinese territory, setting off air-raid sirens and drawing fire from Andong's anti-aircraft guns. The first clash of arms in China's war against America actually occurred on 15 October—ten days before any infantry contact—when Chinese ground fire on the north bank of the Yalu shot down one of the Mustangs. By this date approximately 400,000 Chinese troops from the Fourth and Third Field Armies were concentrated in force in Manchuria, near the Korean border.

Just as it had been for Caesar when he crossed the Rubicon in 49 BCE, the movement of the People's Volunteers across the Yalu River into North Korea marked an irrevocable commitment from which there was no turning back. The columns of soldiers traversed the river at night, some fearing that they were entering 'the gate of hell'. All of the principal Yalu bridges were used for the crossing—from Andong near the river mouth to Manpon over 300 kilometres upstream to the northeast. The cantilevered twin bridges at Andong were the most heavily burdened. At the highest point in the girders there was always a lookout armed with a bugle. On the rail bridge, military engineers laid timber planking to allow trucks to cross at 100-metre intervals. At some crossing points, river barges ferried men and supplies across the water. At others, men walked over water on pontoon bridges constructed by the engineers. In the evenings the autumn temperatures plummeted and ice began to form on the river's surface. By December the ice was so thick there was no need for bridges. In the mornings on the Korean side, frost carpeted the ground and blasted the orchards where the farmers were busy binding straw around the trunks of apple trees in anticipation of the Siberian cold.

The soldiers wore fur caps and reversible padded cotton jackets—khaki on one side, white on the other. Most lacked sturdy boots and had to make do with lightweight rubber and canvas shoes originally intended for use in the Hainan and Taiwan campaigns. Most of them carried a personal weapon and ammunition, a grenade and some basic utensils for eating and cleaning, as well as field rations to last five to seven days. These were usually little more than hard bread or biscuits and a form of stocking filled with dried millet or ground soya bean flour.

In the first echelon, four Chinese armies crossed the Yalu, followed a week later by two more. Each army had three divisions and each division had up to 10,000 infantrymen. The undetected movement of these troops—almost 200,000 men with supplies, vehicles and horses—was substantially completed by 29 October. A truck regiment and a cavalry regiment also came across. It was a prodigious logistical exercise. Civilian rail traffic was suspended throughout north-eastern China. And radio transmission was strictly forbidden, ensuring that the men who manned the British and American radio listening posts never knew of the silent, nocturnal movement of enemy troops. Once on Korean soil, the Chinese were not tied to the roads. Like the Roman legions, they sought to make the shortest distance between two points, sometimes irrespective of contours. Most of them knew only their feet as a means of transport and their backs and shoulders for load-carrying.

All movement was at night except for bivouac scouting parties that went ahead each morning. When dusk fell, the soldiers and porters set off in single file along narrow, stony paths. Out of the shadows North Koreans sometimes appeared to guide them. In the most difficult terrain they held lanterns to point the way. Occasionally white tape was used to mark the route, tied to trees, rocks and bushes. The soldiers walked and trotted noiselessly from early evening until three o'clock in the morning. Then the cooks in the field kitchens began their work, concealing their fires beneath heavy tarpaulins. By daylight all was extinguished and the men stayed under cover, sleeping or cleaning weapons and equipment. No one moved in the open unless the weather was heavy and overcast. No one used radios. Plane spotters with bugles kept watch from the upper slopes. They were an army of ghosts.

Many units had to travel considerable distances from the Yalu to their assembly areas. In one reported case, three Chinese divisions—up to 30,000 men if at full strength—are said to have marched for sixteen to nineteen days over mountain tracks to their designated forming-up places. The author of the United States Army's official history of the first part of the Korean War was impressed. He said—citing Xenophon's account of the retreat of the Greeks—that the Chinese 'march capability and performance equalled the best examples of antiquity'. Not just endurance but also discipline accounted for the success of the Chinese infiltration. Keen-eyed aerial observers saw nothing and aerial photographs revealed naught. Anthony Farrar-Hockley, a British captain who spent two years as a prisoner of war in North Korea, was in awe. He wrote:

> Each division provided air sentries during its night movement. The moment an aircraft was heard a sentry fired his rifle and shouted 'Fijilella!' Every man, horse and vehicle was at once halted, remaining still until the engine noises faded…The success of this simple discipline was absolute. The armies entered Korea without disclosing their presence to United Nations aerial observation.

For this initial stage of the Chinese intervention—known as the first phase—Mao and Peng had resolved to adopt a conservative strategy while they waited for the arrival of Russian arms and ammunition. Their limited objectives were to 'check the enemy's offensive, stabilize the situation [and] cover the northerly retreat and reorganisation of the [North Korean army]'. This meant moving cautiously, constructing containment lines in the mountainous region north of the Chongchon River, fighting defensively and only picking off weaker or isolated enemy units if necessary, but not otherwise engaging in offensive warfare. But as MacArthur's road-bound military units raced each other euphorically to the Yalu—their lines increasingly dispersed and their commanders ever more cavalier—the battlefield situation convinced Mao to abandon his strategy and adopt a more daring approach.

On 21 October, knowing that the entry of Chinese troops into North Korea had not been detected, Mao telegraphed Peng and instructed him to undertake surprise attacks and engage in mobile warfare where possible. The task was made easier because General MacArthur's forces, like those of Hideyoshi in the sixteenth century, had been split in two, diminishing their effectiveness as a single, powerful spearhead. They were not only advancing along two routes but were widely spread along both routes. General Almond's X Corps was approaching from the east coast toward the Chosin Reservoir in the high mountains of the northeast. General Walker's Eighth Army was in the west, heading north in marginally more hospitable country where the mountains were neither as remote nor as high. And between the forces of Walker and Almond there was an eighty-kilometre wide gap. The terrain was rugged but it provided an opportunity for the Chinese to exploit it for flanking attacks.

Warning at Unsan

The first unexpected warning of a considerable Chinese presence in North Korea came on 25 October near the town of Unsan, about thirty kilometres north of the Chongchon River, the last major water barrier in the west before the Yalu. The Chongchon runs from northeast to southwest out of the central mountain range, generally parallel to the Yalu. On the northern side of the river, mountain spurs rise into the hills and extend all the way back to the Yalu, becoming steeper and more remote as they wind into the distance. The spurs provide limited corridors of passage and are a natural barrier to any movement northwards. Unsan is nestled at the base of these spurs, adjacent to one of the Chongchon's tributaries at a fork in the road that runs along the river valley. From Unsan the two branches of the road wend their ways north into the mountains until they reach the gorges of the Yalu. This topography acts like a funnel—the roads converging and the mountain spurs descending to the town's northern perimeter.

As the leading units of the Eighth Army exulted in their triumphal drive north to the Yalu, the Chinese waited patiently in the hills. In the valleys, telltale signs of American overconfidence were everywhere apparent. The mechanised columns, clouds of dust billowing in their wake, were permitted to advance as fast and as far as possible, without close coordination and without reference to gains made by others. A great river of machinery churned up the dirt roads, polluting the air and filling the forests with the nauseous smell of diesel and gasoline. One senior cavalry officer—absurdly 'seated astride a massive cowboy saddle' in his jeep—roared past a British infantry column while the astonished soldiers looked on. Many of the men thought that this was the last brief phase of the war. There was loose talk of parading on Thanksgiving Day and Christmas shopping in Tokyo.

On 24 October, MacArthur casually removed the restriction imposed by Washington on the movement of non-Korean ground forces to the Chinese border. Although the Joint Chiefs felt compelled to ask MacArthur to explain this flagrant insubordination, the end of the war appeared to be in sight and it hardly seemed necessary to countermand his orders. In the field, however, some experienced officers on the drive north were uneasy. The temperature was dropping alarmingly, the terrain ahead was forbidding and, along the route, the roaring and grinding of the armed columns was met by the troubling, contrasting silence of absent villagers and whispering farmers.

Everything changed on 25 October. A South Korean division of the Eighth Army commanded by General Paik was strung out along the road running from the Chongchon River to Unsan. As a tank company of the leading regiment passed through the town and approached the bridge to its northeast, it was hit by concentrated mortar fire, halting the regiment's forward movement. A prisoner was later taken and interrogated. He looked Chinese, spoke Chinese and understood neither Korean nor Japanese. He told his interrogators that there were 10,000 Chinese troops in the hills north and northwest of Unsan and another 10,000 to the east. This chilling information seemed to be corroborated when the second regiment of General Paik's division reached Unsan, turned west and also found Chinese troops blocking its way. The third regiment, bringing up the divisional rear, remained south of the town and out of contact. Paik's entire South Korean division was stalled.

After three days, during which the fighting intensified and the evidence of a well-established Chinese presence grew, a frustrated General Walker, the Eighth Army commander, ordered the American 1st Cavalry Division to leave its position in reserve in Pyongyang, pass through the stalled Korean division at Unsan and continue the approach to the Yalu. This was not exactly what the Cavalry boys were expecting. Most were planning on being back in Japan on 4 November and marching in an Armistice Day parade on 11 November.

The luckless lead regiment was the 8th Cavalry. On 31 October, as its three battalions moved into position to relieve the stalled South Koreans around Unsan, huge smoke clouds filled the air from forest fires north and northeast of the town. They had been started the day before, deliberately lit by the Chinese to mask daylight troop movements and obscure aerial observation. On 1 November, as the smoke and haze continued, the tactical situation worsened. Reports came in of large numbers of Chinese soldiers in a valley southwest of Unsan moving east to cut the road south from the town to the Chongchon River. There were also reports of further enemy columns to the southeast. In the afternoon, radio chatter in the command post stopped when a shocked aerial artillery observer cut in: 'This is the strangest sight I have ever seen. There are two large columns of infantry moving south...Our shells are landing right in their columns and they keep coming.' The Chinese soldiers maintained their momentum, seemingly undeterred, as the ground heaved around them. By the afternoon of 1 November, the escape road south of Unsan had been cut and two rifle companies strongly supported by air strikes were turned back. The stage was now set—Chinese troops were positioned to the north, west and south of the town.

That night the men of the 8th Cavalry were anxious. Word had spread, as bad news tends to do, that there were about 20,000 Chinese in the area—substantially outnumbering the Americans. There had been small-scale probing attacks during the late afternoon but more were expected when night fell. The regiment's first and second battalions, positioned to the north and northwest of Unsan, were dangerously exposed while the third battalion, in a separate area southwest of the town, was wary but not yet vulnerable. As the men at the front stood to for the night and settled in to their positions, a meeting of senior staff officers was taking place in the rear at General Milburn's Corps headquarters. The intelligence reports and operations briefings made it palpable that the 8th Cavalry was likely to be surrounded, isolated and overwhelmed. Milburn reacted by directing the immediate withdrawal of the regiment's three infantry battalions—approximately 2500 men— to a secure position about twenty kilometres south of Unsan. The meeting had commenced at eight o'clock at night and by the time the decision was made and the order passed down the line, the 8th Cavalry had started to fall apart.

The initial attack on the first battalion commenced in the early evening. Musical instruments, like bugles and flutes, could be heard in the hills north of Unsan. Distinctive sounds, unlike anything the Americans had heard before, drifted out of the dark. No one recognised the sequence of notes. All that could be identified was a menacing foreign trilling that some likened to bagpipes—but it was subtler, lighter, not as harsh and more eerie. It was the chilling sound of Chinese entry into battle at night, signalling to one another and striking fear into the enemy. When the music stopped, the Chinese raced through the first battalion's thinly positioned lines, almost at will. There was little effective organised resistance. The speed of the Chinese was so great that some of the stunned soldiers said later that it was 'almost like a track meet'. The first battalion command post rapidly disintegrated. Wounded soon lay everywhere and a sense of chaos grew. When Milburn's order for the regiment to withdraw came through, the first battalion was already pulling out. In the confusion and darkness of the night, under heavy enemy pressure, a convoy of several tanks and about ten large two-and-a-half-ton trucks was put together to take out as many men as possible and any wounded who could be transported.

By eleven o'clock that night the second battalion to the west had also been hit and its situation was getting worse. Both the first and second battalions were now fighting for their lives. They were isolated and withdrawing closer to Unsan, not knowing that the Chinese were in their rear, already in the town. And Chinese roadblocks on the southern edge of Unsan ensured that no relieving unit could reach the town from that direction. As the growing number of fleeing American soldiers and trucks loaded with their wounded approached the town from the north and northwest, they were fired on by the waiting Chinese, causing ever-greater casualties. Millikin, the first battalion commander, ordered two tanks to attempt to crash through, followed by the trucks carrying the wounded. But the first tank was disabled when one of its tracks was blown off. And the second went down the wrong road and became mired in rubble. When its driver emerged, he was shot. A third tank was then sent in to destroy the two immobilised tanks. Millikin did not see the wounded again.

Before long, the pile up of damaged and destroyed vehicles and the escalating Chinese fire made any passage through Unsan impossible. In the disarray and darkness, the Americans began breaking into smaller groups, skirting Unsan, scattering into the hills and looping south on foot to a pre-determined road fork below the town. At the road fork, the level of congestion and confusion was acute. Supply units, artillery and mortar batteries and South Korean soldiers had already been passing through for hours—under constant enemy fire. They were soon joined by survivors from the first and second battalions. All night a steady stream of dazed men arrived at the road fork. By half-past one in the morning the withdrawal had been going on for five or six hours; the 8th Cavalry command post had closed; and effective communication had ceased.

But reaching the road fork brought no redemption. As the first and second battalions abandoned their defensive positions, the Chinese poured through, increasing pressure on the southerly retreat. South of the road fork, along the solitary escape road, they created an ambush zone where the opportunity to bring down overwhelming enfilade fire on the road made it a killing field. When one final push to open the road failed, the position became unsalvageable. There were no choices left and men in small groups began making their own way, disappearing on foot into the hills, gratefully assisted when daylight came by the arrival of American aircraft covering the sky. By noon, most of those who survived had reached the village of Ipsok, south of the Chongchon River, where the regiment had set up a temporary command post. It was 2 November—All Souls Day, as one of the chaplains pointed out.

Conspicuously missing was the third battalion. Its sector had been quiet during the earlier part of the evening when the first and second battalions were assaulted, but the Chinese knew where they were and the relative calm in their sector would not last. After midnight the air exploded with mortar and small arms salvos just as the battalion's many vehicles were being readied for departure. Ormond, the commanding officer, was supervising movement preparations. Firing began almost simultaneously outside the command post and across the battalion area. Within minutes of those first shots, Chinese bugles and pipes were heard above the clamour. There were pockets of resistance that night but nothing effective, nothing structured. The enemy was too fast and too hard-hitting. One soldier, a Private Simon from G Company, 8th Cavalry, reminisced on the unsoldierly mayhem that took over when the Chinese charged out of the gloom. He told Hastings: 'There was just mass hysteria on the position. It was every man for himself...I didn't know which way to go. In the end, I just ran with the crowd. We just ran and ran until the bugles grew fainter.'

When daylight came on 2 November, the Chinese broke off and withdrew into the wooded hills to the west, from where they continued their fire. The third battalion was now besieged. Without relief, its withdrawal was no longer possible. The men who remained did their best to form a defensive perimeter, digging a series of connecting trenches in the open field about seventy metres in front of the command post and positioning three tanks inside the perimeter. But only about 200 men were still combat effective. Another 170 wounded men, including the commanding officer, Ormond, the executive officer and the operations officer, were crowded in the dugout that constituted the command post. The rest of the battalion personnel was unaccounted for. Most had fled on the first night.

A junior officer took charge, expecting a rescue effort from the 5th Cavalry, but as night fell, talk of a relief mission died down. General Gay, the Divisional Commander, then made the hardest decision of his professional career. He left the men of the third battalion alone to fend for themselves and ended all relief operations. The next day a spotter plane dropped a message telling the besieged men to try to get out as best they could. When night fell, the Chinese attacked again and the number of able-bodied men holding the perimeter continued to drop. As ammunition became scarce, many of the defenders were reduced to using Chinese firearms scrounged off dead bodies. Then the last tank departed and with it all radio contact with anyone outside the perimeter. On 4 November a scouting party was sent to find a way out to the east. When two of the party returned and reported on an escape route, the many wounded knew that their fate was sealed. They would be left behind. A brave Captain Anderson, the battalion surgeon, volunteered to remain with the forsaken men at the command post, to surrender to the Chinese. The remnants of the battalion who were fit and able scrambled out that afternoon, escaping as best they could, travelling all night on foot through the hills towards Ipsok. Some made it but a greater number was captured or killed.

By 6 November the battle of Unsan was over—the first and second battalions of the 8th Cavalry Regiment had been mauled and the third battalion had ceased to exist as an organised force. The Chinese then broke contact, vanishing into the dense mountains north of Unsan as mysteriously as they had appeared. In the mountain fastness, away from the battlefront, their military leaders analysed the engagement and drew their tactical lessons. A few weeks later they issued a report entitled 'Primary Conclusions of Battle Experience at Unsan' setting out their analysis of the strengths and weaknesses of the performance of the 8th Cavalry. While giving due recognition to the power of American weaponry and rate of fire, the report's conclusions were unflattering:

[They] abandon all their heavy weapons, leaving them all
over the place, and play opossum...Their infantrymen are
weak, afraid to die, and haven't the courage to attack or
defend. They depend on their planes, tanks and artillery.
At the same time, they are afraid of our firepower. They
will cringe when, if on the advance, they hear firing.
They are afraid to advance farther...They specialize in
day fighting. They are not familiar with night fighting or
hand to hand combat...If defeated, they have no orderly
formation. Without the use of their mortars, they become
completely lost...they become dazed and completely
demoralized...They are afraid when the rear is cut off.
When transportation comes to a standstill, the infantry loses
the will to fight.

Failure of Intelligence

For the men of the 8th Cavalry, the unnerving speed of the Chinese
infantry was all too real. But in Tokyo, MacArthur and his G2, the chief
of intelligence, Major General Willoughby, were unpersuaded. They did
not see it as a warning of things to come. Nor did MacArthur see any
reason to abandon his plans for the Eighth Army's advance to the Yalu.
Three weeks earlier, at an insignificant coral atoll in the western Pacific
called Wake Island, he had assured a troubled Truman that the chances
of Chinese intervention were 'very little...If the Chinese tried to get
down to Pyongyang, there would be the greatest slaughter.' Willoughby
supported MacArthur then and continued to do so after Unsan,
maintaining that there was no major intervention and that the number
of Chinese troops in contact in North Korea was probably only around
16,500 men, possibly up to 34,000. He diminished the significance of the
8th Cavalry's drubbing, reportedly saying that the regiment had 'failed
to put out adequate security, been overrun by a small, violent surprise
attack, and had scattered during the hours of darkness'.

Willoughby was not alone in being loyal to MacArthur, verging
on sycophantic. A seasoned observer described the atmosphere among

MacArthur's general headquarters staff as 'simpering and reverential'. Another described it as 'an insular organisation that rewarded a compliant group of insiders, discouraged divergent thought and blocked outside influences'. And a military historian said that 'MacArthur surrounded himself with men who would not disturb the dream-world of self-worship in which he often chose to live.' The worst feature of this dream-world was that Willoughby presided over an intelligence operation whose primary function seemed to be the delivery of positive reinforcement to MacArthur for his strategic objectives while discouraging independent analysis and criticism. He ensured that MacArthur received the intelligence that he wanted; the intelligence that permitted MacArthur to take his forces where he wanted to take them. The charge to the Yalu would not be the only time in the modern era that fateful military and political decisions were built on limited truths and manipulated intelligence.

The G2 section of the Far East Command was part of the vast and comfortable military bureaucracy that operated from the fortress-like Dai Ichi Sogo building in the Marunouchi district of Tokyo. In that secure and rarefied atmosphere, overlooking the serene waters of the Imperial Palace moat, and an ocean away from the mountains of Korea, Willoughby—who had been born in Heidelberg, Germany, and changed his name from Weidenbach—built and administered a system of intelligence reporting that was essentially circular. The foundation was the G2's critical daily intelligence summary, which Willoughby directly controlled and personally edited. Around that document revolved the entire American system of intelligence reporting and publicity in Korea—the daily releases from the public information officer, the daily Washington situation reports, the daily telephone conferences with the Pentagon and the communiqués issued by MacArthur. Even the CIA's daily Korean summary and the Army Department's joint daily situation report drew on the G2 daily intelligence summary. The Army chief of staff in Washington estimated that Willoughby was the source of ninety per cent of the intelligence that the Pentagon used to develop its strategic planning and policy. And the CIA, while fusing reporting from its own sources, almost entirely derived its daily summary from Willoughby's analysis published by his G2 section.

No one has ever doubted that the burden on a good intelligence officer is heavy. He must work in the darkness and study the unknown; he must strive for objectivity, covering the sensitive ground between prejudice, instinct, cultural bias and reality; and he must try to think like the enemy and understand its history and motivation. But according to one contemporary, Willoughby was 'all ideology and almost never any facts'. He seemed incapable of recognising uncertainty; never understood or respected the Chinese; and was never objective. It was said that 'certitude after certitude poured out of him'. Confirmation bias was part of the problem, but it was more complex than that. MacArthur was, of course, no better and demanded no less. But one of the melancholy roles of a G2 is, and always has been, to tell his superior what he may not want to hear. Some of Willoughby's subordinate intelligence officers were sure he was wrong but they were 'pulled along by the power of the command above'. One said later that the unfolding catastrophe in Korea in late 1950 was 'the saddest thing I was ever associated with because you could almost see it coming, almost know what was going to happen, those young men moving into that awful goddam trap'. Hastings' criticism was trenchant: 'The conduct of the drive to the Yalu reflected a contempt for intelligence, for the cardinal principles of military prudence, seldom matched in twentieth century warfare.'

A number of strategic, operational and tactical certainties confronted Willoughby. All were part of the composite intelligence picture and should have caused alarm bells to ring. One inescapable fact was the multiplicity of explicit political warnings from Beijing, threatening to enter North Korea if American forces crossed the 38th parallel. Willoughby, like Secretary of State Acheson and most of the military and political establishment in Washington, dismissed the warnings as bluff and blackmail. They were ignorant of China's very real fear of American aggression and unable to believe that China would challenge the United States. But Zhou En-Lai's words on 3 October were unequivocal: 'We cannot sit idly by and remain indifferent. We will intervene.' If Zhou's statement was not clear enough, on 10 October Beijing radio broadcast a public declaration to the same effect. And around the same time, an escaped American officer revealed that he had been interrogated in North Korea by three Soviet officers and that one of them, a senior colonel, told him that 'if US forces crossed the 38th parallel new communist forces would enter the war in support of North Korea'.

Another inescapable fact was the undisguised massing of Chinese troops and facilities in Manchuria. Willoughby's daily intelligence summary for 14 October acknowledged the numerical and troop potential in Manchuria, noting that a 'total of 24 divisions are disposed along the Yalu River at crossing points'. Not only did Willoughby know that several hundred thousand troops had been moved from the Taiwan Strait region to Manchuria, but extensive and ongoing infrastructure development was observable near the border in the vicinity of Andong. The improvements included bases, landing strips and expanded air force facilities. The CIA estimated that three airfields at Andong alone could support up to 300 combat aircraft. On 3 November, as the 8th Cavalry was capitulating before the Chinese at Unsan, Willoughby's daily intelligence summary conceded Chinese strength in Manchuria as '833,000 men, of whom 415,000 were Chinese communist regular ground forces'.

At the operational level, consistent intelligence from prisoners captured in the field had started coming in from 25 October. This source of information, always valuable if uniform and aggregated, was treated with scepticism and denial in Tokyo and airily dismissed as 'unconfirmed and thereby unaccepted'. The Chinese prisoners were interrogated intensively in the field. Several were flown to Pyongyang and given lie-detector tests. The first prisoner, a Private Chung San Chien, was even questioned by the South Korean General Paik. He told his interrogator that he was a regular soldier from Guandong; that he was a member of the Chinese People's Liberation Army; that he and his comrades had been sent to Korea to prevent an invasion of China by the United States; and that there were tens of thousands of Chinese in the mountains near Unsan. The interrogation report went on to provide detailed information on the entry by the prisoner's unit to Korea on 19 October across the Yalu River from Andong. The interrogators assessed the information to be fairly reliable but Willoughby responded implausibly by saying that the prisoner was probably a Korean resident of China masquerading as a Chinese—a conclusion he was only able to reach by ignoring four pages of questioning in which the prisoner described in detail his initial entry into the Chinese Nationalist Army in 1949, his capture by the communists in February 1950 and his subsequent training and movement to Manchuria with the People's Liberation Army.

Another prisoner was interrogated by the South Koreans on 26 October. The resulting interrogation report indicated that at least 50,000 troops from the Chinese 40th Army were already in Korea and that they had crossed the Yalu on 15 October. Then there was the account by the American Sergeant 'Pappy' Miller of the 8th Cavalry, who led a patrol on the day his unit arrived at Unsan and came across an old farmer who told him that 'there were thousands of Chinese in the area, many of whom had arrived on horseback'. Yet further corroboration came from interrogations of prisoners captured by the 5th Cavalry near Unsan between 28 and 30 October, which revealed more detail of the scope and intention of the Chinese intervention. And when General Paik looked at the dead on the battlefield around Unsan, he said they were 'all Chinese'. By 30 October, the Eighth Army held ten prisoners who were unarguably Chinese and had identified the presence in Korea of known units of the People's Liberation Army. Willoughby ignored the identification of these Chinese units. He was prepared to concede only that an unknown number of Chinese had been incorporated 'into North Korean units to assist in the defence of border areas'. He added: 'There has been no indication of open intervention on the part of Chinese Communist forces.'

At the same time, on the more mountainous eastern side of the peninsula, where X Corps was advancing to the Yalu from a different direction, General Almond, the commanding officer, personally interviewed sixteen Chinese prisoners on 30 October. They had been captured in the hills along the axis of advance toward the Chosin Reservoir. The prisoners volunteered detailed information about their division's infiltration into Korea, which they said had commenced on 14 October. The X Corps G2 was so concerned that he informed MacArthur and Willoughby in Tokyo that 'integral CCF units have been committed against UN forces'. The added significance of the geographic dispersion of Chinese units—right across the peninsula from positions in the west in front of the Eighth Army to positions in the east in front of X Corps—was now obvious. Yet in Tokyo there was a reluctance to draw any inference that a large-scale Chinese intervention had commenced. Willoughby reported only that 'indications so far point to piecemeal commitment for ostensible limited purposes'.

Nothing would convince MacArthur to change course. And nothing, it seems, would persuade Willoughby to impede MacArthur. He downplayed the quality of proof of individual items of intelligence while ignoring the cogency of the cumulative weight of the evidence. This was an inversion of accepted methodology. For in intelligence gathering, the probability of an overarching inference increases with the number, frequency and consistency of the individual events from which the inference is derived. The result was 'one of the most glaring failures in US military intelligence history'. But years later, Paul Nitze, who had succeeded Kennan at the State Department, offered an unsettling explanation for MacArthur's continued push to the Yalu, despite the intelligence of a Chinese threat: 'Part of the reason he took these excessive risks was to create a situation in which we would be involved in a war with the Chinese communists.'

CHAPTER 8

American Calamity

'I hate war as only a soldier who has lived it can'

MacArthur's troops went deeper and deeper into North Korea, closer and closer to the border with China. Some even reached the Yalu and stayed briefly—but long enough to ceremoniously piss, like schoolboys, in the freezing waters of the river. None of them was aware of Mao Zedong's writings on the art of war and military strategy, which were not published in the West until 1954. One of those uncelebrated and unappreciated works was a treatise called 'On Protracted War', which Mao had composed in 1938 at the height of the Japanese invasion of China. His exposition on the subject of 'luring the enemy in deep' was unknown, as was his telling aphorism, since immortalised in the annals of irregular warfare:

> Enemy advances, we retreat.
> Enemy halts, we harass.
> Enemy tires, we attack.
> Enemy retreats, we pursue.

But such a strategy was exactly what Mao and Peng planned for the 'second phase' of China's war against the American-led forces in Korea.

Lured in Deep

When the sounds of battle abruptly stopped around Unsan on 6 November and an unnatural quiet descended, no one was sure what had happened. The Chinese appeared to have deserted the battlefield. Their surprise onslaught had 'all but destroyed' two South Korean divisions and 'cut to pieces' the American 8th Cavalry Regiment. But the number that had entered the war, their current location and the reason for their abrupt disengagement were all mysteries. When pressed for an explanation by the Joint Chiefs on 6 November, MacArthur's wildly inaccurate estimate of the number of Chinese in the war was 30,000 to 40,000. Any more, he insisted, would have been observed from the air.

In fact, the true number of Chinese in Korea at that time was in excess of 200,000 men and more were coming. Most of them were in the mountains to the north of the Chongchon River, hidden from view, nowhere to be seen. Up there, where the ridges generally run north–south, where the narrow winding valleys splinter in all directions and where many of the peaks exceed 2000 metres, nineteen divisions of Chinese infantry, thousands of animals and countless pieces of equipment were wholly concealed. By late November, six Chinese armies were in place on the western side of Korea opposite the Eighth Army and two Chinese armies were in place above the Chosin Reservoir in the east opposite X Corps. And no one knew they were there. It was the most successful mass infiltration of modern warfare.

Understandably, there had been a degree of official consternation after the debacle at Unsan. Both the Joint Chiefs in Washington and the British government queried the wisdom of continuing the offensive but MacArthur managed to assuage their nervousness. His commitment to the northern advance never really faltered. The Australian mission in Tokyo believed that it understood MacArthur's real objective and was prepared to say so—reporting bluntly on 7 November that 'MacArthur believed that it was time for a showdown with Communism'. The British war correspondent Reginald Thompson was not alone in thinking that MacArthur nursed 'dreams of the conquest of Asia' and that he 'saw himself as a Genghis Khan in reverse, threatening to bring down the world about our ears'.

As relentless daily reconnaissance flights failed to reveal the troops camouflaged in the North Korean mountains, and days passed without contact, an unhealthy, almost delusional confidence rapidly returned. MacArthur insisted to Washington that there was no full-scale intervention by the Chinese. But just in case, he claimed histrionically that his forces were threatened with destruction if the flow of men and materiel across the Yalu were not stopped. And for good measure, he controversially ordered his air force bombers to attack the bridges over the Yalu and to create a wasteland between the front and the Chinese border—destroying from the air every 'installation, factory, city and village'. The worst occurred on 8 November, when the border town of Sinuiju was visited by one of the great apocalyptic spectacles of the twentieth century—a massed formation of B-29 Superfortresses. Seventy-seven of the huge aircraft, glinting silver crosses on the skyline, dropped their deadly payload on the city and its two bridges. But it was too late to prevent the Chinese crossing. Their infantrymen remained undetected and untouched in the mountains. One writer described them poetically as 'a phantom which cast no shadow'. And soon the river would freeze and the bridges would be unnecessary anyway.

While the Chinese consolidated in the mountains, the Eighth Army re-grouped and re-supplied in the valley of the Chongchon River. And X Corps did the same below the Chosin Reservoir in the northeast. The demands of ordnance and logistics were so heavy that the resumption of MacArthur's northern offensive, initially scheduled for 15 November, was put back to the day after Thanksgiving, 24 November. The need for extra time was partly attributable to the vast disparity between the logistical requirements of a Chinese soldier and those of his American counterpart. Typically, for every Chinese soldier forward, there was one man back, while the Americans had nine back to support one forward. And a Chinese soldier required fewer than five kilograms of supply a day, even in the Korean winter, while his American equivalent needed almost thirty kilograms. Extrapolated to the divisional level, the average Chinese division 'required only fifty tons of supplies per day, [and] the average US division 610 tons'.

One difference was in rations—'a bag of millet meal against scores of tins, of candy, Coca-Cola, and toilet supplies'. But there were other contrasts and myriad differences. For example, many but not all American troops were issued with six pairs of woollen ski socks and an ineffective form of waterproof boot known as a 'shoepac'. And on one busy November day, seventeen transport aircraft brought 33,000 field jackets to the front and six more aircraft delivered 40,000 pairs of mittens and 33,000 mufflers.

The timing of Thanksgiving added a surreal dimension to the process of re-supply. On the eve of an unparalleled catastrophe, American army cooks and service personnel were kept busy preparing —and attempting to transport to every remote unit in the field—a wondrous meal of turkey, cranberry sauce, shrimp cocktail, pumpkin pie and fruitcake. Tens of thousands of frozen turkeys arrived from Japan; ration trucks drove off preposterously in every direction to deliver their valuable cargo; and some soldiers hungrily consumed their last supper. At numerous regimental headquarters, in the midst of the ruins of burned-out villages, elaborate menus were printed and tables laid with white cloths and decorated with candles and flowers—while elsewhere 'the slow processions of the stricken refugees toiled painfully in the sombre shadows of the hills'. Such incongruous largesse was not without precedent. In Europe in November 1944, Eisenhower had ordered that every soldier under his command should receive 'a full turkey dinner'.

Bug Out

The morning of D-Day, 24 November, dawned bleak and blustery. The winter cold was already intense—freezing or below—though not as bitter as it would soon become. The whole of the United States Eighth Army, including approximately half of the South Korean Army, lined up to advance to the Yalu across the western side of the peninsula. Approximately 130,000 men with their vehicles, tanks, artillery and supply 'trains' were spread from left to right along a broad front. They were grouped in units in the customary way—by corps made up of divisions, regiments, battalions, companies and platoons. The assemblage had the appearance of a mighty force, but many of the soldiers were accustomed to the life of an occupation army in Japan and were without combat experience. They were overfed and under-trained and most elements were missing some of their winter clothing. Some elements were without it entirely.

The centre-right of the front was beneath Unsan along the Chongchon River. This is where the 2nd Infantry Division was placed. It was the pivotal position in the line, unknowingly facing the heart of the Chinese concentration. Immediately to its right, on the eastern flank, was a South Korean corps consisting of three divisions. Like the American division, it would be eviscerated. The situation was similar to that of the Persian army facing the Greeks at the Battle of Marathon in 490 BCE, except that the Persians had known what was in front of them. In both cases, the invaders were roundly defeated and driven out.

As the ill-fated columns of the Eighth Army lumbered into action, Willoughby's daily intelligence summary from Tokyo reported, tragicomically in retrospect, 'There are some indications which point to the possibility of a withdrawal of CCF to the Yalu River or across the border into Manchuria.' It could not have been more wrong and was simply wishful thinking. MacArthur's communiqué on the eve of the advance was even more unrealistic. It caused experienced war correspondents to despair. One said that it 'filled us with alarm and despondency'. And when MacArthur flew in to oversee the resumption of the advance, he was overheard to say that he expected the boys to be 'home for Christmas'. The Eighth Army was so poorly informed without knowing it, so confident without sound reason, that its generals genuinely expected a quick victory and the rapid extension of control to the Chinese border. The advance, popularly known as MacArthur's 'end of war offensive', barely made twenty kilometres before it was stopped in its tracks and turned around. Within days, amid sickening loss of life, the men of the Eighth Army were fleeing by every means available. By the afternoon of 27 November, the movement had gone from withdrawal to retreat to flight. And the nightmare unfolded.

The advance had started without serious incident, except for the South Korean infantry divisions on the far right that met stiff opposition immediately. But in other parts of the line, the Chinese were luring the Americans into their trap. In some sectors they even encouraged them, ostentatiously withdrawing in front of the advancing army. All changed late on 25 November when the three regiments of the Chinese 120th Division left their assembly areas near Unsan and headed south in a dogtrot to the Chongchon River. Each man carried five days' rations of corn and millet, four grenades and a hundred rounds of small-arms ammunition. Not all carried a firearm. At the river, they stripped and waded across in attack columns, line abreast, holding clothes and weapons dry above their heads. On the other side, some hardly bothered dressing and attacked immediately. They had specified assignments and knew the location of their targets.

By midnight, two more Chinese divisions—the best part of 20,000 more men—had come across the Chongchon River and were everywhere in motion against the frontline units of the American division, hitting hard and moving fast. The latter were outnumbered and unprepared, poorly positioned and inadequately dug in. Some had discarded their helmets for the comfort of warm pile caps; some saw no use for bayonets and had thrown them away; most had made only desultory efforts to dig foxholes and trenches in the rock and shale; and many were shot or bayoneted in their sleeping bags. Frequently the Chinese made straight for command posts, ignoring lesser targets, shooting signalmen and junior officers, knocking out radios and cutting field telephone lines. Some were under orders not to stop, running through the lines and cutting off escape routes to the rear.

On that first night, through the dark hours after midnight, the American infantrymen, occupying frigid, isolated, frontline positions among unfamiliar hills, fought hundreds of small, violent and deadly battles. Most were overrun, leaving behind rations, equipment and ammunition. When the point units fell back, as they invariably did, they found more Chinese in their rear. Shock soon metamorphosed into fear. Chinese infantrymen emerged from the darkness like apparitions, appearing and disappearing. As day followed night, a sense of dread, of desperate danger, grew. Each night was worse than the last. There were, no doubt, individual acts of bravery but the collective response was feeble and some soldiers did not behave like soldiers. One eighteen-year-old private painfully described what happened when somebody shouted 'Every man for himself!' Then, he said, 'there was really chaos. Everybody just bugged out...There was a complete loss of leadership... It was a nightmare, really...I still think about it—the bodies blown up, the Americans run over by [their own] tanks, the panic and shooting in the nights.'

By the second night, 26 November, the 10,000 strong force of the 2nd Infantry Division had been pushed back over three kilometres. On its immediate left, the only African American infantry regiment in the Eighth Army, known as 'Deuce-Four' (24th Infantry), belonging to another division, was also heavily punished. Its sorry story was 'largely one of disorder, ineptness, breakdown of communications, units getting lost in bad terrain, heavy personnel and equipment losses, and a cause of concern to friendly units on its flanks'. To the east, the three divisions of the South Korean corps were pulling out in chaos, abandoning guns, vehicles and equipment. According to one account, they had made 'only a few hundred yards from...their kick-off point' before they crumbled.

The situation became so bad, so quickly, that by 27 November, the centre and right flank of the Eighth Army line of advance had imploded. The British Brigade Commander, Basil Coad, called in from the far-left flank where there was no serious action at that stage, described a level of 'hysteria at IX Corps HQ [that] was quite frightening and [which] did not improve as the days went on' and that by '21.30 hours...general withdrawal was being openly discussed at Corps HQ'. In fact, planning for withdrawal was well underway and was confirmed the next morning by a general order from Eighth Army headquarters issued by radio to all American divisions.

What followed could hardly be described as a 'withdrawal' in the military sense. In the pell-mell race to the south, battalions lost track of companies; companies lost track of platoons; divisions even lost track of regiments; and young men, separated from their units, became ever more frightened in their loneliness. Every kind of military vehicle set off down the rutted, single-track roads. And traffic control was non-existent. Jeeps, light and heavy trucks, load carriers, tankers and engineering plant shamelessly jostled with each other in their self-interested flight from the oncoming Chinese. Often the Chinese were already ahead of them—leading to the unsettling sight of American guns firing wildly in almost every direction, including to the south, in the direction of the withdrawal.

As the withdrawal progressed, the tumult and affright became worse. The whole of the Eighth Army was destabilised—on the move without any clear idea of how far it would go or where it would stop. No serious consideration was given to standing and fighting. The Chinese had established a moral and military ascendancy by their mastery of concealment and surprise, their cross-country marching over mountain tracks, and their persistent attacks in flank and rear. And their resolve only grew as the road-bound columns of desperate soldiers clogged the way south, creating easy targets. It soon became apparent that worse was ahead. On two terrible days—30 November and 1 December— American casualties dwarfed those suffered during any other stage of the war. The 2nd Infantry Division again suffered the most. Not only did it incur the brunt of the initial Chinese assault on 25 November but during the Eighth Army's withdrawal, it made up the rear guard. By 30 November it was the last unit still in contact with the Chinese; the last to run the gauntlet. The war correspondent Reginald Thompson wrote the following poignant eyewitness account:

> Each day the rear guard columns licked their wounds and
> awaited the hideous night. Against this nightmare warfare,
> undisciplined, ill-led, ill-trained troops, even scornful of
> discipline as in some way infringing their rights, could
> find neither defence nor attack. Unaccustomed to march,
> and clinging to their vehicles and equipment, they offered
> themselves as a sacrifice to the enemy. They were not short
> of courage, but of all of the arts of war.

The division's route south from the Chongchon River was along the gravel and dirt road from Kunu-ri to Sunchon, a distance of about forty kilometres. After Sunchon the road was clear to Pyongyang. A ten-kilometre stretch of this road was referred to as the 'gauntlet' and a 600-metre section at the top of a hill was known as the 'pass'. It consisted of a cut made through the hillside, with rock embankments that rose high on either side. At several points along the road and especially at the pass, the Chinese established fire blocks with machine gunners, mortars and infantry. Their existence was known or suspected but their size and extent were not. Nor was it appreciated that the Chinese were pouring in reinforcements by the hour to strengthen and augment the fire blocks. On the morning of 30 November the beleaguered and exhausted men of the 2nd Infantry Division were ordered to 'break through' along this road with the assistance of close air support from fighter-bombers. What followed became known as the 'death ride'. It was one of the grimmest sagas of the war.

All of the unwieldy, mechanised impedimenta of modern warfare, and thousands of anxious men, moved off warily. A whole division's worth of tanks, trucks, jeeps and gun carriages, even prime movers and bulldozers, was packed nose to tail. Frightened soldiers crowded on top of tanks, jammed into trucks and squeezed into jeeps. When enemy fire was encountered, the drivers accelerated and men discharged their weapons wildly, repeatedly, often aimlessly. When vehicles were hit and disabled, blazing wreckages blocked the way forward. Soldiers were flung down, bodies spreadeagled over the road and in the ditches. The vehicles that followed hesitated, then rammed the wrecks in front of them, brutally endeavouring to clear the way, desperate to escape the enemy fire, frequently running over bodies, dead or alive.

Soon the road was a scene of carnage, strewn with just about every piece of equipment the army had in Korea—'every small arms weapon and some artillery pieces, vehicles of every nature, but worst of all men'. Infantrymen dismounted, seeking their own salvation, rarely finding it. All the while enemy fire rained down and screeching fighter-bombers swooped low, strafing the Chinese gunners and spilling napalm, sometimes torching their own men as well as the enemy. Amid the terror and panic, in scenes worthy of Hieronymus Bosch, the agonised screams of burnt and wounded young soldiers were lost in the dust, drowned by the whine of aircraft and muffled by explosions of small arms fire. And as the column moved forward in spurts, dead and wounded were left behind—littered along the road among the useless metal carcasses of trucks, weapons carriers and jeeps.

It was a day of tears. The division was overtaken by a paralysis of command and discipline. Officers and men were numbed; their spirits broken. Order and hierarchy broke down; structure disappeared. The fog and fear of war swamped everything. Panic became infectious. In that barren landscape below Kunu-ri, the morale of the men of the 2nd Infantry Division flickered and died. They were terror-struck by the carnage, intimidated by a superior force and stunned by their reversal of fortune. One writer thought that it was the United States Army's 'most hideous ordeal since the Battle of the Bulge'. The casualties were heart-rending; the loss of equipment staggering. Over 4000 men were killed, wounded or missing in the breakout. And among the untold waste and destruction, three artillery battalions actually lost or abandoned every one of their pieces. The spent and harrowed survivors struggled in to Sunchon on 1 December. From there they joined the general retreat of the Eighth Army, which continued on and on. It ended 'six weeks later when a defensive line was drawn across Korea 300 road miles to the south'.

The retreat had little objective other than to create as much distance as possible from the Chinese. A succession of phase lines was established, then abandoned, then re-established further and further south—from north of Pyongyang, to Pyongyang, to Seoul and then to south of Seoul. The Chinese soldiers kept chasing, pushed unwisely by Mao, even across the 38th parallel. The shameful flight finally stabilised when the Chinese could not keep up. And the term 'bug out' became a new phrase in the English lexicon. It referred to soldiers or units that simply ran away without fighting; who bugged out. The British Commander-in-Chief in Hong Kong, Sir Robert Mansergh, pulled no punches in his secret report to the Chiefs of Staff in London. Referring to the Eighth Army's debacle, he wrote of 'the American lack of determination' and their inability to 'stand and fight'. And he observed, with a wry disdain, that their 'rations, supplies and welfare stores are on such a scale as to be comic if they were not such a serious handicap to battle'. Within days, General Keiser, commander of the 2nd Infantry Division, was relieved of his command and a few weeks later General Walker, who commanded the Eighth Army, lost his life in a jeep crash.

Annihilation

Things were worse, if possible, in the forbidding mountains and frozen wasteland around the Chosin Reservoir in northeast North Korea. At the same time as the Eighth Army was being humiliated on the western side of the peninsula, an understrength infantry regimental combat team belonging to X Corps was being annihilated on the eastern side. Two battalions of infantry, one of artillery and a further artillery battery lost all their equipment and almost all of their men. 'Not a single vehicle, artillery piece, mortar or machine gun was saved.' For five nights and four days they endured sub-zero temperatures and climatic conditions not faced by the United States Army before or since. Appleman, the American military historian, said that 'No American troops have ever fought in an environment as harsh or as hostile', adding: 'There is no other story of the Korean War to compare with it.'

The battlefield was the Chosin Reservoir, located on a plateau in Korea's northeast highlands, approximately 1500 metres above sea level. It is surrounded by jagged peaks—some over 3000 metres high—from which runoff and spring snowmelt cascade into the catchment. On 27 November the combat team was heading north along the eastern side of the reservoir as part of MacArthur's push to the Yalu. The Siberian high-pressure system was exacting its annual toll, generating pitiless winter conditions. The surface of the reservoir was frozen and the surrounding country was blanketed by snow and ice. A wolfish Manchurian wind blew from the north. Cylinder blocks cracked;

rifle bolts and rocket-launcher rounds froze; gun barrels split; tinned food, plasma and water bottles turned to ice; and medics had to thaw morphine syrettes in their mouths. Corpses left in the open were piled high like bags of ice, no longer a sanitation problem. The cold was so intense that wounds were sealed by the cold and blood froze before it could coagulate. It produced the perverse result that normally fatal injuries would not kill outright; the wounded men would only die when brought into the warmth, when their blood started to flow.

The first ominous sign came that afternoon when a reconnaissance and intelligence platoon was sent ahead to establish an outpost near an inlet at the north-eastern extremity of the reservoir. The men, mounted on jeeps with machine guns, headed north into the wind and vanished, never to be seen again. There was no explanation and there were no survivors. The platoon's evanescence was the precursor to a coordinated Chinese attack that commenced that night and continued for the next four. The Chinese came in force, in superior numbers, and infiltrated the frontline positions with ease.

The men were so cold, so inexperienced, so lacking in discipline, that they dozed when they should have been alert. Officers later complained bitterly that they knew the men were asleep but 'If they kicked them to wake them up, they were scared of being shot'. By morning, the Chinese had moved back into the hills, leaving the frontline soldiers rattled, sleepless and ridden with casualties. The two infantry battalions were separated from each other. And after the first night's attack, all three battalions were cut off in their rear.

Late the next night in Tokyo, MacArthur consulted his commanders. The devastating Chinese assault in the west had been ongoing since 25 November and Walker's Eighth Army was in retreat. Now the Chinese had commenced their assault in the east. MacArthur began to speak pessimistically of 'an entirely new war' against 'an entirely new power of great military strength'. He told General Almond, the commander of X Corps, to disengage—to end offensive action and withdraw out of the highlands, away from the Chosin Reservoir; to concentrate his tens of thousands of Marines and infantrymen and their vast array of equipment in the vicinity of the port of Hungnam. But disengagement was easier said than done.

The exposed and separated units of the regimental combat team on the eastern side of the reservoir needed to consolidate, break through the Chinese in their rear and reach a small Marine outpost and landing strip at Hagaru, a village about twelve kilometres to the south, at the base of the reservoir. If they made it that far, they could link up with the Marines retreating down the western side of the reservoir and continue on the road to the port at Hungnam. But it was not to be. Almost all of the infantrymen would perish in the snow and ice before reaching Hagaru. It was an epochal horror. Colonel Maclean, the regimental commander, was lost early—missing presumed dead—and two of his three battalion commanders were wounded and evacuated. Overall command devolved to Lieutenant Colonel Faith, whose assortment of doomed men and machines was dubbed 'Task Force Faith'. For two nights they suffered attritional losses in the crude defensive perimeter they had formed in the snow. Ammunition was in short supply; morphine, bandages and medical supplies were near exhausted; the men had been fighting without sleep for three nights; many had been exposed to extremes of cold they could never have imagined; and more than 500 wounded men needed to be taken to safety.

By 1 December there was little choice other than to attempt to move out. But as the American movement preparations became apparent, the Chinese intensified their fire, adding to the casualties. The wounded were loaded into about thirty trucks that had been emptied of their cargo. Each truck carried fifteen to twenty men laid flat in the back. Many more would be added during the day. The leading vehicles had barely made fifty metres before coming under sustained Chinese fire. Marine air support was called in and flew low over the convoy—only to create a maelstrom. One plane released its napalm tank prematurely, hitting the vehicles in the vanguard. Defenceless, pitiable, already wounded soldiers were set ablaze from head to foot, burned black, staggered and rolled on the ground. One surviving soldier recounted how 'Men I knew, marched and fought with, begged me to shoot them. It was terrible...Men begged to be shot. I couldn't.'

Those who witnessed their agony faltered, and officers had a hard time bringing the troops back to the task. When the trucks moved on, sometimes only at walking pace, they were raked endlessly with fire from Chinese rifles and machine guns. Many of the wounded, lying prone in the back of the trucks, were hit two or three more times. One young man recalled that the 'thud of impacting rounds and the moans of the wounded were unforgettable'. Drivers were especially vulnerable, presenting an easy target to the Chinese on their left, who were firing from the ridge running parallel to the road. And when drivers were shot, or when they abandoned their vehicles, replacements were hard to find—for the job was considered suicidal.

Soldiers were scared to move and 'huddled and crouched around the trucks seeking their protection'. Officers were killed and wounded as they exposed themselves, trying to rally their terrified men along the road or to attack Chinese positions. Surviving officers referred to the 'reluctance, the surly unwillingness' of the men to obey orders. All the while, the excruciating cold wreaked havoc and a deadly storm of lead rained down on the convoy. At every obstacle, the murderous fire increased in intensity. And with each stoppage, men slipped away, taking their chances on foot, seeking to cross the icy reservoir on their right, anything to escape from the Chinese.

When the column reached a blown bridge in mid-afternoon, the trucks laden with wounded were winched roughly across a lumpy, bumpy swamp. One witness recalled 'the wounded screaming in anguish as they were jostled and slammed into one another on the truck beds'. Jangled nerves, edged raw with fatigue and anxiety, were stretched to breaking point by the extreme cold, the unceasing horror and the spectre of death or capture. When Faith found two of his own men—attached South Korean soldiers—hiding under a truck, apparently attempting to tie themselves to the undercarriage, he was so enraged that he pulled out his service revolver and shot them dead, in the snow.

The column ground forward at an agonising pace. With each hour there were more dead and wounded, fewer functioning trucks and ever more desertions. When Faith was struck in the chest by grenade fragments, any remaining discipline went with him. One sergeant recalled that after Faith was killed 'it was everyone for himself. The chain of command disappeared.' The wounded suffered horribly and many could not be retrieved. Those who could be picked up were stacked, suffocatingly, sometimes haphazardly, on top of each other in the back of the decreasing number of trucks. It was a mixed blessing. In a frenzy worthy of Dante, several stalled or abandoned trucks were rammed and pushed aside, spilling and crushing the wounded men inside. Their frantic screams 'seemed like the world gone mad'. When night fell, and the temperature plummeted to thirty degrees below, there was yet another blown bridge, another stoppage and another Chinese roadblock. Five kilometres from Hagaru the pathetic convoy stalled for the last time under a hail of Chinese fire. All hope was lost. Soldiers ran, preferring to take their chances across the ice of the reservoir. Some crawled. Chinese soldiers trotted alongside the trucks, tossing in phosphorous grenades, incinerating men and vehicles. It was the end. A survivor recalled thirty-five years later: 'There was no resistance left in the column...The only sound heard was the moaning of the wounded and dying.'

Marine Escape

A total of 319 men from Task Force Faith was rescued from the reservoir on 2 December and dragged in on sleds to the Marine base at Hagaru. The Marine colonel who led the rescue party said that they were 'a disorganised mob, hysterical with fright, and only a few of them were armed'. A few more stragglers were brought in over the succeeding days. All of them were dazed and disorientated; many carried wounds; many had frostbite; some were delirious with shock and exposure. A Marine patrol the next day estimated that there were approximately 300 charred bodies in the convoy when it finally halted. Thousands of dead or wounded had been left behind on the road, in the ditches and on the hills. Some had been captured. The overall casualty rate was about ninety per cent. Only a minority of officers survived. Appleman said that 'nearly all the officers and experienced non-commissioned officers had been killed or seriously wounded'. The most fortunate of the survivors were evacuated by air while the remainder joined the Marine retreat coming down from the western side of the reservoir.

The withdrawing Marines had a different experience to that of the Army units on the east side of the Chosin reservoir. To start with, they were a more powerful force and constituted a whole division—almost 12,000 men in three regiments. They were well led by Major General Oliver Smith. There were more survivors. They kept their artillery and they brought out most of their wounded. But the physical conditions were extreme and the casualties were high. The ever-cautious Smith was justified when he wrote angrily from the battlefield in mid-November to the commandant of the Marine Corps in Arlington, Virginia, complaining about his orders from X Corps. He stated presciently, 'I believe a winter campaign in the mountains of Korea is too much to ask of an American soldier or Marine, and I doubt the feasibility of supplying troops in this area during the winter or providing for the evacuation of sick and wounded.'

The first men from the withdrawing Marine column to arrive at Hagaru appeared during the evening of 3 December. They had fought their way down the western side of the reservoir from Yudam, under constant Chinese attack for three days. It had been a repetitive blur, contesting hill after hill, ridge after ridge. The most intense fighting was always at night, in darkness, when all that one could see were darting shadows and muzzle flashes; when the cold was so severe that exposed skin stuck to grenades, rifles and shells; when the combination of adrenalin and freezing temperatures deadened pain and enabled wounded men to fight on longer than seemed humanly possible. When they walked in to the perimeter of the base, snow and ice encrusted their helmets, their parkas, their unshaven faces; some stared blankly, dazed and uncomprehending; many winced as swollen, purplish flesh touched the frozen ground. The walking wounded hobbled, leaning on their rifles or clinging to their 'buddies'. Many more wounded came on vehicles, some strapped on litters across the hood, some on the bare metal, many unconscious, perhaps '1,500 of them in all'. Marguerite Higgins from the *New York Herald Tribune* said 'They had the dazed air of men who have accepted death and then found themselves alive after all.'

Hagaru was a respite but it was not a refuge. It was merely the end of the first leg on the torturous journey to the safety of the coast. The column moved out again at dawn on 6 December—headed south through the fog to Koto, a village about sixteen kilometres down the road where Smith had established another small base. By this stage there were more Chinese troops blocking the path to the sea than there were behind the withdrawing column. But Chinese supply lines were primitive and a great many of its infantrymen were now in poor shape—frozen, starved and demoralised—without adequate supplies of food, ammunition or warm clothing. There were skirmishes all the way but the Chinese attacking force had worn itself out and was blunted. After thirty-eight hours of continuous movement by the Marines, without fires for warmth or hot food for strength, the Koto phase of the evacuation concluded, only to be met on 8 December by a snowstorm that blanketed everything. It was the coldest day of the year to date. Many of the Marines had reached the limits of physical endurance. They had lost another 600 men dead, wounded and missing but '10,000 troops and more than 1,000 vehicles [were] safe'.

The last leg of the retreat, from Koto to Hungnam, out of the highlands and down onto the coastal plain, was another agonising, freezing, energy-sapping journey. Along the way, there were grievous mishaps, another blown bridge, and many more casualties from exposure, exhaustion and Chinese fire, but Smith's men eventually reached their destination on 11 December. Their prolonged torment had been 'the worst ordeal in Marine history'—not just because of the men who were killed, wounded and missing in action but also because of the thousands of non-battle casualties. But as bad as the experience was, the Marine division had not been annihilated, unlike Task Force

Faith. The Chinese were disappointed that they had not been able to destroy the Marines but they had over-extended themselves, fighting for too long in savage conditions, without air support, sufficient rations, adequate ammunition or any artillery. Beijing, however, celebrated. The Eighth Army had been routed in the west. And in the east, both the Marine and Army units of the United States X Corps had been repulsed. The American-led incursion into North Korea was over.

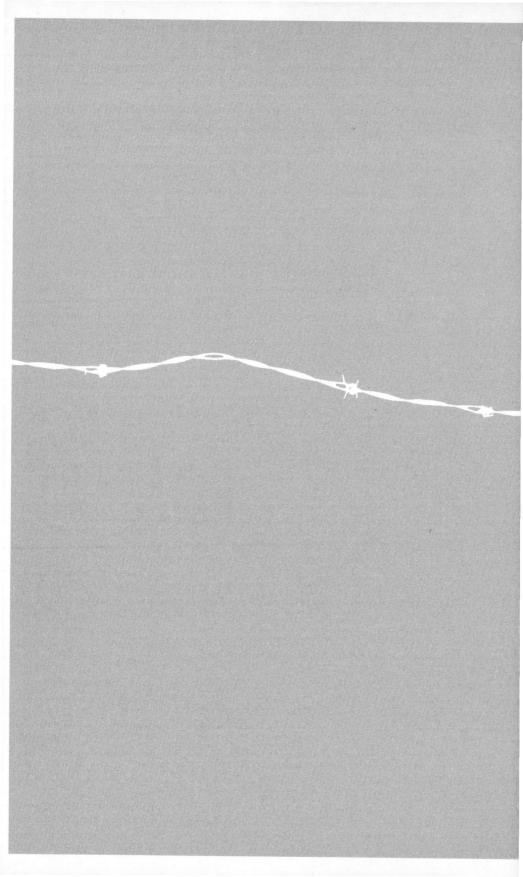

PART 4

The American Response

CHAPTER 9

Indignation and Attrition

'The trumpet shall sound'

As the American units withdrew from North Korea, they left a trail of destruction and waste. Pyongyang and the ports of Chinnampo and Hungnam were singled out for wholesale demolition but almost every village the soldiers went through was set on fire. Even haystacks were burnt. US Defense Department broadcasts, making the best of a bad situation, boasted 'that few buildings [will be] left in which the Chinese Reds will be able to hide from observation or attack'. According to the war diaries of the 24th Infantry Division, the 'razing of villages along our withdrawal route and destruction of food staples became the order of the day'. Some rank and file soldiers enjoyed the process. Others felt guilty and were sickened by the vandalism, the arson, the excess. Much of what they did or witnessed was surreal, nightmarish. The writer Andrew Salmon said that the 'spectacle of a nation put to the torch was lurid, Biblical'.

Retreat and Destroy

The scorched earth policy commenced officially on 2 December as the Eighth Army was chaotically preparing to abandon Pyongyang without a defensive stand. Units were told to destroy everything that could not be evacuated. Surplus rations, winter clothing, gasoline, stockpiles of rice, wheat, barley and millet, not to mention homes and buildings, went up in smoke. One of the last US servicemen to leave Pyongyang recalled that 'In one place, the engineers burned a rations dump about the size of a football field. God, it was a shame to see it in a land of hunger—all the food going up in smoke...I believe we set on fire most of the villages we passed through.' Ostensibly, the destruction was to deny the enemy, but as the harsh winter tightened its grip, its immediate effect was on the civilian population. From 2 to 5 December, explosions and fires proliferated across Pyongyang. The whole city appeared to be ablaze—like Atlanta being burned by General Sherman during the Civil War when 'inhabitants were driven into exile, and their homes... left blackened monuments of barbarism and cowardice'.

One cataclysmic series of explosions stood out above all others. A truck loaded with ammunition from a nearby ammunition supply point caught fire, causing an unstoppable chain reaction of exploding and bursting shells among the stored munitions. The galloping fire and thunderous explosions continued all night—like an out-of-control fireworks display—until '100 tons of British ammunition and 900 tons of American ammunition' were eventually destroyed. Among the losses were over 10,000 rounds of howitzer shells. The waste in all units was unrelenting. When another small explosion erupted in an ammunition car at the main rail yard and temporarily halted rail movements, an American engineering battalion, whose supplies and heavy equipment had been loaded on 185 flat cars pending departure, abandoned the lot. Over at the drill field of the North Korean Military Academy, an area that was about six to eight hectares, a vast collection of US Army ordnance needing repair was collected—including thirty or forty tanks, 200 trucks, 300 weapons carriers and much more. Little could be salvaged and most of it was bulldozed and burnt. And, of course, all the bridges over the Taedong River, newly built by the American-led forces as they had approached Pyongyang only two months earlier, were now systematically demolished as the army reversed direction.

The Pyongyang railway station was a mob scene. Confused and despairing American troops, anxious to head south, sat in stationary passenger cars for two days waiting for a locomotive. Outside the station, frightened and angry Koreans, desperate for food and uncertain of the future, looted and ransacked what they could. When a steam locomotive was finally produced and the soldiers moved out, there was 'a terrible sense of shame'. At divisional headquarters, the panic, the urgency and the fear of the approaching Chinese meant that there was no time to preserve official military records. Thousands of boxes and reams of paper were piled high on bonfires. The past was obliterated and the Eighth Army fled, never to return north of the parallel.

On the east coast, at Hungnam, the destruction was worse. As the Marines and their equipment were evacuated in a convoy of ships that set sail for the southern safety of Pusan, nothing was left for the enemy or the civilians. Food stocks, bridges, boats, locomotives, carriages, signals, rails, port facilities, oil tanks and cranes were blown up, sunk, burnt or destroyed. The orders were simple: the port of Hungnam was to be turned into a wasteland. Civilians became refugees because they had no choice; because there was nothing to stay for. Dispossessed and fearful, they joined long, pitiable queues thronging the icy docks. One said, 'We were afraid of soldiers—Russian, communist or UN—soldiers are soldiers.' The last merchant ship to leave Hungnam was the 455-foot SS *Meredith Victory*. She was registered to carry twelve passengers and forty-seven officers and crew but her saintly captain—a man named Leonard La Rue who later became a Benedictine monk and adopted the name 'Brother Marinus'—allowed 14,000 frightened and tearful Koreans to come on board. He remembered, 'There was a man with a violin, a woman with a sewing machine, a young girl with triplets. There were seventeen wounded, some stretcher cases, many aged, hundreds of babies.' They were all delivered to safety on Christmas Day. La Rue said it was the turning point in his life; his ship became known as the 'Ship of Miracles'.

The destructive culmination in Hungman came on Christmas Eve. It was the 'most spectacular, most terrible manifestation of the... scorched earth policy'. The docks were rigged with tons of explosives, which were ignited; a long line of synchronised explosions was detonated; thunder boomed across the water; and to ensure that nothing was left standing, a simultaneous naval barrage was unleashed from offshore. Everything—quays, cranes, warehouses and lighthouses—was obliterated. The bombardment, led by the USS *Missouri*, rained destruction far inland. Each sixteen-inch shell fired from the turrets of this floating fortress cost the price of a Cadillac. The justification was strategic but in reality it was a display of impotent fury.

Hawks Ascendant

It was the nadir of the conflict. And the circumstances called for a pragmatic re-appraisal—perhaps even the acceptance of temporary defeat with dignity and good grace. China had suffered substantial casualties but it had taught the United States a lesson and dealt a blow to its pride. From Princeton, George Kennan called it 'unquestionably a major failure and disaster to our national fortunes'. At a minimum, Washington should have recognised that the decision to send MacArthur's forces across the 38th parallel and to threaten China on its Manchurian border had been an egregious mistake.

Kennan told Acheson that what counts most is not what happens to a man 'but how he bears what happens to him'. He urged the Secretary of State to accept the blow 'with candour, with dignity, with a resolve to absorb its lessons'. He counselled that if we 'permit ourselves to seek relief in any reactions of bluster or petulance or hysteria, we can easily find this crisis resolving into an irreparable deterioration of our world position'. The advice was ignored. A troubled and belligerent President spoke loosely about using the atomic bomb; rebuffed the ceasefire recommendations of British Prime Minister Attlee; and bizarrely declared a state of national emergency. Overreach in Korea was followed by overreaction at home. The dominant response was indignation. Acheson, who had a well-known aversion to the United States appearing weak or defeated, was determined 'to find a place to hold and fight the Chinese to a standstill'; Truman to 'stay and fight as long as possible'.

Even allowing for his fear of communism, Truman's proclamation of a national emergency on 16 December 1950 was dripping with melodrama and excess. It was a call to arms, summoning 'all citizens...

our farmers, our workers in industry and our businessmen...every person and every community...all State and local leaders' to make 'a mighty effort to meet the defense requirements of the Nation'. The supposed justification was the need 'to repel any and all threats against our national security'. The reference to national security was stretching things—cold war or not. It was the beginning of America's ever-widening concept of a 'threat' to its national security. Dean Acheson articulated it later as any threat to the nation's 'power, position and prestige'. It meant that America could go anywhere on the planet to repel a threat to its national security—real or imagined.

In early December, an alarmed Prime Minister Attlee travelled to Washington for personal consultations with the President. Truman said he would consult before any use of nuclear weapons but was unwilling to put his promise in writing. He was unshakeably opposed to recognising China or giving it a seat on the United Nations as the price of a ceasefire. Nor would he countenance 'cutting loose' Taiwan, where the nationalists led by Chiang Kai-shek constituted an anti-communist buffer of sorts. Truman and Attlee were divided by a combination of ideology and pragmatism. The former clung fervently to the belief that Mao's regime was a tool of Soviet Russia; while the British view, which proved to be correct, was that the People's Republic of China was as much nationalistic as communist. The opposing perspective, shaped by the China Lobby and rooted in the unique world of domestic American politics, made it impossible for Truman to consider either a ceasefire or political concessions to Mao's China. But on this question the United States was out of step with most of the rest of the world. Warren Austin, the United States Ambassador to the United Nations, found that 'most nations shared the British view that China should be bought off with concessions'. In an echo of the future, Richard Stebbins, writing for the Council on Foreign Relations, noted that 'A good many delegations now seemed to consider restraint of Communist China less important than restraint of the United States.'

Within the United States, the impediments to a ceasefire, and pressure for expansion of the war, were everywhere. Aggressive voices in Congress, the Defense Department and among the general public called ever more loudly for 'retaliation' and 'punishment'. Anything less was considered 'appeasement' of China. And there were frequent calls to use nuclear weapons. On 24 December MacArthur submitted 'a list of retardation targets which he considered would require 26 [atomic] bombs'. And he requested '4 bombs to be used on invasion forces and 4 bombs to be used on critical concentrations of enemy air power, both targets of opportunity'. General Bradley, chairman of the Joint Chiefs, was bitter. He urged action against China with the worryingly simplistic statement: 'We used to say that an attack on a platoon of United States troops meant war. Would anyone believe it now if we don't react to the Chinese attack?' The Navy and Air Force chiefs were predictably belligerent, wanting to 'repay the Chinese for their deeds' by blockading the Chinese coast and bombing Chinese cities. And none of these military men cared about the United Nations. Admiral Sherman advocated unilateral action even if the UN did not agree— to which the venerable George Marshall, Secretary of Defense, gave his support, saying that 'we must consider first of all the security of the United States'. He was presumably referring to America's power, position and prestige.

In the State Department, Dean Rusk, whose 1945 pencil line across the map of Korea was, in one sense, the origin of the problem, suggested ambiguously that America 'could try to void China'. John Foster Dulles, another warrior of the period, proposed using Taiwan as a base for covert and even overt activities against mainland China. No one in the State Department, and certainly not in the Defense Department, was prepared to recognise the legitimacy of the People's Republic of China, despite its founding in 1949 and its timely recognition by the United Kingdom and other countries. Nor was any extensive effort made to ascertain the real reason why China had introduced its forces into Korea in such strength. The CIA's wayward speculation was that it was part of a Soviet master plan—thinking that George Kennan, who became United States Ambassador to the Soviet Union in the next year, tried vainly to extinguish. But Truman and Acheson clung to the idea.

The latter famously said, 'We are fighting the second team, whereas the real enemy is the Soviet Union.'

Wrong Way Ridgway

As the new year began, attitudes in the United States hardened. China's demands for a seat at the United Nations and the removal of American forces from Taiwan—which were not unreasonable from a historical perspective—were repugnant to Washington. But for some UN member states, political concessions such as these 'retained considerable appeal in circles which felt that Peking had been unfairly treated in the past and must be conciliated at almost any cost in order to avoid a possible general war'. Prime Minister Attlee urged 'a supreme effort' to consider China's perspective—'to see clearly into each other's hearts and minds'. But he and Truman were vastly different men, with divergent perspectives. And in early January, when Mao demonstrated his own hubris by sending his armies across the 38th parallel in pursuit of the Eighth Army, the fires of American indignation and aggression reached a new intensity.

The indignation coincided with a pivotal change in the military command. General Walker—harried, despondent and much criticised for the Eighth Army's uncontrolled 'bug out'—died in the field two days before Christmas. His replacement was General Ridgway, a man known for his no-nonsense, hands-on approach. Ridgway breathed new life into a dispirited army, touring frontline units in freezing weather and writing later of his first impressions: 'Every command post I visited gave me the same sense of lost confidence and lack of spirit. The leaders, from sergeants on up, seemed unresponsive, reluctant to answer my questions.' Ridgway stiffened their resolve, bringing about a 'toughening of the soul as well as the body'. He dismissed generals, engaged in the wholesale relief of senior officers and disabused the enlisted men of any hope that they might evacuate the Korean peninsula. Not surprisingly, they called him 'Wrong Way Ridgway'. Strangely, he always carried a grenade strapped to his chest, reminiscent of the silver-plated revolver constantly at General Patton's hip during World War II. But whatever the reason for this showmanship, Ridgway successfully transformed the Eighth Army.

Reluctantly, slowly, the Eighth Army cranked up, turned around and headed north again. Its progress was now made easier by the steady lengthening of China's supply lines and the inevitable weakening of the fighting capacity of its armies—just as Peng had warned an overly impatient Mao. Seoul was recaptured in early March. At the end of the month, the front was re-established more or less along the 38th parallel, where it remained for more than two years of further conflict—like a grim remnant of the trenches on the Western Front during World War I.

Once back at the border where the hostilities had started, some understandably thought that the conditions for a ceasefire now existed. A truce on the basis of a rough parity of military positions looked possible, 'and signs were that the Soviets in particular, but also the Chinese, agreed that the time was right for talking rather than fighting'. But from the American perspective, there was little chance of a truce at that stage. The restoration of the status quo that existed before the North Korean invasion might have appeared rational but it would also have deprived the United States of the opportunity to deflate the military prestige of the Chinese. Truman, Acheson and the Joint Chiefs would not let go of their desire for political and military retribution. And Truman's pugnacious side, even in his personal life, had become painfully and publicly obvious. On 6 December, he wrote to Mr Paul Hume, the music critic for the *Washington Post* who had given an unfavourable review of a performance by his daughter Margaret, saying, 'Some day I hope to meet you. When that happens, you'll need a new nose, a lot of beefsteak for black eyes, and perhaps a supporter below!' Hume made the letter public.

While Ridgway was re-organising the Eighth Army, Truman played his major political card—despite initial opposition and anxiety from European and Commonwealth governments, even from a number of Asian, Arab and Latin American countries. He sought a UN resolution condemning China as an aggressor in Korea, principally for having advanced south of the 38th parallel. The irony of doing so when, only four months earlier, the American-led UN forces had crossed the parallel in the opposite direction seemed to be lost. Acheson's lobbying for the resolution among member states was eventually effective but it was heavy handed and threatening. He told Bevin, the British Foreign Secretary, that 'UN failure to recognise China as an aggressor would not only mark the beginning of the end of the United Nations as a collective security organisation but also set off a wave of isolationism [in the US] which would jeopardize...the Atlantic Pact countries'. There was little practical choice. The bullying succeeded and the aggressor resolution was passed on 1 February. It put an end to indirect and tentative discussions that had taken place in January between Beijing and Washington.

And the prospect of further discussions in the short term was derailed by an unauthorised and hard-line intervention by MacArthur. It was deliberate sabotage. He did not want a truce but an all-out effort to carry the war to China and thus 'save Asia from...engulfment'. A few weeks later Truman relieved him of his command and sent him home—into the arms of his conservative supporters, who greeted him as a returning hero and urged him to run for president. In New York, twice the number of people turned out to see MacArthur as had honoured Eisenhower on his return from Europe. MacArthur's self-adulatory message to Congress was broadcast over a nationwide radio network 'into every community and often into every school in the community'. But at the Congressional hearings into his dismissal in May and June 1951, he was put in his place by the Washington heavyweights—Acheson, Marshall and Bradley. And by the time of the 1952 Republican national convention his star had begun to fade. It is wrong, however, to attribute the failures of the Korean conflict to MacArthur. The fault was broad-based and institutional and others were also to blame. MacArthur's fear of China and his determination to be aggressive toward it were, and remain, a pervasive American characteristic.

Russia salvaged the situation in June when Jacob Malik, the Soviet ambassador to the United Nations, called for a ceasefire including the mutual withdrawal of forces from the 38th parallel—prompting the formal start of armistice negotiations on 10 July 1951. It was the beginning of a tortuous process. The negotiations concluded on 27 July 1953—two years, two weeks and millions of deaths later.

The Pentagon Way

The armistice negotiations were accompanied by ever-expanding and more punitive US bombing—in the belief that the bombing would lead to concessions at the truce talks. Military operations were intensified across the board and the defence budget expanded exponentially. The first surge in the intensity of the bombing came in late July 1951 when the Joint Chiefs approved Ridgway's plan for an air strike on an almost desolate Pyongyang using 370 medium and light bombers and fighter aircraft—on the condition that 'no publicity be given to the mass nature of the raid'. A few weeks earlier, and only three days after the start of armistice negotiations, the Joint Chiefs had demonstrated their collective short memory, as well as their preference for military pugilism, by recommending that permission be given—once again—to advance north of the 38th parallel. Truman demurred.

Official policy was nonetheless to continue 'strong efforts to deflate Chinese Communist political and military strength and prestige by inflicting heavy losses on Chinese forces in Korea'. Deflating Chinese prestige was seen as central to the maintenance of the power, position and prestige of the United States. There was much boyish talk of 'retribution' and restoring 'credibility'. Washington was motivated, as it still seems to be, by a 'baser concern with showing Asia that the United States could inflict a military defeat on China'. This crude goal became a controlling factor in the armistice negotiations and in the continuing disposition of the war; a war that had grown out of control from its humble origins as a successful UN police action, which had achieved its objective after three short months.

As ever, Washington's foreign policy was dictated by domestic political sentiment. The febrile politics of the era ensured a considerable public lust for expanding the war. Most wanted to 'get peace or hit harder'. In one poll in April 1951, the majority of respondents favoured bombing Manchuria. And a third of the respondents urged a general war against China. Another poll found that sixty per cent of respondents wanted the United States to give Chiang Kai-shek's nationalist forces 'all the help they needed to attack the Chinese Communists'. American antipathy toward Mao Zedong's regime was resolute, as was resentment at the supposed 'loss of China'—a concept that was unique to Americans.

During the congressional enquiry into MacArthur's dismissal, General Marshall predicted strenuously that 'Taiwan would never be allowed to fall into the hands of the Communists or the PRC allowed to assume a seat in the United Nations'. The ties between the United States and the outlawed nationalist regime on Taiwan were becoming ever more tightly bound—giving rise to a self-created core issue that continues to sour Sino-US relations. And Dean Rusk's hard words, which seemed almost designed to sabotage the armistice negotiations, revealed another misconception. He called the regime in Beijing 'a colonial Russian government—a Slavic Manchukuo on a larger scale', adding bizarrely that 'It is not the Government of China. It does not pass the first test. It is not Chinese.' Even Truman was troubled by Rusk's assertions. It is no wonder that the British ambassador observed that Washington's policy in the Far East seemed to be 'drifting...in the direction of that espoused by General MacArthur'.

Many in the military establishment favoured the expansion of the war into China. Numerous proposals were put forward to increase military pressure and harass China, not always with allied approval or knowledge. One proposal, with echoes of modern tilting in the South China Sea and the Sea of Japan, involved the mounting of a large and disturbing naval operation—twenty warships and 140 aircraft—as a 'show of force' in the Taiwan Strait. Another included the expansion of covert operations in China 'to increase the problems of control all over China...divert more of the regime's resources to internal security problems...and somewhat weaken Communist military capabilities'. Another recommended 'US involvement with guerrilla warfare on the mainland as a prelude to larger overt operations using Chinese Nationalist forces'. Naturally, the up and coming CIA found itself in the thick of things.

The Joint Chiefs pushed for military expansionism. In April, they recommended 'immediate preparations for naval and air action against the Chinese mainland'. And a few weeks later, they secretly embraced a request from Ridgway 'to attack enemy bases in Manchuria and the Shantung peninsula following any major air attack from... behind enemy lines'. Ridgway was given carte blanche to attack at his discretion 'without further reference to the JCS or higher authority'. Acheson, who was mindful of inevitable British concerns, protested and the matter was taken to Truman, who resolved it in favour of the military, while adding an ambivalent qualification about 'minimising' allied dissension.

Truman now sided increasingly with the military. And the State Department gradually gave ground to the Defense Department. The hawks were in the ascendant. Within months, the Joint Chiefs boldly proposed a further widening of Ridgway's authority so that the bombing of Chinese air bases could be pre-emptive and not merely responsive. And when Ridgway sought the removal of restrictions on the bombing of Rashin on the Russian border, Bradley promptly gave his approval, subject to the President, notwithstanding that he had given a contrary assurance at the MacArthur hearings. By the end of 1951, a Pentagon paper canvassed the option of all-out war against China because it would 'provide a significant strategic opportunity, perhaps the last opportunity, for the United States to weaken and undermine the Soviet Union's principal ally'.

Acheson managed to hold the line against these more excessive aspirations of the military establishment. But, as the armistice negotiations continued, the only course that Truman could see was to steadily increase the infliction of military punishment. He favoured military force over diplomatic compromise as the preferred method of resolution. And as the negotiations became prolonged, he decided in favour of greater force. In early 1952, a petulant Truman revealed his dark inner feelings in a private jotting—unwisely retained—in which he wrote that unless Moscow changed its policies, there would be all-out war. 'It means,' he mused, 'that Moscow, St Petersburg, Mukden, Vladivostock, Peking, Shanghai, Port Arthur, Dairen, Odessa, Stalingrad and every manufacturing plant in China and the Soviet Union will be eliminated.' The future, he thought, was either an end to hostilities in Korea or 'the complete destruction of China and Siberia'. To use a phrase famously coined by the *New York Times* journalist James Reston in the context of the bombing of North Vietnam, it seemed as if it were 'war by tantrum'.

Washington's War

It was no surprise that when General Mark Clark replaced Ridgway in May 1952, Truman authorised new levels of bombing and destruction. Clark was a well-known supporter of MacArthur's apocalyptic strategy for ending the war. He duly orchestrated a marked increase in the frequency, intensity and harshness of the bombing campaign over North Korea—even though there were fewer and fewer legitimate targets. The stepped-up bombing raised international concerns that the military was exercising too great an influence on Washington policy; and consternation that if it were permitted to dominate policy, the inevitable culmination would be the extension of the war to China. An associated concern was whether Washington, or its military leaders, could be trusted. These widespread anxieties were expressed by Nehru, the Indian Prime Minister, when he said that he was 'disturbed at the thought that the future of the United Nations and of war and peace... might ultimately depend on the discretion of military commanders who would naturally think more of local military objectives than of large questions affecting the world'.

There had been allied concerns about trust during MacArthur's tenure as Supreme Commander and they were always just below the surface, but they re-emerged with the first major bombing raid on Clark's watch. In early June 1952, he ordered attacks on all North Korean power installations except those located on the Yalu River, which the allies had agreed were proscribed targets. Despite that prohibition, the Joint Chiefs could not resist the opportunity to extend Clark's plan to include the Suiho power station on the Yalu, justifying it to the Defense Secretary on the basis that it was the largest and most important of all Korean hydro-electric plants. The United States Air Force was only too happy to oblige and the first massive sortie of approximately 500 aircraft took off on 23 June. That raid and those following 'caused a power blackout in North Korea for 15 days'. Of greater international significance was the direct effect on China. The bombing 'resulted in the loss of 23 percent of Manchuria's power requirements for 1952'.

Contrary to protocol, the British government, led once again by Winston Churchill, had not been informed of the intended operation. And Churchill's new Foreign Secretary, Anthony Eden, afterwards pleaded with Acheson for 'no more surprises'. More troubling was the fact that the defence minister, the illustrious Lord Alexander—Viscount, Field Marshal and former Governor General of Canada, who had only recently been a personal guest at Clark's headquarters—had been kept in the dark, as if he were a member of the 'mushroom club'. Acheson apologised glibly for the error and described it unconvincingly as a 'snafu': situation normal all fucked up. But Washington was seen to be dissembling and the raids undermined the Truman administration's credibility with its allies. In particular, the Foreign Offices of London and Ottawa believed that consultations with them had been deliberately avoided 'for fear that the allies would raise objections'.

Acheson attempted valiantly to keep the allies on side, to maintain the appearance of a United Nations crusade rather than as a narrow pursuit of American national interests. He was genuinely concerned about allied cohesion; Truman less so; and the Pentagon barely at all. This was the first modern 'coalition of the willing'. In reality, it was an American show from first to last, and the alliance was uneasy and unequal. The senior command structure was entirely American and all of the foreign units were subordinated and integrated into American corps under the command of US Army generals. Each of them reported to the Eighth Army commander, who in turn reported to the Supreme

US Commander in Tokyo, who in turn took instructions from the Joint Chiefs at the Pentagon, who in turn advised the Secretary of Defense and the President, who was the Commander-in-Chief. The United Nations organisation was not part of the military chain of command. Everyone knew that:

> for all the great and sincere efforts that were made by senior
> Americans to cloak their efforts in Korea in the mantle
> of the United Nations, from beginning to end the conflict
> could never be other than Washington's war, to which other
> states provided token contributions chiefly for the diplomatic
> appeasement of the United States.

Fifteen surprisingly disparate countries answered the call to provide combat forces: Australia, Belgium, Canada, Colombia, Ethiopia, France, Greece, Luxembourg, the Netherlands, New Zealand, the Philippines, South Africa, Thailand, Turkey and the United Kingdom. All contributions were relatively minor, at least compared to that of the United States; and most countries wanted something in return—money or treaties or both.

The peak number of American ground forces during the conflict was in the order of 330,000 men. This was more than ninety per cent of total allied ground forces. The United Kingdom, Turkey and Canada sent brigades (3500 to 5000 men) while most other non-American forces were battalion size (about 1000 men or less). South Korea was a separate case and Australia eventually provided a second battalion in 1952. Many of the soldiers from lesser nations were actually clothed, armed, equipped, ammunitioned and fed by the United States—which each of those countries was notionally obliged to repay at the rate of $14.70 per man per day in the field.

In the skies, the United States Air Force, supplemented by the Marine and Navy air units, was overwhelmingly dominant. Australia and South Africa each initially provided a fighter squadron of propeller-driven Mustangs and the British provided a Sunderland flying boat squadron, each of which was absorbed into 'wings' of the US Air Force. But these contributions were minuscule compared to the huge numbers of American aircraft, pilots, navigators, bombardiers and ground crew that were sent to Korea. There were losses—on some occasions considerable—caused by Russian-built MIG jet fighters or improved anti-aircraft defences, but it remained true that the Americans ruled the skies. Fighter pilots could go 'weeks, even months, without glimpsing an enemy aircraft'. And unless the bomber boys flew over 'MIG Alley' in the northwest corner of North Korea near the Yalu River, 'flak seldom troubled them' and most days 'they saw no sign of enemy fighters'.

CHAPTER 10

The Bombing Campaign

'For behold, darkness shall cover the earth'

The air superiority of the United States ensured that the bombing campaign in North Korea was 'long, leisurely and merciless'. And no name is more closely associated with it than that of the cigar-chomping Curtis LeMay, the 'father of overkill', who maintained his views to the last and went so far in the next decade as to contend that North Vietnam should be bombed 'back to the Stone Age'.

The Mind of the Bomber

LeMay came to prominence in World War II as the Air Force general who orchestrated the massive incendiary attacks on sixty-six Japanese cities in the last months of the war, taking the United States into a new era of warfare. The greatest of these was the firebombing of Tokyo on the night of 9 March 1945 by 300 B-29 Superfortress heavy bombers. It was the single most destructive bombing raid in human history and the deadliest of World War II—greater than Dresden, Hamburg, Hiroshima or Nagasaki. The raid killed more than 100,000 civilians, displaced over a million, destroyed 250,000 buildings and incinerated forty-one square kilometres at the centre of the world's most densely populated city—an area far larger than that destroyed by the first atomic bomb.

Truman once pointedly said that the fire bombing of Tokyo—before he became President—'was one of the most terrible things that ever happened'. More people were killed, slowly, more agonisingly, than in the atomic bombings of Hiroshima and Nagasaki. Aircrews at the tail end of the bomber stream reported that the stench of burned human flesh permeated their aircraft when over the target. One recalled: 'At 5,000 feet you could smell the flesh burning. I couldn't eat anything for two or three days...it was nauseating really.'

Much the same happened in North Korea—only more often, over more towns and cities, and for a longer period. And LeMay, as head of Strategic Air Command, was again responsible; and Truman was his commander-in-chief. LeMay was the world's foremost practitioner of obliteration bombing. The Luftwaffe's Herman Goring and the Royal Air Force's 'Bomber' Harris 'weren't even in the same league'. When LeMay reminisced on his achievements in Korea, he remarked with unflinching casualness that 'Over a period of three years or so, we killed off—what—twenty percent of the population of Korea as direct casualties of war, or from starvation or exposure?' He added that we 'eventually burned down every town in North Korea anyway, some way or another, and some in South Korea, too'.

LeMay's attitude to civilian casualties was morally indefensible by any standard. 'There are no innocent civilians,' he said. 'It is their government and you are fighting a people, you are not trying to fight an armed force anymore. So it doesn't bother me so much to be killing the so-called innocent bystanders.' His attitude was a familiar refrain among flyers—who engaged in 'an impersonal, abstract form of violence'—but it was less common among soldiers on the ground who faced death at close quarters. LeMay's estimation was that 'we killed off over a million civilian Koreans and drove several million from their homes'. He conceded, however, that 'I suppose if I had lost the war, I would have been tried as a war criminal.'

He was probably right on the last point. When the Charter of the International Military Tribunal at Nuremberg was agreed in August 1945, it formulated four crimes for which Nazi leaders—not allied leaders—would be tried. Two of them were 'wanton destruction of cities, towns or villages not justified by military necessity' and 'inhumane acts committed against any civilian population'. It was said that these were not new crimes and that the Nuremberg tribunal was 'an instrument of enforcement', giving effect to the customs, usages and practices of civilised nations. In the period 1945 to 1949, the protection of civilians and the morality of urban area bombing were much debated—primarily because of the British bombing of German industrial centres and the American bombing of Japanese cities.

The international discussions led to the 1949 Geneva Conventions, the fourth of which addressed the issue of the protection of civilians in time of war. The first additional protocol, not finalised until many years later, but even today not ratified by the United States, prohibits indiscriminate and disproportionate bombing. This includes attacks not limited to specific military targets; attacks that strike military objectives and civilians without distinction; bombardments that treat cities, towns and villages as a single military objective; attacks that are excessive in relation to the 'concrete and direct military advantage anticipated'; and the bombing of dams and dykes.

Targeting Cities and Towns

North Korea presented unique difficulties for an effective bombing campaign. In addition to its mountainous terrain, it was relatively undeveloped, with only a fraction of the identifiable and worthwhile industrial targets that had existed in Germany and Japan. When the war commenced, Truman was mindful of the international debate and ordered that bombing should be 'not indiscriminate'. Initial targets were therefore military and strategic, but few were large enough to justify attack by medium and heavy bombers in the massed formations in which they were accustomed to fly. The Far East Air Force Bomber Commander, Major-General 'Rosie' O'Donnell, even complained that in the first six months, 'We were not at that time permitted to…go to work on burning five major cities in North Korea to the ground'. But he added, 'We did it all later anyhow.' And air force historian, Robert Futrell, explained that in the first months of the war the 'Joint Chiefs would generally disapprove massed air attacks…if such attacks could possibly be interpreted to be against the civilian population of North Korea'.

This moral circumspection was short-lived; its demise influenced by the cult of overwhelming air power that was popularised in American culture by, of all things, an animated Walt Disney film called *Victory Through Air Power*. Even Roosevelt was taken by it. So 'When China intervened...and the United States began to lose', the bombing strategy moved progressively to 'urban area bombardments'. MacArthur ordered the Air Force to 'destroy every means of communication, every installation, every factory, city and village' north of Pyongyang, from the Chongchon to the Yalu rivers. O'Donnell gave this testimony to the MacArthur hearings in June 1951:

> *Senator Stennis*: Now, as a matter of fact, Northern Korea has been virtually destroyed, hasn't it? Those cities have been virtually destroyed?
> *General O'Donnell*: Oh, yes; we did it all later anyhow...I would say that the entire peninsula is just a terrible mess. Everything is destroyed. There is nothing standing worthy of the name...Just before the Chinese came in, we were grounded. There were no more targets in Korea.

Committee Chairman Russell then commended O'Donnell, telling him: 'I think you have demonstrated soldierly qualities that [have] endeared you to the American people.'

When Clark replaced Ridgway in May 1952 and the armistice talks stalled, the Joint Chiefs requested, and Truman approved, an increasingly heavy-handed bombing strategy. All American commanders who were engaged in fighting on the peninsula 'recognised that they could now take more forceful action'. More and more targets became substantially civilian—dams, reservoirs, hydro-electric stations, power installations, irrigation systems and other works, not to mention cities and towns. One United States Air Force general even controversially announced over Seoul Radio the names of seventy-eight North Korean towns 'scheduled for destruction'. The avowed purpose of this change in combat operations policy was to induce a 'more cooperative attitude' at the truce talks. In reality, this was a euphemism that concealed an absolutism. It meant simply that the object of the bombing was to compel agreement on the terms of an armistice that the United States demanded. Civilians came to be seen 'as a strategic target not as incidental casualties'. Clark saw heavy bombing of towns as a means of 'undermining the morale of the people of North Korea and their ability to wage and support a war'.

The British questioned the legitimacy of such bombing but Truman was determined to adopt a tougher stance, notwithstanding the effect on civilians. His urgent desire to end the conflict meant that the lives of hundreds of thousands of Asian people were treated as dispensable. There were similarities in this respect with his decision to use the atomic bomb in August 1945. Truman's purpose then had been to strike a psychological blow to Japanese morale in order to induce an unconditional surrender. Hiroshima was predominantly a civilian target and had never been included among the thirty-three targets on 21st Bomber Command's priority list. The US Strategic Bombing Survey noted that 'all major factories were on the periphery of the city—and escaped serious damage'. As had been the case in Japan in 1945, so it was in Korea.

As the armistice talks ground on into 1952 and 1953, the bombing campaign in Korea became a form of psychological warfare designed to influence the outcome. One operation was actually called Operation Insomnia. Most of North Korea was levelled—'systematically bombed town by town'. Cities and towns were razed, leaving a landscape pockmarked by piles of bricks and the foundations of buildings. MacArthur had already said in 1951: 'The war in Korea has almost destroyed that nation. I have never seen such devastation…If you go on indefinitely, you are perpetuating a slaughter such as I have never heard of in the history of mankind.' Dean Rusk said that the United States bombed 'everything that moved in North Korea, every brick standing on top of another'. One captured American soldier taken north by his captors recalled that 'everywhere we marched we saw total devastation. The Air Force must have bombed their targets over and over again.' Air Force records themselves noted that 'virtually no structures remained above ground in the cities of Hwangju, Kunu-ri, Sariwo and Sinanju'.

By late 1952 the population of Pyongyang was down to about 50,000 people from half a million before the war. The few officials who had not moved to safety at Kanggye in the north operated from underground bunkers; many women and children had been sent to China; and those who remained lived a troglodyte existence in caves and holes in the ground. Robert Lovett, who succeeded Marshall as Secretary of Defense, made the American objective clear: 'If we keep on tearing the place apart, we can make it a most unpopular affair for the North Koreans. We ought to go right ahead.' The notorious double agent George Blake explained that he changed sides because of:

> the relentless bombing of small Korean villages by
> enormous American flying fortresses. Women and children
> and old people...It made me feel ashamed of these
> overpowering, technically superior countries fighting
> against what seemed to be defenceless people. I felt I was
> on the wrong side.

Others shared his point of view but there were few protests and little knowledge of what was really happening.

In July Operation Pressure Pump began with practically every operating air unit in the Far East let loose in a savage assault on Pyongyang. In the first attack, the Air Force flew over 1200 sorties, losing only three aircraft. Radio Pyongyang reported that the strikes destroyed 1500 buildings and inflicted 7000 casualties. An even heavier bombardment occurred on 29 August when more than 1400 sorties were flown. Massed formations of silver bombers appeared on the horizon, roared and growled across the night sky and descended on the city. Pyongyang was pounded and pulverised with relative impunity. Resistance was weak and ineffective.

Ghastly, frightening, murderous scenes were played out across the city. A Marine squadron of aptly named Skyraider fighter-attack aircraft flew at almost zero feet down the main street, while tens of thousands of rounds of ammunition were employed in 'strafing at low level'. One pilot reported that 'The town was blowing up all over. The smoke was the blackest I have ever seen.' It was a scene from Hades. According to one account, only two buildings were left intact. According to another, 'almost no buildings were left standing, and an entirely new capital had to be rebuilt after the war'. The purpose of the bombing was to maintain credibility—and to shock and awe—but it lacked any sense of proportionality. Then and now, the military and foreign policy establishment in Washington had a fetish for 'credibility' at the expense of proportionality.

In September 1952, restrictions were selectively lifted to allow the bombing of an oil refinery close to the Russian border and a chemical plant on the Yalu River—to which the State Department agreed, but only if 'no immediate publicity was given to [the bombings]…and that the British were informed'. On 23 September the gloves came off. The Joint Chiefs cabled Clark to prepare for the 'removal of all restrictions [except for] attacks on USSR proper [and the] use of atomic and chemical weapons'. The latter were, it seems, available. Clark was so enthused by this invitation that despite the stated exclusion of atomic weapons, he pressed for their use 'against appropriate targets including those of opportunity'. He also recommended that, once again, military forces drive north of the 38th parallel and that there be air and naval attacks on mainland China. By November, rumours were circulating widely that the United States intended to expand the hostilities. The UN Secretary-General, Trygve Lie, was told that the Americans were not interested in the resumption of the armistice negotiations 'because they were all set for a big offensive, especially an air offensive, which they thought might end the war'.

As the bombing increased, aircraft production for the Air Force reached new heights. Public opinion polls showed that a majority of Americans wanted to 'stop fooling around and do whatever is necessary to knock the Communists out of Korea once and for all'. One Congressman declaimed: 'Never in the history of our Nation have our Armed Forces suffered defeat in war. Never has the United States set out to gain an objective through armed conflict and abandoned that objective before the battle was fought and decisively won. Never, that is, before Korea.' Many seemed to think the truce negotiations amounted to appeasement of Communism. One young senator—by the name of Richard Nixon—made some of the most risible accusations, charging Truman with 'losing 600 million to Communism'.

Eisenhower's Legacy

When Truman's presidency came to an end in November 1952, his negotiating legacy was one of ever-widening bombing unrestrained by a sense of proportionality and not confined to military targets. His successor, Dwight D. Eisenhower, an old soldier surrounded by men who wanted to expand the war, had no compunction about continuing the same approach. He believed that nothing less than unrelenting military pressure would bring an end to the conflict. He had even criticised the decision to enter into the truce negotiations, which he described as a 'trap'. And Dulles, his Secretary of State, actually favoured the repudiation of 'provisions in the armistice which we had agreed earlier'. In early February 1953, on the eve of his State of the Union message, Eisenhower approved the largest attack on enemy forces for more than a year, causing B-29 bombers to drop tons of high explosives on frontline troop positions. This was followed in May, as the truce talks neared their conclusion, by an ignoble and cataclysmic campaign to destroy irrigation dams and rice fields, with the object of breaking enemy morale, obliterating the rice crop, increasing civilian unrest and ultimately causing famine.

Five major dams, including the Toksan reservoir, were targeted. The official war history records that: 'Buildings, crops and irrigation canals were all swept away in the devastating torrent.' Villages were submerged, and farmers and domestic animals drowned. The plunging floodwaters 'wiped out rice paddies, railroad lines, bridges and highways'. The system that irrigated seventy-five per cent of North Korea's rice farms was torn apart, resulting in 'starvation and slow death'. The month of May was chosen because 'the rice crop could be almost completely destroyed'. Earlier doubts about the moral and political implications of attacks on dams were put to one side; the bombing now supposedly justified on the ground that 'the resultant floodwaters would interdict the enemy's lines of communication'. But there was no question that the rice crop was the primary target. One of the strategic considerations was that the destruction of the dams 'could cause famine in North Korea among both civilians and the Communist armies'.

It was disturbingly reminiscent of the conduct of Arthur Seyss-Inquart, the Reich Commissioner for the Occupied Netherlands, who was convicted and hanged at Nuremberg. The charges against him included breaching the dykes in order to slow the Allied invasion, resulting in the flooding of agricultural land, the killing of civilians and the destruction of food production. Attacks on dams and dykes— causing the release of 'dangerous forces' and 'severe losses among the civilian population'—are now specifically prohibited by the first additional protocol to the Geneva Conventions, which the United States has not ratified. Blaine Harden of the *Washington Post* had a point when he wrote of the bombing in North Korea that the American people 'never really became conscious of a major war crime committed in their name'.

Napalm Nightmare

What made the bombing campaign in North Korea so ruthlessly effective was napalm. It was the United States' most devastating single weapon, the one that actually caused more death and destruction than anything else. It came into its own in Korea, well before television footage from Vietnam made it notorious. Napalm is a sticky incendiary gel that burns at an extremely high temperature. Its name was coined, apparently incorrectly, from two chemical compounds, napthenate and palmitate. Marines referred to it as 'cooking oil' and aircrews described napalm-filled incendiary explosives as 'hell bombs'. In John Ford's 1951 propaganda film *This is Korea!*, footage of napalm being deployed is accompanied by John Wayne's chilling commentary: 'Burn 'em out, cook 'em, fry 'em.' The *New York Herald Tribune* acclaimed it with the headline: 'Napalm, the No. 1 Weapon in Korea.'

Napalm's efficacy in Korea as an instrument of terror and destruction for cities, towns, villages and troops was unsurpassed. It is now prohibited by international convention, although the position of the United States is qualified. When it finally ratified the convention on President Obama's first full day in office in 2009—almost three decades after its adoption by the UN General Assembly—it made an express reservation of 'the right to use incendiary weapons against military objectives located in concentrations of civilians where it is judged that such use would cause fewer casualties and/or less collateral damage than alternative weapons'.

The inventor of napalm was a Harvard professor of organic chemistry named Louis Feiser, whose forbears had come from a village outside Heidelberg. His father was an engineer and his grandfather once owned and published the first German-language newspaper in Ohio. By 1942 Feiser was head of a top-secret research project coyly listed in Harvard's register as 'Anonymous Research No. 4'. It was a collaboration between the university and the Chemical Warfare Service, a unit of the United States Army. Harvard continued to pay Feiser's salary but he was relieved of teaching responsibilities and devoted himself full time to incendiary weapons development. His wife, also an organic chemist, was his enthusiastic assistant. She once equipped him for a trip to Germany with a swagger stick that had been modified by a friend in the OSS to conceal a dagger.

Oversight of Feiser's project came from a little-known committee of the Council of National Defense, part of the Executive Office of the President. Money was practically unlimited and there was a direct reporting line to Roosevelt who created, in effect, 'a small company of scientists and engineers acting outside established channels, [who] got hold of the authority and the money for the program of developing new weapons'. Feiser's work at Harvard was only one of hundreds of secret weapons projects funded and supervised by the committee at universities and institutions around the country. The most famous was the Manhattan Project, which developed the atomic bomb—on which many brilliant physicists worked, but not Albert Einstein, who was considered a security risk.

The first field test of a napalm bomb took place on Independence Day in 1942 in an experimental pond built on a picturesque Harvard sports field. It was, by all accounts, an idyllic summer day. Tennis players in whites gathered on the nearby courts, unaware of what was about to happen. And behind the field, the golden dome of the Business School Library sparkled in the sun. When Feiser flipped a switch, a spectacular, billowing, 2100-degree Fahrenheit fire cloud rose over the field. Lumps of searing, flaming napalm splashed into the water and continued to burn. Gobbets of gel hissed, flickered and died. And the pungent aroma of phosphorous mixed with the oily smell of gasoline hung in the air. The disconcerted tennis players dispersed but the field test had achieved what Feiser had hoped—'a bomb that would scatter large burning gobs of sticky gel'. The napalm bomb was born.

The Chemical Warfare Service conducted final qualification trials, pitting Harvard's napalm against products from DuPont and Standard Oil. Napalm was clearly superior. Further trials took place at the Dugway Proving Ground in Utah, using full-scale replica Japanese and German residential dwellings. No expense or effort was spared to achieve authenticity. Noted architects with years of practice in Germany and Japan were hired; a Hollywood studio provided faithful designs of German furnishings; and soldiers watered the newly constructed buildings to simulate the mists of Japan and the winter rains of Germany. Fully furnished Japanese duplex houses were built to replicate the urban row-house dwellings of workers. And three types of German house were constructed—one with a slate roof in the style of a Rhineland residence, another with a central German tiled roof and a third of East German design. There was no modelling of industrial or commercial buildings, let alone of military materiel or establishments. And as for people, shaved white Cheshire pigs were used as substitutes because their skin was thought to resemble most closely that of humans.

The Utah findings confirmed napalm's devastating destructive capacity. Feiser and his team returned triumphantly to Harvard and transformed their secret laboratory into a 'design centre for special napalm weapons worthy of James Bond's Q Branch'. Their eager clients were the OSS and the armed services, which initially used the product in flamethrowers—first in Sicily in August 1943 and subsequently in the Pacific in December. Air bombardments soon followed. Requests multiplied as commanders began to appreciate the 'stopping' power of napalm. It was used to a limited extent on the Normandy beaches and on the Siegfried Line. In the Pacific islands, it was used on Japanese troops. From March 1945, it was used in the area bombing of Japanese cities. Five years later in Korea, it came into its own, reaching new levels of fiery devastation. A relentless barrage of napalm and conventional explosives rained for over three years. And the brunt was borne by North Korean cities, towns and villages.

Napalm's prodigious effectiveness in urban areas was a consequence of its unique features. Combustion occurred wherever the gel made contact; it produced a viscous liquid fire that ran between buildings and down into trenches, cracks and crevasses; it burned slowly at an extremely high temperature; and, being liquid, it spread and kept burning. Pliny the Elder noted a similar phenomenon with flaming mud, which was used against the Romans in 69 BCE. The substance, he said, 'adheres to every solid body which it touches, and moreover, when touched, it follows you if you attempt to escape from it...It is even set on fire in water.' The result in urban areas was often widespread and total: 'A shattered structure can perhaps be repaired, but an incinerated facility, its contents vaporized, melted, warped or reduced to ash, is ruined.' A US Air Force textbook from the 1960s explained that 'large targets (as an entire city) suffered more damage per ton of [incendiary] bombs than small targets, because fires had more opportunity to spread widely'.

As for napalm's effect on human beings, observers in Korea were shocked, although public awareness remained limited. Worldwide public revulsion at the horror of napalm only really developed two decades later during the Vietnam War when the image of a naked and terrified nine-year old, Kim Phúc, was caught by an Associated Press photographer and beamed around the world. She was still burning, stripped by flames and running from her village. There were similar incidents in Korea—and many were much worse—but no such dramatic photographs accompanied them.

Only a few war correspondents attempted to convey the cruelty of napalm in Korea. One was René Cutforth from the British Broadcasting Corporation. In early 1951, he was summoned by a doctor at a British field hospital who wished to complain about injuries caused by the 'new weapon'. Cutforth wrote that he was shown a 'corpse bolt upright...hideously grinning, and smouldering all over' and another figure with 'no eyes, and the whole of his body...covered with a hard black crust speckled by yellow pus'. Another correspondent, George Barrett from the *New York Times*, described a macabre village—like Pompeii—where the inhabitants 'were caught and killed and kept the exact postures they held when the napalm struck—a man about to get on his bicycle, fifty boys and girls playing in an orphanage, a housewife strangely unmarked, holding in her hand a page torn from a Sears-Roebuck catalogue'. And Walter Karig, a former naval captain and prolific author, wrote that pilots came back to their ships after low-level napalm drops setting fire to villages occupied by men, women and children, 'stinking of the vomit twisted from their vitals by the shock of what they had to do'.

The elderly Winston Churchill was privately appalled by the effect on civilians and wrote: 'I do not like this napalm bombing at all...No one ever thought of splashing it about all over the civilian population. I will take no responsibility for it.' But there was little sympathy in Washington. Barrett's piece in the *New York Times* only caused Dean Acheson to suggest that censorship authorities be notified so that this kind of 'sensationalised reporting' could be stopped. And Bradley,

Chairman of the Joint Chiefs, irritated by rumblings in the House of Commons, complained that British objections 'would harm Anglo-American relations' and 'requested permission to issue a statement that confirmed UK support for US napalm attacks'. No statement was ever issued. Nor was there any let-up in the deployment of napalm.

Among the combatants, there was no weapon that the Chinese and North Korean infantrymen feared more. But some of the most distressing and frequently bitter recollections were of friendly fire incidents. An American soldier who witnessed the accidental release of a napalm bomb on his fellow troops on the east side of the Chosin Reservoir, recounted: 'Where the napalm had burned the skin to a crisp, it would be peeled back from the face, arms, legs...like fried potato chips.' In another incident, British soldiers watched in disbelief as American Mustang fighter-bombers dropped their load squarely on the men of B Company of the Argyll and Southern Highlanders Regiment. As the napalm burst among them, a black cloud tinted with amber whooshed into the sky, followed by a wave of orange-flamed lava that tore along the hilltop, spewing rivulets of liquid fire down the sides of the ridge. An incomprehensible heat and deadly flames engulfed the pitiable men. Burning figures writhed, staggered and fell into charred heaps. Others were horribly disfigured, their skin hanging off in strips. Men screamed as the napalm gel stuck and burned into them. The skin on the face of one young soldier 'had come off like a surgical glove'. One junior officer, skinned alive, took twenty minutes to die. And a smouldering, dying Argyll, given a smoke by a mate, did not notice that when he removed the cigarette, his lips came with it.

A Shattered Land

MacArthur was right about the devastating effect of the bombing in North Korea—'a slaughter such as I have never heard of in the history of mankind'. By the time an armistice was agreed in July 1953, civil society was broken. Conventional explosives and napalm had achieved their intended effect. Not only were more bombs dropped on Korea than in the whole of the Pacific theatre during World War II—635,000 tons as against 503,000 tons—but more of what fell was napalm in both absolute and relative terms. Over a million sorties were flown, mostly in North Korean air space behind the front line; the amount of napalm used was about double that dropped on Japan; and except for opposition from MIG-15s in the vicinity of the Yalu River, resistance was limited. At the beginning of the war about 21,000 gallons of napalm hit Korea every day. When China intervened, that number more than tripled. An Eighth Army chemical officer said that on an 'average good day' United Nations pilots dropped 70,000 gallons of napalm: 45,000 by the United States Air Force, 10,000–12,000 by the Navy, 4000–5000 by the Marines and some by Australian and South African Mustangs.

By the end of the war, North Korea's industrial infrastructure had been knocked out. Electricity generation was only 17.2 per cent of its 1949 output; coal was 17.7 per cent; steel was 2.8 per cent; and cement was 5 per cent. A report from the United States embassy in Seoul stated that everything was flattened and that the 'air bombing was so devastating that rebuilding North Korean industry is largely a problem of new construction rather than rehabilitation'. Little remained standing in Pyongyang. And the casualties were heart-rending. On one account, the number was 'two to four million...most of it non-combatants'. According to another, 'about three million Koreans were killed, wounded or missing. Those whose families were broken up by the war numbered an astounding ten million...civilians accounted for over 70 percent of all Korean casualties.' The damage to the people of North Korea was incalculable—in lives lost, families broken, property destroyed and psychological dysfunction. By the end of the war, the country's total population had declined by 1.3 million people, a great number of whom had been able-bodied men.

The immediate cause of this human and material wreckage was the prolonged exercise of overwhelming air power directed at cities, towns and installations. The bombing campaign continued relentlessly for nearly three years after the North Korean invasion had been repulsed in September 1950. And it kept going for fifteen months when the only outstanding issue at the truce talks was the question of the release and repatriation of prisoners. Dulles liked to call it 'massive retaliation'. Even when peace was in sight, Dulles had misgivings about letting up on the bombing campaign. He did not want an armistice 'until we have shown—before all Asia—our clear superiority'. He would probably never have agreed to the modern statement of proportionality in the first additional protocol to the Geneva Conventions. It prohibits an attack that may be expected to cause incidental loss of civilian life if the attack 'would be excessive in relation to the concrete and direct military advantage anticipated'. Over 170 countries have ratified the protocol. The United States is one of a handful that has refused to do so. Others include Israel, Iran, Pakistan, India and Turkey. The United Kingdom and Australia have not merely ratified the protocol but enshrined its principle of proportionality in their domestic law.

It is poignant to recall the opening address to the Nuremberg Tribunal by Justice Robert Jackson, Chief Prosecutor for the United States, who spoke eloquently and memorably:

> If certain acts of violation of treaties are crimes, they are crimes whether the United States does them or Germany does them, and we are not prepared to lay down a rule of criminal conduct against others which we would not be willing to have invoked against us…We must never forget that the record on which we judge these defendants is the record on which history will judge us tomorrow.

CHAPTER 11

Nuclear Near Miss

'Since by man came death'

There was another dimension to the bombing campaign in North Korea, a hidden side whose origins lay in certain secret military and industrial projects commenced by the United States during World War II. One of these was the Manhattan Project, which resulted in the successful production of the atomic bomb and its detonation over Hiroshima and Nagasaki in August 1945. The other was the even more secret biological warfare project—so secret that service personnel recruited for work on biological warfare were exempted from overseas service for fear they might be captured by the enemy and forced to reveal the existence or content of the project.

Einstein's Warning

Not everyone was comfortable with the atomic bomb, especially Albert Einstein. In 1947 he issued his dire warning to the world that the release of atomic energy was 'the most revolutionary force since the prehistoric discovery of fire' and that 'there [was] no possibility of control except through the aroused understanding and insistence of the peoples of the world'. A few years later, he deprecated America's increasing militarisation under President Truman and criticised the 'disastrous illusion…that it is possible to achieve security through armaments on a national scale'. But Einstein's pacifism, not to mention his criticism, made him suspect and the President had a different attitude. The atomic bomb clearly meant a lot to him.

Henry Stimson, Secretary of War, said that the successful testing of the atomic bomb in New Mexico in July 1945 caused Truman to be 'tremendously pepped up'. Winston Churchill thought that he became 'a changed man'. And Peter Townsend, distinguished squadron leader in the Battle of Britain, royal equerry and later a successful author, was unusually cutting when he wrote: 'It was natural. The former bankrupt haberdasher from Kansas City, with the atom bomb in his pocket, was now the most powerful man on earth.'

Over the next five years, the President increased America's atomic weapons stockpile to almost 300 Mark 4 plutonium bombs. In January 1950, he announced a further development—the building of a thermonuclear device known as a hydrogen bomb, which used fusion in a chain reaction rather than splitting atoms by the process known as fission. There was opposition to this decision, including from a committee of the Atomic Energy Commission, which argued presciently that the only prospective use for a fusion weapon with such a high explosive yield would be for 'exterminating civilian populations'. But Truman was undeterred.

When the Korean conflict erupted, the President's thoughts turned immediately to the atomic bomb. His first wartime meeting with senior advisors was on Sunday night, 25 June 1950. There were fourteen men in the room and eight of them were military. Truman had returned urgently to the capital that afternoon from his home in Independence, Missouri. Sometime between the first call from Dean Acheson on the Saturday night and touchdown in Washington on the Sunday afternoon—perhaps during the flight on his personal DC-6 aircraft named *The Independence*—he leaped to the conclusion that the North Korean invasion was the first stage in a broad Soviet offensive across all of Asia. When told at the meeting that Air Force planes with atomic bombs could 'take out' Soviet bases, he promptly ordered the preparation of plans for a nuclear attack on Soviet territory when it entered the conflict. No one at the meeting voiced an objection.

A week or so later, still apprehensive that Soviet Russia would enter the conflict, the President decided that it was necessary to 'let the world know we mean business' and that 'nuclear strength must be used to demonstrate [our] determination to prevail in Korea'. In a reprise of 'the B-29 feint' during the Berlin blockade, he conceived the 'bombers to Britain' operation. Curtis LeMay was ordered to deploy from Strategic Air Command two bomber groups consisting of nuclear-configured B-29s and fighter escorts. The bombers carried 'Russian target materials'—presumably maps and charts, prioritised target lists and radar-scope information—and fully assembled Mark 4 atomic bombs without their fissile cores. The plan was that they would land ostentatiously at air force bases in East Anglia. The object was to demonstrate America's resolve and send a signal of deterrence to Moscow.

But the hasty deployment nearly caused a diplomatic incident when the Royal Air Force refused the American request for landing permission on the ground that there might be 'wide consequences' and that Moscow might regard the show of force as 'an unfriendly act'. The issue went up the line, across the Atlantic and back to London—from the Air Force Vice Chief of Staff to the head of the British Joint Liaison Mission in Washington, then to the British Chiefs of Staff, the Prime Minister and the Cabinet. Overnight, Washington must have spoken in forceful terms to its ambassador in London, for the next morning he called on Prime Minister Attlee without an appointment, insisting that the latter be called out of a cabinet meeting so that the deployment proposal could be put to him personally. Attlee did not like the idea at all but agreed to put it to his cabinet colleagues. After considerable debate, the Cabinet relented and on 11 July the B-29s with their fighter escorts crossed the Atlantic to Britain.

Three weeks later, at the end of July, Truman ordered a similar deployment of ten B-29s across the Pacific to Andersen Air Force Base on the island of Guam. They were to be accompanied by the prepositioning of tankers and support aircraft. Once again, each bomber carried an assembled atomic bomb without its fissile core. When one of the colossal propeller-driven, heavy bomber aircraft crashed in California shortly after take-off, killing the prospective commander of the nuclear strike force, the explosion was so huge that some local newspaper accounts speculated that atomic weapons might have been on board. They were close to the truth.

In late September, when the feared Russian intervention did not materialise, the atmosphere softened. Cool heads in the State Department argued that 'the probable costs [of an atomic strike]— measured in terms of shattered UN unity, decreased respect in Asia and possible war with China—far outweighed any possible military gains'. In November, however, when China entered the conflict in force, the public and congressional pressure on Truman rose once again. Louder and louder voices demanded tougher action, including the use of nuclear weapons. Deliberations took on a renewed vigour. And there was much loose talk of reprisals.

The Truman Show

In times of heightened anxiety and elevated tensions, indeed at any time, Washington's deployment of nuclear weapons and its readiness to implement a nuclear attack are never admitted, revealed or publicly discussed. The subject is never commented on. Not, that is, until 30 November 1950. On that day, as the United States appeared to be facing an entirely new and unexpected war, an anxious President Truman succumbed to the pressure of the moment. The historian Clay Blair said it was 'one of the worst blunders of his presidency'. The Eighth Army in Korea had crumpled and retreated before the advancing Chinese. The President held a news conference at the White House hoping to mollify public concerns but it concluded with the following unfortunate exchange:

> *The President*: We will take whatever steps are necessary to meet the military situation just as we always have.
> *Question*: Will that include the atomic bomb?
> *The President*: That includes every weapon that we have.

Question: Mr President, you said 'every weapon that we have'.
Does that mean that there is active consideration of the use
of the atomic bomb?
The President: There has always been active consideration of
its use.

The exchange did not end there. Truman went on to say, 'The military
commander in the field will have charge of the use of weapons, as he
always has.' The implication was that America was not only actively
considering the use of the atomic bomb in Korea but that the Pentagon,
not Truman, would decide whether the targets would be civilian or
military; and that MacArthur himself—the mad satrap—had 'charge of
the use of [such] weapons'. There was a later attempt to backtrack but
it had little effect. Truman's statements provoked worldwide foreboding
and intensified an already tumultuous and fearful atmosphere in
Washington and at the United Nations. The next day he added fuel to
the fire by asking Congress for supplemental defence appropriations of
$16.8 billion. A fortnight later he declared a state of emergency. Only
five years after Hiroshima and Nagasaki, the world waited and held its
collective breath.

Anthony Farrar-Hockley, who ultimately became Commander-
in-Chief of NATO's Allied Forces Northern Europe, said 'Some
diplomatists were so convinced that a world war was about to start that
they had tears in their eyes during discussions in offices and corridors.'
The United Kingdom and France were already anxious about
America's threatened extension of hostilities to China and Truman's
comments turned their anxiety to alarm. Seventy-six members of the
House of Commons signed a statement of protest. And the French
Prime Minister René Pleven and Foreign Minister Maurice Schumann
went immediately to London to meet with Prime Minister Attlee. They
agreed that 'America had to be restrained'.

When Attlee landed in Washington a few days later for urgent
meetings with Truman and Acheson, he represented 'the fears and
doubts of all the states which had supported the original decision by

the UN to resist the North Korean attack'. His mission, said the *New York Times*, was to 'get Truman's finger off the nuclear trigger'. But the relationship was uneasy and he came away with little. Acheson was disparaging of Attlee, and Truman refused to put in writing a promise to consult before considering the use of the atomic bomb. Truman and Acheson resented the British intrusion and were determined to resist any pressure 'to share command and control over both Korean operations and any possible use of nuclear weapons'.

Battlefield Expectations

On the battlefield, MacArthur never doubted that nuclear weapons would be available to him. In early December, as the Marines were being evacuated from Hungman on North Korea's east coast, he informed the Joint Chiefs that 'he desired commander's discretion to use atomic weapons'. A few weeks later, he submitted 'a list of retardation targets' for which he needed twenty-six atomic bombs. Truman held back. Acheson thought that the threatened use of nuclear weapons would 'frighten our allies to death'. But there were rumblings from the director of the CIA, who said that America's nuclear superiority was 'a wasting asset best used before the Soviet stockpile grew'.

MacArthur's characteristic views were already known. In July, a few weeks after the North Korean invasion, he had told Air Force chief of operations Bolte of his plans for handling any potential Chinese or Russian intervention. He said that he would 'cut them off in North Korea...I visualise a cul-de-sac. The only passages leading from Manchuria and Vladivostok have many tunnels and bridges. I see here a unique use for the atomic bomb—to strike a blocking blow—which would require a six-month repair job.' In a Mephistophelian touch, he told Bolte to 'Sweeten up my B-29 force'.

Not everyone thought MacArthur was delusional, certainly not in the Pentagon, but there was definitely a surreal quality about his utterances after the war. On one occasion he said that he would have 'dropped 30 or so atomic bombs...strung across the neck of Manchuria' and created 'a belt of radioactive cobalt...[with] an active life of between 60 and 120 years' from the Sea of Japan to the Yellow Sea. With customary brio he added: 'For at least 60 years there could have been no land invasion of Korea from the North. My plan was a cinch.' Journalists, scientists and historians alike have since argued that Cobalt 60 has more than 300 times the radioactivity of radium and that one 400-ton cobalt H-bomb could wipe out all animal life on earth.

Neither of MacArthur's successors, Ridgway or Clark, was as cavalier as their predecessor, but both assumed that their weaponry should include atomic bombs. When Ridgway succeeded MacArthur in late April 1951, the air was thick with rumours of 'Enemy planes parked wingtip to wingtip on Manchurian airfields; Soviet submarines concentrated at Vladivostok; and a sizable Soviet force…on Sakhalin'. Over-anxious national intelligence estimates asserted that Soviet Russia had the ability to 'expel the US from Korea…and attain air superiority over Korea, the Sea of Japan and probably Japan proper'. And the Pentagon continued to insist that Korea was 'just one phase of [this] battle' between Moscow and Washington. The British challenged Washington's assessment of the threat but Acheson chose not to refute the challenge or to seek British concurrence.

In response to the perceived emergency, the President spoke anxiously to the chairman of the Atomic Energy Commission, painting an ominous picture and convincing him to authorise the transfer of nine atomic bombs to Air Force custody, this time complete with fissile cores. No such thing had happened since 1945. The warheads, ready for immediate operational use, were transhipped across the Pacific to the American Air Force base on Okinawa, the Japanese island in the Ryukyu chain occupied by the United States military. On Okinawa the nuclear weapons were prepositioned for action. A few weeks later, the President approved a second movement of nuclear-configured aircraft to Okinawa. It was followed by the despatch to Tokyo of a command and control team to coordinate nuclear operational plans and the grant of authority to Ridgway to launch atomic strikes against air attacks originating from beyond the Korean peninsula—an authority that Truman had not been prepared to give MacArthur.

In preparation for the contemplated strikes, American jet reconnaissance aircraft overflew airfields in Manchuria and Shantung to obtain photographic and other target data. And Washington sent an emissary to China whose mission was to 'contact persons capable of getting [a] message to PRC leaders'. The gist of the none-too-subtle message was that Chinese leaders should be aware of Washington's ability to 'lay waste their cities and destroy their industries'. For its part, China was not concerned about the threat of a nuclear attack. It remained insouciant. General Nie Rongzhen, who went on to head the commission that developed China's own atomic bomb, told the Indian Ambassador K.M. Panikkar: 'the Americans can bomb us... but they cannot defeat us on land. We have calculated all that. They may even drop atom bombs on us. What then? China lived on farms.'

Nothing eventuated, but the posturing continued even after the B-29s and their nuclear cargoes returned home. In late September 1951 the President approved simulated atomic strikes in North Korea. The exercise was known as Operation Hudson Harbor and involved B-29 aircraft undertaking bombing runs over North Korea from the Strategic Air Command base on Okinawa. The B-29s carried dummy nuclear explosives and replicated an actual nuclear strike. The object was part intimidation, part practice run and part information gathering. The information gathering demonstrated that 'timely identification of large masses of enemy troops was a rare occurrence'. This was a critical issue because troops safely below ground level in underground tunnels or foxholes would not be affected—'the atomic blast would go right over them'. Live testing in the Nevada desert with soldiers and animals later proved this conclusively. It meant that the viability of strategic nuclear bombing of enemy forces by the slow-moving and cumbersome B-29s was questionable, leading to a recommendation for the development of 'a ground to ground vehicle capable of delivering atomic missiles'. This was 'tactical' as opposed to 'strategic' nuclear bombing and resulted in the next frightening step in weapon systems delivery—the ability to fit nuclear warheads to artillery shells and missiles.

As 1952 dawned, there was a growing desperation to force a settlement in Korea by whatever means. Truman was dangerously frustrated. In January, he wrote his disturbing private rant about the destruction—meaning nuking—of 'Moscow, St Petersburg, Vladivostock, Peking, Shanghai…and every manufacturing plant in China and the Soviet Union'. In April, a committee of the Joint Chiefs known as the Joint Strategic Survey Committee recommended additional military measures to force a settlement, including the 'tactical use of atomic weapons'. And in October, when the armistice negotiations were suspended, Clark formulated an ambitious military plan for the Joint Chiefs that involved an offensive well beyond the current battle line—to the narrowest part of the peninsula another 100 kilometres or so into North Korea. It was to be accompanied by amphibious assaults and air and naval attacks in China and Manchuria. Clark's recommendations included the rider that 'nuclear weapons would be essential' and that unless atomic bombs were deployed, an armistice 'on US terms was not realistic'.

Eisenhower's Resolve

Still, Truman held back. His nuclear threats, feints and practice runs had very nearly made it onto the battlefield but the United States was no longer the world's only nuclear power and the possibility of a reprisal caused him to pause. When the burden of office was almost behind him, he revealed a certain ambivalence in his farewell address to the nation when he said, 'Starting an atomic war is totally unthinkable for rational men.' In truth, Truman was more pragmatic than moral. He never resiled from his 1945 decision—when there was no prospect of retaliation and the targets were predominantly civilian—to detonate atomic bombs over Hiroshima and Nagasaki. His reservations at the end of his presidency were not prevalent among the Washington establishment. Few shared his concerns about starting an atomic war and many were deeply disappointed by his farewell hesitancy—but they were soon heartened by the resolve of the new President.

Eisenhower introduced an altogether different, more frightening dimension—one that treated nuclear weapons as though they were like any other weapon, except more powerful; as if they represented a quantitative rather than a qualitative difference in methods of destruction. He made clear that he had no compunction about using the atomic bomb to compel agreement on the armistice terms that the US negotiators demanded. This difference of approach was embraced by the military establishment in the Pentagon, whose enthusiasm was bolstered by advances in nuclear weapons and delivery systems: America's stockpile of atomic bombs had grown to over a thousand units; the first test of a hydrogen bomb—codenamed Ivy Mike—had been successfully carried out; and a smaller atomic warhead of a size suitable for use as a tactical battlefield weapon had been successfully detonated.

As Presidents do, Eisenhower brought like-minded men into his fold. He appointed John Foster Dulles as his Secretary of State and plucked Allen Dulles from covert operations and made him the new director of the CIA. The brothers were unabashed hawks who were given full licence under Eisenhower. The former had cut his ties with the Truman administration before taking office and published his own foreign policy manifesto labelled 'A Policy of Boldness'. It advocated the threat of instant and massive retaliation with atomic weapons and strategic air and sea power. Dulles' willingness to let slip the dogs of war was manifest. In February he addressed a National Security Council meeting at which he emphasised the need to make nuclear weapons more acceptable; to deal with 'the moral problem and the inhibition on the use of the A-bomb'; and to respond to 'the Soviet success to date in setting atomic weapons apart from all other weapons'. Both Eisenhower and Dulles wanted to 'break down this distinction'. They were 'in complete agreement that somehow or other the taboo which surrounds the use of atomic weapons would have to be destroyed'.

This more pragmatic, utilitarian approach to the role of nuclear weapons resulted in a new recklessness, even encouraging Dulles to wish for the re-opening of issues that had already been agreed in the armistice negotiations and generating unrealistic talk of 'voiding the armistice'. Atomic bombs were returned to Okinawa. And Clark's plan for an offensive with nuclear weapons to establish a demarcation line further north than the 38th parallel was worked over—to 'achieve a substantial victory over the Communist forces and…get a line at the waist of Korea'. Dulles even contended, somewhat extraordinarily, 'that if the Communists refused a truce along this line, the United States would take it as a sign that they were not acting in good faith'. One eminent historian called it 'misguided self-righteousness'. It was certainly absolutist.

In the end, Eisenhower did not have to implement his choice. His timing was fortunate. Stalin died on 5 March and the dynamics changed. Dulles remained unstoppable, however. On the day of Stalin's death, he terrified the British Foreign Secretary by saying that 'it might be necessary to expand the war in order to end it'. And to Indian Prime Minister Nehru, he later said: 'if the armistice negotiations collapsed, the United States would probably make a stronger rather than a lesser military exertion, and that this might well extend the area of conflict'.

Throughout that Washington spring, during the last desperate dying months on the battlefield, the National Security Council and the Joint Chiefs pored over a contingency plan for ending the war if the armistice talks collapsed. The plan involved nuclear strikes against China. On 20 May Eisenhower approved the plan as 'the most likely to achieve the objective we sought' if the United States was forced into 'an expanded effort in Korea'. And on the eve of the truce, he authorised the transfer of completed nuclear weapons to military custody for overseas deployment. There was no doubting Eisenhower's conviction but the long-running armistice talks finally reached a resolution and the conflict ended in July 1953 without resort to nuclear weapons. The world dodged a bullet but the same cannot be said with certainty about the use of biological weapons.

CHAPTER 12

Secrets and Lies

'Behold, I tell you a mystery'

On Truman's last day in office, he felt obliged to write to the head of the Atomic Energy Commission, who was distressed by the President's farewell remark to the nation that 'Starting an atomic war is totally unthinkable for rational men'. The Commissioner complained that such thinking coincided with 'the invalid reasoning of the Russians'. Truman's irritated response included the observation: 'It [the atomic bomb] is far worse than gas or biological warfare because it affects the civilian population and murders them by the wholesale.' The President's comparison with biological warfare was not random. At the time of the exchange between the Commissioner and the President, the alleged use by the United States of biological weapons in China and North Korea was a topic of considerable and controversial interest. It remains one of the most enduring and notorious allegations of the war. Predictably, the official denials continue to be loud and long. Much, however, is relatively clear.

Biological Warfare Program

The United States commenced a biological warfare program during World War II. Like Japan, it had refused to ratify the 1925 Geneva Protocol banning 'bacteriological methods of warfare'. The program grew to become 'one of the largest war-time scientific projects in American history, second only to the Manhattan Project'. It was well funded and enjoyed top-priority status. And when the Korean conflict commenced, the program accelerated with greater funding and expanded facilities. By the end of the war, it employed many thousands of people—over 3800 military personnel and a hundred civilians at one site alone. Most of the wartime work was carried out by the Special Projects Division of the Chemical Warfare Service at a classified site known as Camp Detrick, deep in rural Maryland, surrounded by over 280 hectares of forest and farmland, to which a further 200 hectares were added in 1952. The site was chosen both for its remoteness and its proximity to Washington DC. Its nickname was 'Fort Doom' and its operations were cloaked in the deepest secrecy. In time, the Chemical Warfare Service became the Chemical Corps and Camp Detrick was upgraded to Fort Detrick.

The wartime program was overseen by George W. Merck, scion of the German family that had founded the world's oldest pharmaceutical company, Merck, in Darmstadt near Frankfurt in 1668. The company had pioneered the production of morphine and dominated the commercial cocaine market. George Merck became the Secretary of War's 'special consultant for biological warfare'. The scientists at Fort Detrick focussed initially on anthrax and the toxin that causes botulism, one of the most lethal biological substances known. By the end of World War II, a cluster bomb that spread anthrax in a cloud of spores was operational. And, at an isolated biological weapons testing site on Horn Island, Mississippi, in the Gulf of Mexico, intriguing studies with insect vectors had been secretly carried out. Despite these advances, the American program was behind that of Japan, which had started earlier and had much to offer the United States.

Japanese Unit 731

Japan had utilised plague-infected fleas and cholera-covered flies during its invasion of China in 1937–45. Various methods of dispersal were tried, including dropping bombs carrying infected insects. The headquarters of the Japanese biological warfare operation and its principal research and development centre was known as Unit 731. It was located on the southern edge of Harbin in Manchuria, near the

Pingfan railway station. It is now a museum and has been proposed for inclusion in the UNESCO World Heritage List. The site once covered six square kilometres with approximately 150 buildings, among which were laboratories, operating theatres, workshops, factories and prison cells. Unit 731's euphemistic official name was the 'Epidemic Prevention and Water Purification Department'. In reality it was the Imperial Japanese Army's notorious covert biological research and development unit, whose operations were more extensive than those of Dr Josef Mengele at Auschwitz.

The senior officer was General Shiro Ishii, who supervised medical trials on tens of thousands of prisoners of war, mostly Chinese. Many types of gruesome experiments were conducted. Some involved human vivisection, live dissections and organ removal without anaesthetic; some subjected prisoners to deliberate wounding with firearms or assault by flamethrowers; others tested the limits of human resistance to cold, frostbite and extremes of air pressure. What was thought to be most helpful to the development of America's biological warfare program were the experiments that exposed prisoners to lethal bacteria. The process was unfathomable—a phantasmagorical nightmare in which Japanese medical scientists infected helpless prisoners with anthrax, plague, cholera, typhus, dysentery, botulism, brucellosis, staphylococcus, tularaemia, meningitis and smallpox, while monitoring and meticulously recording the effects on their vital organs as they slowly expired. And in adjoining workshops and factories, valuable work on delivery systems for bacteriological weapons was carried out. General Ishii himself had a special enthusiasm for plague bacilli spread by fleas. The estimate of the number of Chinese soldiers and civilians killed by Japanese bacteriological warfare on the battlefield is in the hundreds of thousands. An estimate of prisoner deaths in laboratory experiments at Unit 731 is 'as many as ten thousand'.

American interest after the war was almost immediate. Within months, the head of the Massachusetts Institute of Technology was despatched as President Truman's emissary to review Japanese scientific development, including its offensive biological warfare work. Scientists from Fort Detrick followed. They could not contain their professional excitement at the records and testimonies of biological warfare development that they obtained, including more than thirty-five reports, 800 slides and lengthy autopsy results from deathly experiments. Dr Edwin Hill declared enthusiastically that 'Evidence gathered in this investigation has greatly supplemented and amplified various aspects of this field' and that the cost of obtaining the information 'was a pittance against the millions spent by the Japanese'. The Japanese data on human experiments was unmatched and their work on delivery systems and the use of insect vectors was significant. General Willoughby, MacArthur's loyal G2 at Far East Command, was readily persuaded of the value to the United States. He insisted: 'The utmost secrecy is essential in order to protect the interests of the United States and avoid embarrassment.'

Although the Soviet army put twelve men captured from Unit 731 on trial at Khabarovsk for war crimes and sentenced them to terms of imprisonment, the United States Far East Command took a different course. In June 1947 Truman, MacArthur and the Commander of the Chemical Corps jointly recommended that all information from the investigation of Unit 731 'be held in intelligence channels and not used for the War Crimes program'. Willoughby duly closed investigation and prosecution files relating to events at Unit 731. He said it was 'for the benefit of the United States in [this] critically serious form of warfare'. None of the evidence of atrocities gathered by American investigators was presented to the International Military Tribunal in Tokyo. And General Ishii and twenty-one senior officers and scientists were given an amnesty as well as cash payoffs pursuant to a secret arrangement that only became public three decades later. Men who might otherwise have been executed as war criminals were let free to resume their previous careers and went on to dominate Japanese medical and scientific research for a generation. When the truth of this travesty emerged, the last surviving judge on the tribunal, the Dutchman Justice B.V.A. Roling, wrote movingly: 'It is a bitter experience for me to be informed now that centrally ordered Japanese war criminality of the most disgusting kind was kept secret from the court by the US government.'

An Offensive Capability

Within days of the onset of the Korean conflict in late June 1950, an influential report landed on the desk of George Marshall, the Defense Secretary, calling for urgent action and renewed urgency on the biological warfare program. It stated that no 'useful distinction can be made between weapons on a moral basis'; warned that the 'United States is not prepared for biological warfare'; and counselled that 'not enough is being done to explore the offensive potentialities of this mode of warfare'. Despite the existence of a formal retaliation-only policy, the Secretary adopted most of the report's recommendations. The immediate result was a breathtaking escalation in budgeted expenditure for research and development and associated test and production facilities. The biological warfare allowance for the years 1951–53 was increased to $345 million—about seventy times the paltry $5.3 million spent in the 1950 fiscal year.

The flood of government money precipitated a military-industrial feast. And by the end of 1951, a growth industry had developed in the biological warfare field. Fort Detrick was expanded and a new biological weapons facility was added at Pine Bluff, Arkansas; contracts with businesses, universities, medical schools and public institutions proliferated; many of the country's outstanding biological experts were enlisted; and leading industrial companies worked on munitions and delivery systems for biological weapons. In addition, field testing of select species of bacteria and fungus, using simulants, was carried out on unsuspecting citizens. Amid clouds of secrecy, residents of the San Francisco Bay area, workers in Virginia and a group of uninformed African Americans were all deliberately and unknowingly exposed.

But it was not enough—not for Lovett, the new Defense Secretary, nor for the Joint Chiefs. In September 1951, a study conducted for the Joint Chiefs expressed concern at the state of biological warfare readiness and the absence of 'large-scale realistic trials under warlike conditions using hot BW agents'. And in December, the Secretary issued an urgent directive to the three military departments and other defense agencies, stressing that 'actual readiness be achieved in the earliest practicable time'. More telling was the response to the study by the Joint Chiefs. In a top-secret memorandum, they approved the immediate acquisition of 'a strong offensive BW capability'; its employment 'without regard for precedent'; and 'a more vigorous test program including large scale field tests...to determine the effectiveness of specific BW agents under operational conditions'. Their final recommendation was that the United States 'be prepared to employ BW whenever it is militarily advantageous'. It has been rightly described as an 'enthusiastic' endorsement.

The Joint Chiefs' memorandum is dated 25 February 1952. It belongs to Record Group 218 in the National Archives, described as 'Records of the Joint Chiefs of Staff'. By 2006, 1431 declassified pages from this category, mostly from the Korean War and early cold war era, had been removed from the shelves and re-classified as top secret. The *New York Times* reported that 9500 documents had been restored to classified status, including more than 8000 after President George W. Bush took office. The largest category belonged to the Defense Secretary. The process was carried out at the instigation of government agencies, primarily the CIA and the Defense Intelligence Agency, and approved by the President. The *Washington Post* called it 'a secret government program to disappear historical documents from public view'. One scrutineer observed that the choice of documents seemed to be guided by a reflex 'to cover up embarrassments, even if they occurred half a century ago'.

Shadows and Mischief

It is not difficult to understand the sensitivity about the Joint Chiefs' 25 February 1952 memorandum. Uncannily, a day or two before it was issued, Mao Zedong informed Stalin, and Zhou Enlai informed the world, that the United States had carried out air drops in northeast China of several kinds of insects infected with plague, cholera and other diseases. And two weeks later, Zhou claimed that between 29 February and 5 March American aircraft had conducted further sorties in northeast China, dropping germ-carrying insects.

It seems likely that security in the Pentagon had been compromised and that Washington's plan for offensive biological warfare readiness had become known to Zhou and Mao, who then milked it for propaganda purposes. Simon Winchester said that Zhou's 'intelligence staff told him of America's memorandum about biological warfare'. There was certainly time and opportunity for leakage, as the issue had been receiving prominent consideration within the Pentagon for some months before the Joint Chiefs' enthusiastic endorsement. And there was a healthy precedent for such a security lapse. During the first year of the Korean War and until their sensational defection in May 1951, British double agents Guy Burgess and Donald Maclean channelled classified information to Moscow about America's war effort in Korea and its nuclear program. Burgess was second secretary at the British embassy in Washington and Maclean was head of the American desk at the Foreign Office. The 'third man' was Kim Philby, a British intelligence officer in Washington from 1949–51, who had access to CIA and FBI files.

Zhou's public allegation that infected insects were dropped by American aircraft was accompanied by a ferocious and theatrical Chinese propaganda campaign designed to cause maximum embarrassment to the United States. It is conceivable that the Chinese claims were just a cynical concoction, far removed from the truth, built on what the Japanese had done in China and encouraged by the revelation that the Joint Chiefs had endorsed the offensive use of biological weapons whenever it was militarily advantageous. On the other hand, it is also conceivable that Zhou's allegations, exaggerated and embellished perhaps, were derived from actual events. Cluster bombs containing insect vectors may have been surreptitiously dropped—if only in covert operations to test the effectiveness of 'specific BW agents under operational conditions', as the Joint Chiefs had directed.

Fragmentary documentation of irregular provenance obtained from the Russian Presidential Archive in 1998 purports to indicate that in several cases, unidentified 'false areas of exposure' and 'false plague regions' were prepared. And there is little doubt that the Chinese took advantage of the situation. But the letters in this cache were mostly created by Lavrenty Beria or came into existence at his instigation during the byzantine power struggle after Stalin's death. They were tools in his witch-hunt against Khrushchev's protégé, Ignatiev, and their cogency and motive are questionable. The brutal Beria, murderous head of the NKVD, the secret police, was capable of anything. He even claimed responsibility for the death of Stalin. After Beria's execution by firing squad, Khrushchev ordered that his body be burnt and his ashes symbolically thrown to the four winds. The Russian documents are not as persuasive as some would like to think.

Agents and Vectors

The truth is that the American biological warfare program involved considerable work on agents and vectors for the transmission of infectious diseases. During World War II, the potential use of insect vectors was investigated at the Horn Island weapons testing site in Mississippi. And, after the war, the Japanese experience was carefully examined. Weapons and munitions for the deployment of insect vectors and other agents were the subject of tests and experiments at a remote proving ground in Utah known as Dugway. And joint field trials were carried out at a northern outpost in Alberta, Canada, known as Suffield Experimental Station, where, as in northeast China, winter temperatures drop to minus 15 degrees Celsius.

Among Fort Detrick's shadowy and incomplete historical records, there are numerous references to the advantages of fleas, lice, flies, ticks and mosquitoes; and revealing glimpses of project descriptions concerned with insect vectors, insect bombs and 'arthropod dissemination in biological warfare'. One project description specified 'a more effective vehicle for the offensive use in BW of insect borne pathogens'. The Special Operations division at Fort Detrick was even commended for its work on 'devising means and mechanisms for the covert dissemination of bacteriological warfare agents'. Its Device Branch worked closely with the CIA on suitable dissemination systems for biological agents. Their secret collaboration on this and many other matters was the stuff of spy thrillers, leading incidentally to a mind-altering substance that was thought likely to become a valuable new espionage tool—lysergic acid diethylamide or LSD.

In Korea, the United States Air Force had the primary operational role in the biological warfare program and covert operations were conducted by its Psychological Warfare Division, with assistance from the CIA. A much-used weapon of the psychological warfare units was a 500-pound cluster bomb, which was adapted and standardised for use as a biological weapon designed to release lethal agents over the war zone. The primary function of a cluster bomb was the distribution of warnings and propaganda leaflets. Warnings were distributed for humanitarian reasons prior to bombing raids so that non-combatants might have an opportunity to disperse. When the bombs burst in mid-air, the leaflets fluttered to the ground like over-sized confetti.

Officially, the first standardised biological weapon was the M33, which had been developed by 1952 as a 500-pound cluster bomb to carry the *Brucella* bacteria. But it was also tested with other agents and vectors. The dropping of cluster bombs filled with insect vectors, specifically one bomb known as the M105, was a prominent feature of the Chinese allegations, which may well explain why so much documentation is now limited or non-existent. For a brief period, the M105 cluster bomb was actually described as a 'biological bomb' in a publication of the United States Air Force Materiel Command. But soon after publication, the study was withdrawn without explanation and its author transferred to another position.

More revealing perhaps is the tangled and implausible mess in which Colonel Moore found himself during a formal investigation of allegations that biological bombs were dropped in North Korea in May 1952. Moore was the commanding officer of the 3rd Bomb Wing. China specifically accused the 'US Air Force 3rd Bomb Wing of using 500-lb leaflet bombs, model number M105, for biological warfare purposes'. There was no dispute about the mission or the dates and Moore admitted—disingenuously it seems—that: 'The group did fly leaflet missions, the purpose of which was to warn non-combatants in the areas adjacent to military targets that those targets were subject to attacks by USAF, thus enabling civilian personnel to avail themselves of an opportunity to escape injury and fatalities.'

Unfortunately, Colonel Moore's express reliance on leaflet drops 'to warn non-combatants in the areas adjacent' seems difficult to reconcile with his operations order, which stipulated daytime bombing runs by thirty-six F-84 fighter-bombers from 3rd Bomb Wing, followed by further attacks during the night by four B-26 bombers. The order concluded with these words: 'with the last aircraft carrying two leaflet bombs'. The attacks commenced in the early morning and continued all day and through the night. Forty aircraft were involved. Only the last B-26 carried leaflet bombs. Its bomber mission report, signed by pilot, navigator and bombardier, asserted that the aircraft carried two 500-pound 'leaflet canisters'.

As Colonel Moore quite properly explained, the purpose of humanitarian warnings was to assist civilians before a bombing raid 'to escape injury and fatalities'. Dropping cluster bombs with supposed leaflet warnings at night and after an all-day attack made no sense. Dropping bombs containing bacteriological agents after degradation by conventional explosives is more likely—in order to prolong the damage by contaminating the bombed area. Regrettably, this happens to accord with the Chinese allegations. And it is consistent with a prevailing American military culture at the time that regarded itself as having 'only one moral obligation' in Korea in connection with biological warfare, which was 'to develop at the earliest possible moment that [biological] agent which will kill enemy personnel most quickly and most cheaply'.

Cover Up and Concealment

The picture is clouded, deliberately so. Documents, whether potentially incriminating or possibly exculpatory, have been destroyed, concealed or classified. And in some cases, de-classified documents have been re-classified. Some Air Force units flying regular classified missions adopted a deliberate process of document destruction, using a 'burn barrel' for sensitive and classified documents. Very few surviving operations orders have come to light. Combat mission reports, especially of those flyers who were shot down and made confessions, have been removed from files. After the armistice, as if to underscore the secrecy and sensitivity of these matters, Far East Command ordered that a wide range of potentially incriminating documents be withheld from public view, including those relating to 'military operational policies, plans and directives dealing with the offensive employment of BW against specific targets'; 'specific living agents standardised for offensive military employment'; and information about 'processes and plants involved in the large scale production of living BW agents'.

In Washington, there was a disarming frankness about the need for deception. Memoranda in early February 1952 to the Joint Chiefs addressed the topic of 'Deception in the Biological Warfare field'. When the issue was raised in the United Nations, the Defense Department briefed the US Ambassador to the UN, Benjamin Cohen, telling him that a statement saying that 'the United States did not intend to use bacteriological warfare—even in Korea—was impossible'. And as late as 1975, CIA Director William Colby acknowledged to a Senate Committee that because of the paucity of written records, 'some of which were destroyed in 1973', he could not rule out that bacteriological weapons had been 'used in an aggressive way against someone to kill someone'.

And then there was the heavy-handed treatment of the airmen who were shot down, captured and signed statements confessing to their involvement in America's biological warfare program. Thirty-eight of them, all Air Force and Marine officers captured in early 1952, made confessions. When they were released after the armistice, they were subjected to a different sort of coercion. All were initially classed as hospital patients, kept under close surveillance, shadowed by the FBI and subjected to intense political, public and military pressure to recant. Most repatriates returned home on ships that were 'floating laboratories overrun by psychiatrists, criminal investigators and intelligence agents'. Some were segregated, guarded by military police and promptly despatched to Valley Forge, Pennsylvania, to be sequestered in a sealed psychiatric ward, continually surrounded and attended by intelligence officers and military psychiatrists.

The United States Attorney General stated publicly that 'prisoners of war who collaborated with their Communist captors in Korea may face charges of treason'. He was hinting at the death penalty, which was the fate suffered by Julius and Ethel Rosenberg in June 1953. The Secretary of Defense said that 'those who collaborated and the signers of false confessions should be immediately separated from the services under conditions other than honourable'. A storm of venomous public opinion brewed around the disconsolate men, who became the object of an ill-informed popular prejudice, like the modern-day aspersions against John McCain by Donald Trump: 'I like people who weren't captured.'

Those looking for an excuse to explain the behaviour of collaborators associated the returned prisoners with all that was wrong with American society. They were said to be symbols of an 'effete and indulgent society' and were 'linked to deep anxieties about the American character'. Popular cinema even blamed the supposed loss of manly vigour on 'an overwhelming feminine force that threatens American manhood/nationhood'. Mothers were said to be to blame. The film *My Son John* (1952) explored an unhealthy relationship between mother and son that eventually turned John into a communist.

In this noxious environment, and under the inevitable threat of court-martial, the airmen who made confessions while in captivity were sat down with officers from the Pentagon's Office of Special Investigations, given pen and paper and a list of leading questions, and prompted to write retractions. They all did, but in circumstances that led the State Department to express 'concern about the credibility of retractions under such publicly orchestrated pressure'. In reality, neither the confessions nor the retractions of the American airmen had any serious probative value. On both sides, they were tainted documents whose foremost objective was to serve the political and propaganda purposes of those who extracted them.

Intriguingly, decades later, the airmen's principal interrogator in Korea, the wily, genial and elderly Zhu Chun, who became an English-speaking professor and senior official of the China Institute for International Strategic Studies, provided an insight into the slender evidentiary value of the confessions that he obtained. 'Let me tell you something about the personality of American officers,' he said. 'Over the years, I met many of them. They are very malleable. They don't need a lot of pressure to change their minds…The English officers, now they are different.'

It seems likely that the full story of the United States' involvement in biological warfare in Korea has not yet been told. The search for the truth is bedevilled by secrecy and obstruction. As long as the whole picture is hidden, official denials ring hollow. They remind one of the observation by Hamlet's mother that 'The lady doth protest too much'. Although few serious commentators accept the fantastic detail of the Chinese claims, the most articulate defender of the United States Air Force only goes so far as to deny the possibility that the Air Force could have conducted '*the major BW operations* described in communist allegations'. (emphasis added) While its most thoughtful critic says that it engaged in the covert and experimental testing of bacteriological agents. Selig Harrison, the veteran *Washington Post* bureau chief, agreed with both of them. He was satisfied that in February and March 1952, 'US forces did not carry out *systematic biological warfare*' but 'in all likelihood did conduct large-scale field experiments with biological weapons in North Korea and China'. (emphasis added)

The Needham Report

Finally, it has to be said that the answer to the question of American involvement in biological warfare in Korea does not lie in the 1952 enquiry and report of the International Scientific Commission led by British biochemist Joseph Needham. In war, as in life, the truth is often many layered—usually more so. Needham could hardly have been more unsuitable for the task. He was handpicked by the Chinese after they had dismissed a proposed investigation by the International Red Cross on the ground of Western bias. Needham's team consisted of scientists and biologists from Europe as well as one from Sao Paulo and another, Zhukov, from the Soviet Academy of Medicine. Zhukov was the only apparently political member of the commission and had participated in the Russian trial of Japanese scientists from Unit 731 at Khabarovsk.

The commission did not have legal advice or assistance, or any member with judicial experience. No one attempted to ensure that the evidence presented to them was credible and reliable. The members of the commission exhibited no natural scepticism and they were naïve. They accepted what was presented to them by Chinese scientists and officials without verification and did not conduct their own independent scientific investigation. The report itself was only sixty pages in length. Its bulk—over 600 pages—consisted of appendices, schedules, alleged confessions and statistics that were simply presented to the commission, and accepted by it with blind trust.

Needham himself was compromised. He had many good and humane qualities but he was not impartial. He was a committed socialist who was active in radical politics at Cambridge; who detested the vulgarity and individualist materialism that American society represented; who had a natural willingness to believe the worst of American policy; who was the first president of the communist-backed Britain-China Friendship Association; and who had travelled extensively in China, had many friends there and had a profound respect for China's ancient culture and science. He was distressed by Western ignorance and racism toward Asian peoples, whom, he believed, were too often treated as 'experimental animals...not as equals and brothers'. Those who knew him described him as 'gentle and somewhat mystical and unworldly'. He was a Cambridge don straight out of a C.P. Snow novel—brilliant, charming, eccentric, in love with his Chinese research assistant, whom he would eventually marry, and a Morris dancer to boot. He was the perfect receptacle for Chinese propaganda, which he swallowed without question or hesitation. Joseph Needham's unsound report was never going to be the end of the matter. It was only the beginning.

CHAPTER 13

Propaganda Prisoners

'Behold, and see if there be any sorrow'

Against the backdrop of daily bombardment with conventional explosives and napalm, constant nuclear threat and controversy over the use of biological weapons, the armistice negotiations developed a life of their own. They commenced within months of the battle line settling around the 38th parallel, and continued interminably for over two years and 575 meetings. The United States' inability to prevail on the battlefield was matched by its frustration at the conference table. Success was hindered by the Pentagon's negative attitude toward the negotiations and its aggressive attitude to the continuation and expansion of the war. Significant members of the military establishment in Washington and Tokyo would have preferred that the United States 'cross the 38th Parallel [again], roll back Communism, and demonstrate its power and the Communist bloc's impotence'.

A Cultural Problem

Many wanted to take the war to China—'to teach China a lesson, to destroy its military prestige'. These men—angry, middle-aged, white, mostly military—regarded the armistice negotiations as a test of America's will, of its ability to prevail. They were of a certain cast of mind—one that associated negotiation with appeasement; that was intolerant of ambiguity; that glorified strength and denigrated weakness. They tended to envisage the outcome of a negotiation in terms of winners and losers, and were unable to see that 'the language of machismo denied the value of the softer art of compromise or exchange'. Fundamentally, they believed that change would only come from coercion not conversation.

The negotiations were three-way—between Chinese, North Korean and UN Command military teams. China was the senior member on the communist side; the United States represented the UN Command. Political issues were off the table. It was to be—if it could be achieved—a battlefield armistice confined to military issues. The American military delegates were, as has often been remarked, not well suited to the task. They were not practised in the art of negotiation nor adept at the bargaining process. Nor were they trained to keep cool during offensive harangues about themselves or their country. They exhibited all those qualities that are custom-designed to undermine a process of negotiation: moral rectitude, a lack of attachment to compromise, a combative style and an unshakeable sense of right.

The outcome was vitriol and intemperateness, intransigence and inflexibility, marked by an unwillingness to understand the communist side or to respect its point of view. China was not without fault and was proud of its ancient civilisation but its ideology always had a certain pragmatism; and for at least the last two centuries it had learned to accept the need for accommodation at times of relative weakness. In contrast, the political beliefs of the American negotiators were unyielding. They were imbued with a deep-rooted sense that only the values and ideals of the United States could guarantee universal peace and prosperity; that only the terms that they proposed were fair and just. The fact that their country, a nation dedicated to winning, had been held to a stalemate on the battlefield and been forced to negotiate a settlement, was a source of deep resentment.

None of this made for an easy negotiation to end the hostilities, at least one predicated on reciprocity and compromise. Among the American public, within the military and in Congress, there was deep dissatisfaction with the very idea of bargaining with an ideological adversary and dismay at the prospect of having to accept a military stalemate. Some even queried how America could 'compromise with the Communists, who were evil'. A standoff was incompatible with the American propensity to think of war as a pursuit to total victory and unconditional surrender—as had eventually happened against Japan. Participation in the Korean armistice talks was therefore grudging; compromise was distasteful; the notion of bargaining uncomfortable. This ambivalence resulted in an aggressive negotiating style that usually amounted to little more than a 'firm and clear commitment to a position, which would be put forward in the form of an ultimatum, in the [fanciful] expectation that the opponent would be forced to recognise the "fairness" of the position'. In truth, it was a non-negotiating style; the antithesis of reasonableness.

And time and again, the dysfunction and bitterness were magnified by the habitual characterisation of the Chinese and North Korean negotiators in hostile and racist terms. Ridgway called them 'treacherous savages'; General Harrison, the chief UN negotiator in 1953, described them as 'common criminals'; and Admiral Libby said they had 'the quality of talking animals'. Their prevailing opinion was that the Chinese and North Koreans were 'sons of bitches and outside the pale of normal gentlemanly humanity'. The corollary on the battlefield was the misguided theory of Generals Ridgway and Clark—endorsed in Washington—that the Chinese and North Koreans could be encouraged to accept American peace proposals 'if only they were bombed enough'.

It was not just a contrast in styles but a clash of cultures. The Chinese, in particular, had no interest in inflexible ultimatums. They desired equality of status and sought to 'arrive at parallel advantages by offsetting mutual risks, gains and losses'. They expected respect and equivalence, not condescension and belligerence. On the other hand, the Americans did not want to be there; they were disillusioned by the armistice's tortuous process; and they believed only in increased military pressure and greater firmness. When General Clark signed the armistice agreement in July 1953, it was the darkest day of his life.

Reneging on Key Issues

On the first issue of crucial importance in the armistice talks, the American delegation reneged. The Chinese had assumed, with considerable justification, that the demarcation line would be the 38th parallel. It had been fixed in 1945 by the Americans and agreed to by Soviet Russia; it had constituted the effective border between the two fledgling Korean republics since 1948; it had been crossed three times during the conflict; and in 1951, during the high-profile Senate enquiry hearings into MacArthur's dismissal, Secretary Acheson and each of Generals Marshall, Bradley and Collins had advocated a ceasefire at the parallel.

The Chinese paid particular attention to Acheson, who said on 2 June that a settlement at or near the parallel 'would accomplish the military purposes in Korea'. On the previous day, Trygve Lie, the UN Secretary-General, had announced that a ceasefire along the parallel 'would fulfil the main purposes of the United Nations'. A few months earlier, Ridgway had stated publicly that 'it would be a tremendous victory for the United Nations' if the war ended on that line. And in late June, the Western world greeted with relief the statement by Jacob Malik, the Soviet ambassador to the United Nations, that was the basis for commencing the armistice talks. He had called for a ceasefire and the mutual withdrawal of forces from the 38th parallel. On the strength of Malik's intervention, Ridgway was instructed to open discussions with his opposing field commanders.

The UN Command team knew that the Chinese and North Koreans considered a ceasefire at the 38th parallel to be a foundational premise that had been tacitly understood before the negotiations. Yet conservative forces in American politics would not accept it. Nor would the military in Washington. Richard Nixon was one of the senators who claimed that a truce at the 38th parallel would be an 'appeasement peace'. And Paul Nitze, the hawkish senior State Department official, explained that a settlement at the 38th parallel would give the 'impression' that the Chinese and North Koreans had been able to achieve 'somewhat more than an even military result'.

The reluctance to agree to the 38th parallel had much to do with pride and resentment and little to do with reasonableness. The battlefront had recently crept above the parallel in the mountainous east and the Joint Chiefs had no intention of returning to the old dividing line. Any small concession on territorial gains was anathema. It was inconsistent with the official policy objective of doing everything possible to deflate 'Chinese Communist political and military strength and prestige'.

The Chinese and North Koreans had no idea of what was coming. After the first seventeen days spent painstakingly settling the agenda, the American delegation announced its 'minimum negotiating position' on the demarcation line—not along the 38th parallel, nor along the current battle line, but even further north along a line running through Pyongyang itself, the capital of North Korea. It is said that the team experienced 'a strong sense of guilt in advocating a line so far north of the battle area'. Even if that were true, the proposal was provocative, if not also foolish, and lacked any sense of reciprocity, let alone any credible argument to justify it.

The result was an immediate collapse of trust and confidence, from which the negotiations never recovered. The Chinese and North Korean negotiators were stunned, shocked and silenced. They felt tricked—'as contemporaries recognised and Acheson belatedly acknowledged'. The atmosphere and language deteriorated. Admiral Turner Joy, the lead American negotiator, could not see that he had overreached; did not want to bargain; and wished to present his position as an immutable principle. His opponent repeated fourteen times that the proposed line cut deep into current communist positions. On 10 August the two sides sat facing each other in sullen silence for two hours and eleven minutes, in total deadlock on the issue.

It was not Joy's fault alone. He took his orders from Ridgway, whose temperament and attitude were significant factors in worsening the discord. The qualities that made him an eminent general in the field were not those required for the successful conduct of negotiations. Washington tried to restrain Ridgway but he tended to believe that 'a display of US power, represented by inflexibility at the talks and military pressure, would better secure the US global role and the optimum outcome for Korea'. Ridgway's unbending will, his unremitting drive and his unflinching confidence in the correctness of his views exasperated even his own superiors. On one issue the Joint Chiefs instructed him to delete from an intended communication the 'purple adjectives which give it an unnecessarily truculent tone'. On another, General Bolte was moved to remark that Ridgway was 'resisting making concessions'—an observation with which General Bradley agreed, adding grimly that Ridgway had 'decided not to follow our views'. On another, Ridgway beseeched the Joint Chiefs to show 'more steel and less silk, more forthright insistence on the unchallengeable logic' of his position—without ever recognising that his own logic might possibly be challengeable.

Slowly, eventually, and with much weeping and gnashing of teeth, the Chinese and North Koreans agreed to a demarcation line along the military line of contact rather than the 38th parallel. This was a substantial concession but the price of extracting it was high. The mutuality of interest that should have existed between the two sides had been undermined; what should have been reasonably debatable was rendered extraordinarily contentious; and what should have been resolved within a reasonable time was extended beyond all expectation. The consequence of this dysfunction was agonisingly slow progress—mired in distrust—on everything. But on no issue was the outcome more tragic than on the last remaining substantial question—the release and repatriation of prisoners. It was an issue that should have been straightforward; an issue that was governed by the 1949 Geneva Convention on Prisoners of War.

For fifteen months from May 1952 to July 1953, after all other questions had been resolved, the resolution of the prisoner repatriation issue was grotesquely prolonged. It was the sole reason why the war continued. Instead of straightforwardness there was complexity. Instead of compliance with the Convention, there was rationalisation of its avoidance. Washington, professing to be motivated by humanitarian concerns but determined to achieve a propaganda advantage, ignored the Convention. All the while, men on the line on both sides endured the privations of war and the miseries of battle; prisoners suffered and died in captivity; countless civilians and combatants lost their lives or their homes or their families; and the US Air Force 'attacked all structures and anything that moved' in North Korea.

The Geneva Convention

Article 118 of the 1949 Geneva Convention on Prisoners of War stated that prisoners 'shall be released and repatriated without delay' once hostilities have ceased. The United States had signed but not ratified the Convention and was not strictly bound by it, but had played a leading role in the international negotiations that had led to its adoption and had announced that it intended to abide by its terms. It was inconceivable that it would not do so. The unqualified obligation to repatriate prisoners of war had been debated, discussed and ultimately agreed by all participating nations. The use of the imperative—'shall be repatriated'—was and remains a time-honoured mechanism for stipulating the mandatory nature of an obligation. It represented the collective agreement of civilised countries.

The context in which the compulsory repatriation of prisoners came to be embodied in the 1949 Geneva Convention was well known. Following the end of World War II, the international community was alive to disturbing aspects of the repatriation of Soviet prisoners. On their return to the Motherland, many who had been held as German prisoners of war were promptly transported to the Gulag. This was not really surprising given that the Red Army field manual assumed that a loyal soldier was either fighting or was dead and that surrender was tantamount to treason. Repatriated prisoners who had defected or who were accused of collaboration or treason faced a worse fate. The penalty for defection or surrender 'not necessitated by combat conditions' was death by shooting. Naturally, there were many instances of brutal and peremptory Russian retaliation against their own men, some of which were later dramatised by novelists such as Alexander Solzhenitsyn and Nikolai Tolstoy. Among the Russian defectors who were forcibly repatriated was an entire regiment of Cossack Cavalry, a great many of whom were executed or committed suicide.

By the time of the Korean conflict, the issue was familiar and its resolution had been settled. The British set the precedent for compulsory repatriation in Greece as early as 1942. The British War Cabinet made the policy official in 1944 and Roosevelt's administration soon followed suit. At the Yalta Conference in February 1945, while Churchill, Roosevelt and Stalin discussed the postwar division of Europe, their military representatives negotiated a repatriation agreement that adopted the principle of mandatory return of prisoners of war. In May, a formal repatriation agreement gave effect to the Yalta accord. And from May to September the Allies forcibly delivered over two million Soviet citizens or almost ninety per cent of all Russians held in Western occupation zones.

When the fate of a tragic minority of Soviet returnees became apparent, there were misgivings and General Eisenhower requested the State Department to re-examine the question. Dean Acheson was one of the State officials in 1945 who, at that time, opposed the use of force to repatriate Soviet citizens. He would later change his mind twice. He warned then that there was 'growing reluctance among British and American troops to carry out this distasteful task'. The arguments went back and forth but the policy did not change. In the following years, the matter was re-examined in the negotiations leading to the Geneva Conventions. The International Committee of the Red Cross drew attention to the 'distressing cases of prisoners of war repatriated against their will (which sometimes led to suicide)'. In 1947, a Conference of Government Experts prepared the first draft of the Geneva Convention but did not consider that there should be any provision to cover the concerns highlighted by the Red Cross. The next year, the Seventeenth International Red Cross Conference in Stockholm adopted the same approach and decided against any departure from the principle that repatriation of prisoners shall be effected as soon as possible after an armistice.

In 1949 the issue was considered one last time in the final negotiations leading to the Geneva Conventions. Austria proposed an amendment to enable prisoners of war 'to apply for their transfer to another country which is ready to accept them'. A substantial majority, including the United States, rejected the amendment on the ground that 'the general principle of repatriation of all prisoners of war of a given country to that country' should be maintained. In support, the Soviet delegate expressed the view that 'a prisoner might not be able to express himself with complete freedom when he was in captivity'. This was prescient given the fearful circumstances that would come to exist in the American-controlled UN Command prisoner-of-war camps in South Korea.

The UN Camps

The justification for the Russian concern that prisoners might not have freedom of expression in captivity was never clearer than in Korea. One of the most deplorable aspects of the entire conflict was the way in which the prisoner-of-war camps administered by the United States Army in South Korea were allowed to become cesspits of violence, intimidation and lawlessness; where Chinese and North Korean prisoners were politicised and subjected to inflammatory indoctrination; where the ideological campaign to exploit prisoners and encourage defections went badly wrong; and where prisoners in fear of their lives had no genuine freedom of expression. A United States Army study confirmed the lack of freedom of choice—stating that the conditions were such that an individual Chinese or North Korean prisoner of war could not make 'an un-coerced, unintimidated, informed choice' about repatriation. This imbroglio was the major factor in the ensuing impasse that stalled the armistice talks and prolonged the war.

None of this is to say that the prisoner-of-war camps conducted by the Chinese and North Koreans were without criticism. Many prisoners died through neglect and violence in the early temporary camps run by the North Koreans, although once the Chinese took overall control, in 1951, there was an improvement. Food was usually sufficient, guards more professional and methods of indoctrination subtler. Attempted escapes or other infractions resulted in punishment but 'systematic physical torture was not employed in connection with interrogation or indoctrination'. However, the UN Command camps were in a special category. The largest and most infamous of them was on the island of Koje-do, a fishing community off the southern tip of the peninsula, a short distance across the water from the port of Pusan. It was established in 1951 when the number of captured Chinese and North Korean soldiers reached new heights after Mao's overly ambitious spring offensive. Over 150,000 prisoners were crowded into four vast wired enclosures. Each enclosure was subdivided into compounds. Each compound contained 5000 to 8000 inmates. The density was 'four times greater than that tolerated in US federal penitentiaries'. And outside the wire, if one writer is to be believed, a shifting population of about 8000 prostitutes congregated–'for whose services so many sentries were accustomed to abandon their posts'.

It must be said that the guards were the 'least impressive manpower in the US and [South] Korean armies'. They were the war trash, the ones who could not make it on the line, the dregs and cast-offs. They treated the prisoners like animals, with casual brutality and with hostility and contempt. No serious attempt was made by officers to impose discipline or to exhibit leadership. 'Gambling, drink and local whores' were the only diversions. Knife fights and brawls were commonplace. It was a damning historical precedent for bad behaviour fifty years later by another generation of the United States Army at Abu Ghraib, Bagram and Guantanamo Bay.

One medical orderly at Koje-do recalled: 'We ended up with the scum of the army—the drunks, the drug addicts, the nutters, the deadbeats. I found the whole place was a living hell—I was in fear constantly. There were fights in the barracks, fights in the compounds.' And the guards 'were very rough on the prisoners, often beat them up very badly...just waiting for trouble'. The situation was made worse because for approximately every 200 prisoners, there was only one American guard. Some South Korean guards filled out the ranks but they were considered to be 'below even the American dregs'. The inadequate ratio of guards to prisoners meant that gangs took control, guards rarely went inside the wire, and camp authorities did not seem to care. The compounds were effectively no-go areas.

When the American authorities began a concerted program of exploiting prisoners for psychological warfare purposes to influence opinion and encourage defections, the volatility and violence in the compounds rose to new levels. Prisoners became deeply politicised. President Truman's newly formed Psychological Strategy Board regarded the Chinese and North Korean prisoners as a resource offering tantalising possibilities in the propaganda battle for hearts and minds. Washington stipulated that the treatment of prisoners of war 'shall be directed toward their exploitation, training and use for psychological warfare purposes'. These tasks were enthusiastically performed by the Army's counter-intelligence corps and the men of the civil information and education section.

This organised defection program commenced in earnest in the spring of 1951 and intensified over the next two years. Anti-communist agents were planted in the compounds; linguists and instructors from Taiwan and Seoul—in reality often undercover agents or secret police—were recruited; Christian missionaries were brought to the island; classes were held on the lives of people in the free world and on democracy versus totalitarianism; outside broadcasts from the Voice of America bombarded the compounds; and prisoners were required to read translations of news releases from the United States Information Service. The Taiwanese and South Korean instructors were 'vigorous propagandists for not going home'. Ideological debates about repatriation turned into a life and death issue. *Time* magazine reported that: 'Each compound seethes with intrigue—half figuring ways to escape, the rest pressure groups fighting each other. Killings? Plenty of them. The victims are usually beaten to death with tent poles.'

For those loyal Chinese communists who had helped to build Mao's People's Republic in 1949 and who had hounded the United

States out of North Korea during the first winter of the war, it was intolerable. For the nationalist Chinese who had been impressed into Mao's army, it reinforced their partisanship. The ideological barrage and the competing political alignments between inmates created so much tension, terror, torture and violence that the International Red Cross recommended that the political elements of the American program be eliminated. But there was no chance of that happening. It was part of a concerted campaign to turn as many Chinese and North Korean prisoners as possible against repatriation to their homeland. As one historian noted: 'the psy-warriors could not have realised how much their program would impact the course of the war.'

Flawed Policy

When the armistice talks opened, there was no hint of the furore that would later blight the negotiations and prolong the war. Ridgway's instructions were clear—to seek an exchange of prisoners on a one-for-one basis until all American and other UN Command prisoners had been returned, after which he could repatriate the remaining Chinese and North Korean prisoners. There was a certain churlishness about this approach, arising from the fact that the number of communist prisoners to be returned was far greater than the number of Americans who would be received. Some in Washington thought this was inequitable, as if the mutual repatriation of prisoners after the cessation of hostilities should be numerically equivalent. But at least at that stage it was intended that all of the Chinese and North Korean prisoners would go back.

The impetus for a change in approach came from General Robert McClure, the chief of psychological warfare—the army's top 'psy-warrior'. He was one of those military types for whom psychological operations were all that mattered. And he had made a career of it— as head of the psychological warfare branch at Allied headquarters in North Africa and then in the same position at Allied headquarters in Europe. In Korea, regular soldiers referred somewhat disdainfully to McClure's branch of the army as the 'loudspeaker and leaflet brigade'.

McClure was the first to propose that the United States' public commitment to abide by the terms of the Geneva Convention should be questioned, and that the obligation to repatriate Chinese and North Korean prisoners should be ignored.

The pretext for McClure's proposal—for pretext it really was—was an assumption that any returned Chinese or North Korean soldier not loyal to his communist homeland would be 'severely punished, sentenced to slave labour or executed', just as some Soviet citizens had been after World War II. This was pure speculation on which not everyone agreed and no one could be sure. And it was not borne out by subsequent events. Nor was the suggested parallel with Soviet Russia sound. The Australian ambassador was forthright in criticising the American assumption that repatriated prisoners would have their lives jeopardised. And one experienced British official claimed that it was 'debatable whether any prisoner of war would return to certain death or slavery'. In his view, the majority of prisoners 'might only be subjected to intensive re-education'.

This was not popular thinking in America. A fixed idea took root that opposition to compulsory repatriation was a great humanitarian cause; that to repatriate Chinese and North Koreans against their will was contrary to a basic moral principle of political freedom; that the terms of the Geneva Convention should not be allowed to prevent the United States taking a stand to save lives, even if they were Chinese and North Korean lives and even if, by doing so, the lives of American and allied prisoners would be jeopardised and sometimes sacrificed. This reasoning, which had more than a whiff of cant about it, was driven by morality, ideology and domestic politics. In reality, its proponents in Washington 'savoured the [expected] propaganda victory when the Communist troops refused to return home'. And most statements invoking humanitarian principles were coupled with another that revealed the true purpose of the policy—the prospect of a powerful psychological victory; the importance of encouraging defectors; or the serious effects on American psychological warfare operations if prisoners were compulsorily repatriated.

There were few who dared to speak the truth. At first Dean Acheson did so. In late 1951, he insisted that the interests of the United States were best served by 'strict observance of the provisions of the Geneva Convention' and that 'the possible psychological advantages of the proposed policy' could not be achieved without conflict with the provisions of the Geneva Convention, 'which the United States as the Unified Command has expressed its intention of observing in the Korean conflict'. State Department officers also warned against violation of the Geneva Convention and cautioned that the administration did not know of the size of the problem; that 'moral factors against leaving our own POWs in enemy hands indefinitely' had not been sufficiently taken into account; and that there had been no consideration of the 'thousands of additional casualties' that would result if the negotiations broke down or were 'prolonged 6–7 months'. Little did they know how much longer the delay would be or how many millions of additional civilian and combat casualties would be suffered.

The watershed event was President Truman's personal involvement. He took a simplistic stand, which one historian cruelly described as a classic example of 'the president's tendency for premature cognitive closure'—a disposition toward eliminating ambiguity and arriving hastily at definite, sometimes unsound, conclusions. The President thought that an all-for-all exchange was 'not an equitable basis'. And he was fixated by a belief that Americans and South Koreans in the current conflict, and Germans and Japanese in the last war, had been done away with. He wrote melodramatically in his diary: 'Are they murdered or are they in slave labour camps?' As ever, he equated China with Soviet Russia. And adherence to the Geneva Convention did not seem to enter his consciousness.

This was not Acheson's initial view. He was joined by General Ridgway and Admiral Joy, both of whom had a strong practical military preference for exchanging all prisoners as soon as hostilities ceased. But Acheson was biddable and his successful working relationship with the President was based on his willingness to respond favourably to his predilections. Truman's keen interest in the issue became pivotal. And senior officials and agencies, including the CIA, whose primary interest was propaganda not principle, added to the pressure. They wanted to stand fast against compulsory repatriation and to allow prisoners to make a choice, even if it resulted in China and North Korea breaking off the armistice talks and American and allied prisoners languishing longer in Chinese POW camps. It was all about a propaganda victory. To give way on voluntary repatriation 'would undermine the whole basis of psychological warfare since neither soldiers nor civilians would defect from Communist rule if they thought they would be returned'.

So Acheson found a way to reverse himself. His departmental officers invented a new and implausible interpretation of the Geneva Convention, despite the plain language of Article 118 and its known context. They argued that since the 'spirit' of the convention was to protect the rights of individuals, forced repatriation was impermissible. As a senior State official unconvincingly said: 'Well, we have rationalised our position in such a way so that we can at least say...' It was artificial. Worse, it also offended Article 7, which specified that prisoners could not renounce their right to return. But Acheson had changed sides and now unashamedly pandered to the President's preference; pitching the issue as part of the global struggle between freedom and totalitarianism; advising him that the forced return of prisoners 'would be repugnant to our most fundamental moral and humanitarian principles of the importance of the individual'; and adding as always, that it 'would seriously jeopardize the psychological warfare position of the United States in its opposition to Communist tyranny'. Acheson was an experienced attorney. The phenomenon of senior lawyers telling presidents and prime ministers what they want to hear, and sometimes reversing themselves in order to do so, is not new.

Thugs and Lists

With presidential support, the defection program became a core strategic element of the armistice negotiations. If Washington could not get triumph on the battlefield, it wanted a moral victory on repatriation. Voluntary repatriation became the remaining, solitary, all-consuming issue, sacrificing everything in its ideological wake—notwithstanding the Geneva Convention and Acheson's initial opposition. For the last fifteen months of the war, while the UN Command refused to release and repatriate all of the Chinese and North Korean prisoners it held, terrible casualties mounted on the battlefield—approximately 125,000 Americans and their allies, over 250,000 Chinese and North Koreans, and a vast unknown number of civilians. And it was all based on wholly unreliable numbers for would-be defectors, located in compounds run by thugs, where terrified prisoners were tortured and coerced into opposing repatriation.

Washington salivated over the illusory prospect that there might be up to 80,000 Chinese and North Korean defectors prepared to give up their families and their homeland for Western 'freedom'. But the inflated numbers were deeply compromised and the opportunity for independent choice was virtually non-existent. In many compounds, anti-communist barracks bosses—who even the American ambassador labelled 'Gestapos'—conducted anti-repatriation drives, systematically beating and torturing those who would not sign and threatening them that they would 'remain in the POW camp indefinitely'. They viciously tattooed prisoners on their chest, back or arms with slogans such as 'Down with communist dogs', 'Fuck Communism' and 'Jesus my Saviour'. Most prisoners had no political beliefs and just wanted to go home. Cowering and petrified, they succumbed to tattoos or were coerced by petition drives. Some Chinese learned to survive by saying the only word of English they knew—'Taiwan'.

US Army camp administrators facilitated the intimidation—with acquiescence 'if not outright assistance'. They connived at beatings, torture and threats of punishment; allowed the Chinese nationalist flag to fly over compounds and even on American army trucks; and were transparently partial toward non-repatriates. Conversely, guards came down hard on communists, sometimes 'shooting them for relatively trivial offences such as singing, shouting insults and throwing stones'. British and Australian observers were aghast. Former US Private Scarsalleta told Max Hastings: 'I couldn't get over how cruel we were to the prisoners'. Clark issued a general instruction that 'prisoners who throw or attempt to throw rocks should be shot while in the act'. He added: 'I will be much more critical of your using less force...than too much.' In due course, on the third anniversary of the establishment of the People's Republic, when Chinese communist prisoners were 'milling around', singing and flying their national flag, guards opened fire. Fifty-two men were killed and over a hundred wounded. It was not the only massacre.

Senior American officials knew of the internal warfare in the compounds and were informed that the freedom of choice of prisoners was compromised by systematic terror, yet they ignored the criticisms and compiled lists and counted numbers as if they really meant something. Admiral Joy was told of appalling scenes and that 'the results of the screening were by no means indicative of the POWs real choice'. Ridgway ordered a re-screening but it never eventuated. It 'marked a step into dreamland'. Investigating State Department officials reported as forcefully as they could that the primary reason for the number apparently refusing repatriation to China was physical terror by anti-communist leaders, including 'organised murders, beatings, threats before and even during the polling process'. The information went up the line to Acheson. A 20 May memorandum, marked as having been read by him, listed the facts, including: 'Chinese Nationalist influence prior to screening' and 'Prisoner-to-prisoner brutality preceding and during the course of screening'. In a masterpiece of understatement, it added that 'there is some doubt as to the full desirability of full public disclosure at this time'. Nitze described the facts in the memorandum as the 'firecrackers under the table'.

The President and his advisors would not, or could not, see the irony of the situation that they had created. Despite their appeal to humanitarian principles, there was a very short supply of 'human rights, maintenance of dignity and UN Command protection' in the camps run by the United States Army. And perversely, the anti-communist thugs who ruled the violently totalitarian compounds were 'the actual objects of [US] concern'. The dominant consideration was the tantalising psychological warfare advantage that the administration expected. The anticipated 'refusal of some 80,000 Communist POWs to return except at rifle or bayonet point' was seen as hitting China 'in a most sensitive and vulnerable spot'. And until the world protested, nothing would change. But eventually the world did protest and Washington finally altered its position, with misgivings.

A State Department official started the debate that had to happen. He suggested that New Delhi assume responsibility because of its known humanitarianism and that the United States no longer be directly concerned. A Democrat senator floated the idea of military representatives from neutral nations stepping in. In Britain, both *The Economist* and *The Times* called vigorously for impartial intervention. In the United Nations General Assembly, Mexico called for non-repatriates to be sent to neutral countries; Soviet Russia proposed an eleven-nation commission; Peru called for an independent commission; Iraq called for the transfer of unwilling prisoners to a neutral nation; Indonesia called for an independent supervisory committee; and India proposed that the non-repatriates be dealt with by a repatriation commission made up of the four states designated to serve on the armistice supervisory commission—Sweden, Switzerland, Poland and Czechoslovakia. The common theme was that responsibility for prisoners classified as supposed 'non-repatriates' had to be removed from American hands.

America's allies increasingly came out on the Indian side. But Washington was in a state of denial and 'struggled to block other nations from trying to end the war by compromising on voluntary repatriation'. Acheson became ridiculous. He thought that India had 'seduced America's allies into an unprincipled conspiracy'; he dubbed key allies as 'the conspirators'; and he resorted to threats and blackmail, warning that 'divisions among us on this essential matter would bring grave disillusionment in the United States regarding collective security, which would not be confined to Korea but would extend to NATO'. In late October, he introduced a resolution boldly calling on the Assembly 'to support and commend the UN Command's efforts at Panmunjom together with its policy of non-forcible repatriation'. The armistice negotiations were suspended. Truman and Acheson were personally and politically locked into a position that they deemed an inflexible moral principle. But by the end of the year, they were gone from office.

Stalin revelled in the quagmire in which the United States found itself in Korea, even encouraging Beijing to remain resolute. But eventually, a few weeks after Stalin died, China was the first to move. On 30 March 1953, Zhou En-lai proposed the exchange of those prisoners who wished to be returned and the handing over of the remainder 'to a neutral state so as to ensure a just solution to the question of their repatriation'. He insisted, as so many states and diplomats before him had suggested, that the supposed non-repatriate prisoners be placed 'outside the control of the detaining power', namely the United States.

The British, Canadians, Australians and Indians all urged that China's offer be followed up. When the United States moved in repsonse, the negotiations at last resumed. Over the next few months, a resolution fell into place that reflected the essence of the Chinese and Indian proposals—a five-nation Neutral Nations Repatriation Commission consisting of Czechoslovakia, Poland, Sweden, Switzerland and India; a ninety-day 'explanation period' under neutral authority, free of intimidation, during which prisoners' true desires would be determined; supervision of explainers and persuaders by the Indian military; and a thirty-day cooling-off period. India agreed to chair the commission and the UN Command agreed to relinquish possession of the prisoners for four months. This was enough to secure the armistice.

But American psy-warriors did their best to corrupt the process to the last. They devised stratagems to prevent prisoners in Indian custody from changing their minds under the influence of Chinese and North Korean explainers. A report to the Psychological Strategy Board stated that the utmost effort was being exerted to assist prisoners by 'protecting them from Communist explainers' and that 'the objective was to have anti-Communist PWs remain firm in their decision not to return...thus bringing about one of the greatest propaganda victories'.

The sad outcome was that the process was not allowed to succeed. It failed the prisoners. One historian calculated that 'less than one-sixth of the North Koreans and barely 2,000 out of 14,700 Chinese ever got near the north door'—to return home. When its job was done, the commission concluded with great sadness that 'any prisoner who desired repatriation had to do so clandestinely and in fear of his life'. On one account, as many as 40,000 of them, who 'would have seen their families if it had been safe', were withheld.

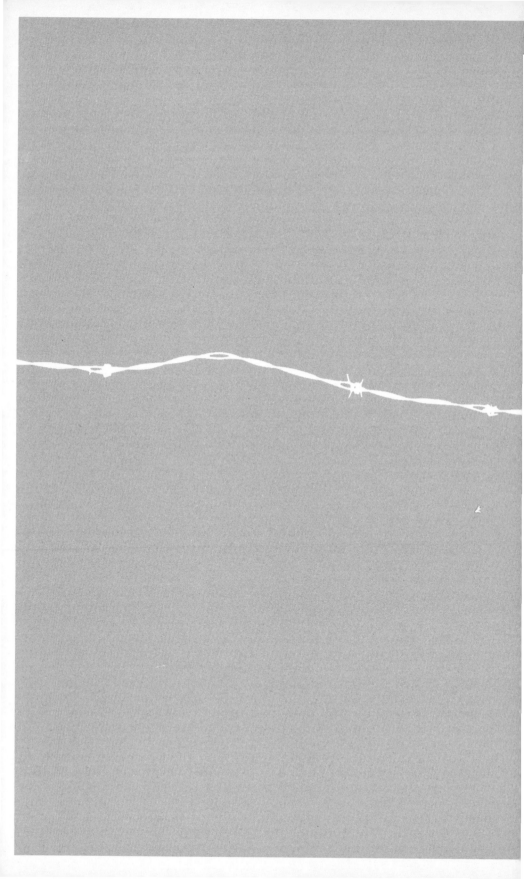

PART 5

The Legacy

CHAPTER 14

New World Order

'All we like sheep have gone astray'

The ill-tempered Korean armistice did not end the war, it only caused a cessation of hostilities. It did not solve the political issues, it merely hardened them. The United States resented the drawn outcome; refused to accept the legitimacy of China; treated North Korea as a pariah; and funded, and still does, the nationalist regime on Taiwan. And from a leadership perspective, it forfeited the moral high ground—never able to comprehend the long-term effect of its devastating bombing of North Korean cities, towns and villages and the killing of millions of civilians.

In retrospect, the Korean conflict was a crucible. Everything changed after it. The assumptions and precepts that the war engendered, and the manner of the war's conduct, established a precedent that Washington has chosen to continue—no more clearly demonstrated than by Secretary of State Madeleine Albright's jarring statement that: 'If we have to use force, it is because we are America; we are the indispensable nation.' As one diplomatic historian noted sombrely: 'Korea's legacy is practically incalculable...in terms of the cost of the arms race, the international isolation of China, and for the impact on American political development.' Half a century after Korea, Gore Vidal described with biting and uncomfortable cynicism the foreign policy trend that has been followed ever since: 'We honor no treaties. We spurn international courts. We strike unilaterally wherever we choose...we bomb, invade, subvert other states.'

American Century

The war gave oxygen to the Truman doctrine; removed the postwar cap on military spending; restored and enlarged the American military apparatus after nearly five years of demobilisation; unlocked the riches of NSC-68; and defined the modern world in a way that pitted the United States against any movement wherever it saw a perceived threat to its strategic or economic interests or even its credibility.

And it deepened and continued Washington's antagonism toward China. At the Geneva conference in 1954—held to agree on the terms of a peace settlement to follow the ceasefire—it was clear that there was no prospect for the political resolution that the armistice contemplated. The United States denigrated Beijing and refused to recognise the status of the People's Republic of China. And when Zhou Enlai extended his hand to US Secretary of State Dulles, the latter turned his back, refused to shake it and walked away. It was an astonishing display of disrespect by Dulles, whose behaviour was a portent of worse to come. Two years later, the United States announced that it intended to introduce nuclear weapons and missiles into South Korea—notwithstanding the concerns of its allies and the State Department's unambiguous legal advice that to do so would be a violation of the terms of the armistice. The consequence of this provocative decision was to render nugatory the work of the Neutral Nations Supervisory Commission, whose job it was to ensure compliance with the treaty. The commission was relegated to insignificance and obscurity; the architecture of the armistice was undermined.

No one can deny the validity of the initial decision to repel the North Korean invasion and restore peace and security at the 38th parallel; or that the ensuing three-month conflict was a just war. But the fateful decision in October 1950 to invade North Korea was driven by an ideological objective—to defeat communism and impose social, political and regime change. Like the slow-burning consequences of interventions in the Middle East, it has engendered a deeper and longer-lasting conflict, one that is exacerbated by the continuing festering presence of American troops on the peninsula, from which they have never left. It is not difficult to understand why there is still no peace treaty with China or North Korea. Nor is it difficult to understand why the Korean peninsula has become the world's most volatile crisis point.

In 1941 Henry Luce coined the phrase the 'American Century' as part of his swaggering call for the United States 'to exert upon the world the full impact of our influence, for such purpose as we see fit and by such means as we see fit'. The abortive invasion of North Korea was the first serious misstep of the American Century. Washington's inexorable wars and interventions of the last six decades can be traced to the attitudes, prejudices and policies revealed during that conflict. What started as the first serious clash of arms for the Truman doctrine, metamorphosed into a failed attempt at regime change and became in reality the beginning of America's perpetual wars. When Dean Acheson said that 'Korea saved us', he meant simply that the war justified, and persuaded President Truman to approve, the monumental leap in defence expenditure that NSC-68 proposed. But just as George Kennan feared, the principle of containment soon became militarised and globalised, and American foreign and defence policy never looked back. Threats to national security, often chimeric or merely ideological, usually geographically distant, began to be pursued relentlessly all over the world. The process was once vividly described as 'perpetual war for perpetual peace'.

Regime Change

If Korea was the first serious misstep of the American Century, Vietnam was the second. The line was direct and immediate, and the pattern was the same. So were the mistakes and the overreach. Only two months after Kim Il-sung's invasion on the Korean peninsula, American military advisors were dispatched to the Indochina peninsula to assist the French. They were on the ground in Saigon as early as 3 September 1950. It was the beginning of another foreign adventure. Three years later, Washington 'was underwriting about 80 percent of France's war in Indochina'. When the French were defeated at Dien Bien Phu in 1954 and subsequently withdrew from Indochina, they were supplanted by more American aid, more American military advisors and, as the 1960s rolled on, a swelling tide of hundreds of thousands of bewildered and sometimes stoned US conscripts. It was all for nothing. The United States was forced out of Vietnam just as it had been from North Korea. With the wisdom of age and the benefit of experience, former Defense Secretary Robert McNamara rued the decision to go to war. His remarks are as pertinent to Korea as they were to Vietnam, and almost every conflict since. He observed that: 'Where our own security is not directly at stake...We do not have the God-given right to shape every nation in our own image.'

No one in Washington adhered to such views during the Korean conflict or dared to express them. And despite the failed foray into North Korea, ideologically driven attempts at regime change soon proliferated. The CIA went immediately to work. It came of age in Korea, which vitalised it and provided a fertile field for a wide variety of clandestine actions and all sorts of subversive, sometimes nefarious, covert activities. When war broke out on the Korean peninsula, the CIA was still a fledgling organisation that had progressed little from its modest beginnings in 1947. The conflict and its associated cold war apprehensions generated a growth surge that has never really stopped. Covert operations quickly became the CIA's stock in trade and regime change became its byword. By 1952, the number of personnel in the covert operations section of the CIA had expanded from about 300 in 1949 to almost 6000; the budget had risen from $4.7 million to $82 million; and overseas stations had grown from seven to forty-seven. The CIA became a juggernaut, and in time, 'a rogue elephant'. Its director from 1953, Allen Dulles, decided that it 'must reach into every corner of the world'.

One celebrated but unsavoury operation during the Korean conflict deserves particular mention. In that first winter of legendary ferocity, as the Chinese army became stretched and exhausted from being pushed too hard and too fast by an ebullient Mao, sickness became rife. Scores of thousands of soldiers in the mountains, without adequate shelter, in snow and sub-zero temperatures, 'lay immobilized by pneumonia and intestinal diseases...in disease-producing misery'. China persuaded Nehru's government to provide medical supplies and medical personnel for its sick and dying soldiers. India had adopted a humanitarian approach to the Korean conflict, contributing an ambulance unit to the United Nations Command but not being prepared to become involved militarily, and opposing the crossing of the 38th parallel by American-led forces. Its 60th Parachute Field Ambulance provided a valuable service and remained in Korea longer than any other unit, even staying as part of the post-armistice custodian force.

In January 1951 a Norwegian freighter chartered by the Chinese loaded a huge cargo of medical supplies and personnel at the port of Bombay and sailed for the Far East. The shipping manifest included supplies for three full field hospitals, assorted drugs, surgeons, physicians, nurses and other medical personnel and equipment. Washington learned of the Indian medical mission from one of its agents inside the Indian government. An intelligence assessment stated in horror that there were 'enough [drugs] to give at least three shots of penicillin to every enemy soldier north of the 38th parallel'. A chilling directive was sent to CIA stations in East Asia, informing them that the ship and its cargo must be stopped from reaching the enemy 'at any cost'. The humanitarian aspect of the shipment was not a consideration. The message came to Hans Tofte at Atsugi, Japan, a CIA station that later became notorious for mind-control experiments. The operation to prevent the delivery of medical supplies was called Operation TP-Stole and authorised Tofte to spend up to $1 million without further recourse to Washington. He took this to mean that stopping the ship was 'definitely an act-first-and-talk-later proposition'.

Tofte sought the assistance of Chiang Kai-shek, the nationalist leader in Taiwan, who offered the services of his coast guard. Soon afterwards, a flotilla of nationalist gunboats, guided by United States Navy communications, intercepted the Norwegian freighter north of Taiwan. Boarding parties took command of the freighter and systematically pillaged the medical supplies, while CIA agents remained below decks and out of sight. The operation had all the appearance of an attack on the high seas by Asian pirates. Tofte allowed the nationalists to keep the medical supplies as a prize of war, while the dedicated nurses, doctors and other medical personnel on the ship were never heard of again. One can only guess at their fate. The freighter resumed its voyage without them.

It is not difficult to see why some commentators have described the CIA as 'a personal, secret, unaccountable army of the president'. One of its directors once likened the agency's ethos to that of 'an order of Knights Templar'. Dulles himself 'prized zeal rather than balance'. Only a month after the Korean armistice, he authorised—with presidential approval—the CIA's first known coup d'état. Kermit Roosevelt Jr, grandson of former President Theodore Roosevelt, led the brutal operation in August 1953 that toppled the democratically elected government of Prime Minister Mossadegh in Iran and installed the Shah on the Peacock Throne. Regime change in Iran was followed by a dazzling array of other 'successes'—all now acknowledged—including Guatemala (1954), Congo (1960), the Dominican Republic (1963), Brazil (1964), Indonesia (1965) and Chile (1973). None of them was legitimate by conventional legal and moral standards.

Even when Nicaragua won a famous victory against the United States in the International Court of Justice in 1986, the lessons were not learned. Congress seemed to think that the CIA intervention was justified because the government of Nicaragua had taken 'significant steps towards establishing a totalitarian Communist dictatorship'. The Court was puzzled by this logic, saying: 'However the regime in Nicaragua be defined, adherence by a State to any particular doctrine does not constitute a violation of customary international law; to hold otherwise would make a nonsense of the fundamental principle of State sovereignty.' It added that it was beyond contemplation that one state could intervene against another simply 'on the ground that the latter has opted for some particular ideology or political system'. The reaction in Washington to this straightforward and obvious proposition was indignant and dismissive—the United States withdrew its consent to the court's jurisdiction; refused to recognise the judgement; and blocked its enforcement in the United Nations Security Council. The similarity with China's reaction to the decision in the South China Sea arbitration in 2016 has not gone unnoticed.

Force Projection

A foreign policy that sought to project American power around the world was the last thing contemplated by the Founding Fathers. George Washington had warned against foreign 'entanglements' and foreign alliances but John Quincy Adams encapsulated it best. On Independence Day 1821, the classically educated future President gave a memorable speech explaining that the United States was 'the well-wisher to the freedom and independence of all'. But he added importantly it 'goes not abroad, in search of monsters to destroy'. Neither Washington nor Quincy Adams would have approved of an interventionist and militarist approach to world affairs. All changed in 1898 when the United States burst onto the Asia-Pacific region as an imperial power. At issue was the fatal attraction of China and its market potential. After initiating a brief war with Spain and invading Cuba—on a pretext that owed more to jingoism than reality—the Philippines became, for a relatively nominal sum, a colony of the United States, and Guam became and remains one of its territories. In fact, Guam's location west of the International Date Line ensures that it is still the place where America's day begins. Both acquisitions, but particularly the Philippines, were regarded as stepping-stones to the riches of China.

General Arthur MacArthur, father of Douglas, made no bones about it. He marvelled at the strategic location of the Philippines, saying that the country was 'unexcelled by any other position in the globe'; not only were the Philippines 'relatively better placed than Japan' but the China Sea was 'nothing more than a safety moat'. No one better expressed the prevailing rationale for America's first steps into the Asia-Pacific region than Senator Albert Beveridge, the Asia expert who told Congress in 1900: 'The Philippines are ours forever... And just beyond the Philippines are China's illimitable markets...We will not abandon our opportunity in the Orient...The Philippines give us a base at the door of all the East.' Naturally, there was opposition from anti-imperialists such as Mark Twain, who famously said that he was 'opposed to having the eagle put its talons on any other land'. But the Washington establishment thought differently—the prospect for market expansion was too enticing, the lure of unimaginable riches too great. And, bizarrely, President McKinley thought that American colonisation would 'Christianize' the heathens of the Philippines, apparently not appreciating that they had long ago been converted to Catholicism by Spain.

Half a century later, the next generation of MacArthur—General Douglas MacArthur—had no doubt about the military rationale for American force projection into the Asia-Pacific. In top-secret remarks in Washington in 1948, he stated: 'The strategic boundaries of the US were no longer along the western shore of North and South America; they lay along the eastern shores of the Asiatic continent.' Beijing is approximately 10,000 kilometres from California and about as far away from New York as is Antarctica. MacArthur's thinking may have seemed excessive to some but it quickly became the prevailing view—as if the whole of the Pacific Ocean were or should be an American lake. It is reflected in the longstanding strategic objective of the United States in the Asia-Pacific 'to prevent the rise of any other hegemonic power in the region that could threaten its interests by seeking to obstruct American access or dominate the maritime domain'.

The urgency generated by the Korean conflict rapidly transformed MacArthur's aspirations into reality. From 1950 to 1954, the United States embarked on the creation or expansion of an unparalleled series of military bases and strategic alliances across Northeast Asia—motivated by China's ascension to international prominence, a dread of worldwide communism and the bitter aftertaste of the Korean stalemate. Money, arms, ships, aircraft, troops and CIA officers poured into Japan, South Korea, Taiwan and the Philippines. One treaty after another was signed with authoritarian, undemocratic, anti-communist political regimes; huge American military bases and airfields were built or extended throughout the region; and the Seventh Fleet became a permanent floating sentry, patrolling from Subic Bay in the Philippines to all corners of the North and South China Seas.

Today an empire of American military bases and installations girdles China's eastern flank, extending from the western fringe of Australia to the northern reaches of Japan. In fact, there are 'US affiliated encampments and weapons on every Chinese frontier except the one bordering Russia'. In South Korea, there are more than eighty American installations, including huge, self-contained military encampments that are islands of American culture. In Japan, there are more than a hundred. And Guam exists almost solely for its vast naval and air force bases. The American bases in the Asia-Pacific region represent about a third of the approximately 800 foreign military installations that the United States maintains around the world. Each of the United Kingdom, France and Russia has only a handful of foreign bases. In the Western Pacific, the islands of Okinawa and Guam have become crucial components of American force projection—secret enclaves of military airfields, submarine pens and intelligence facilities, congested with American service personnel and their families and bristling with the most sophisticated armaments, aircraft, ships, weapons and missiles. Okinawa, the poorest prefecture in Japan, is host to almost seventy-five per cent of all American military installations in Japan. Tiny Guam, one-fifth the size of Rhode Island, has forty-seven military installations, leaving little room for anything else.

Okinawa was considered so strategically vital when the terms of the Japanese peace treaty were negotiated in 1952 that it was held back by the United States and did not revert to Japan for another twenty years. From Okinawa and Guam, heavy bombers once rained destruction on North Vietnam. Guam now hosts nuclear-capable long-range strategic bombers in deployments that the Pentagon likes to call 'BADD'— bomber assurance and deterrence deployment. These awesome aircraft, together with surveillance drones, nuclear-armed ballistic missile submarines and more aircraft carriers than any other country has at its disposal, provide extended nuclear deterrence for America's allies in the Asia-Pacific region. Most of these 'allies' were signed to treaties during the frenetic diplomatic shuffle that commenced in late 1950, led by John Foster Dulles, first in his role as Truman's special consultant and then as Eisenhower's Secretary of State. Money, arms, attention and promises of security were lavished upon them.

Now the tide is turning. The prodigious extension of American military capacity in the Asia-Pacific region has become a source of maritime and political tension. China wants its 'just measure of Pacific lebensraum' and regards a heavy United States military footprint in the western Pacific as disproportionate to its proximity. That heavy footprint is sometimes said to date from 1945 but its effective practical commencement was in 1950, when the Korean conflict erupted. Some now suggest that the United States should 'withdraw to its natural sphere of geographic influence in the eastern Pacific'. China, for its part, believes that the United States is suffering 'a long-term overstretch of power in pursuit of global domination' and that this overstretch is 'politically, economically and financially unsustainable'. China has a naval plan to achieve equivalence in the Pacific Ocean—'absolute material and strategic equality'—by 2049. That year happens to be the centenary of both the foundation of the People's Republic and the People's Liberation Army. The plan, which has 'firm goals, set dates, political will and a commitment of money and machinery', extends as far as the 'Third Island Chain', a line that runs from the Aleutians through the Hawaiian Islands to Samoa. The curtain is falling on the American Century.

Treaties and Allies

For the time being, the strategic architecture of Northeast Asia remains substantially in place. The United States set about establishing it within days of the start of the Korean conflict. Taiwan was immediately targeted as an American ally. President Truman ordered the Seventh

Fleet to the Taiwan Strait almost before anything else. Until that moment, Washington had considered Taiwan to be outside its defence perimeter and the State Department had informed its embassies that the island held 'no special military significance' and was expected to fall to the Chinese communists. The startling and provocative naval movement of the Seventh Fleet to a position off China's coastline, almost 1500 kilometres from the Korean war zone, immediately injected the United States into the Chinese civil war, saved the Chinese nationalists from annihilation and accelerated Chinese distrust of American intentions. In one stroke in late June 1950, Truman created the ongoing 'Taiwan issue'. Six months later, he publicly vowed that the United States would not allow Taiwan to fall into communist hands. The defence of Taiwan suddenly became an article of faith. Taiwan's current anomalous existence—unrecognised by the United Nations, defended by the United States and claimed by China—has its origin in those first days of the Korean conflict.

Almost three decades later, when Congress eventually recognised the legitimacy of the People's Republic of China, it passed the Taiwan Relations Act, doggedly affirming continuing American military support for Taiwan against 'force or other forms of coercion that would jeopardize the security, or the social or economic system, of the people on Taiwan'. The unfortunate corollary is that, despite having adhered to the One China policy since 1979, the United States is bound by law to defend Taiwan. It still sends arms shipments to Taiwan, and the Pentagon has developed a top-secret comprehensive military operational plan, designated 'OPLAN 5077', to defend Taiwan against China, if necessary by the use of nuclear weapons. The Korean conflict was Taiwan's salvation.

Japan's story is the same, yet different. The Korean conflict was also its salvation and also ensured its long-term military security and economic prosperity. Japan collapsed into American arms as soon as the war erupted. It was said to be the only real casualty of the domino theory. When the Japanese Prime Minister, Yoshida, heard of the North Korean invasion, he exclaimed, 'It's the Grace of Heaven.' And the

Governor of the Bank of Japan, Ichimada Naoto, called it 'divine aid'. The ensuing procurement boom transformed Japan into 'one huge [American] supply depot, without which the Korean War could not have been fought'. The war expedited the finalisation of a peace treaty between Japan and the United States; gifted it with a security treaty that transformed its status from occupied former enemy to grateful ally; enabled the establishment of hundreds of American military bases on Japanese territory; and fortuitously provided Japan with the markets, stimulus and economic opportunities that guaranteed its prosperity.

There is, however, an excruciating irony about Japan's situation. Its pacifist constitution, which had been imposed on it by the American occupying force in 1946, has always been regarded as a hindrance to an effective military alliance with the United States. Article 9 provides that the Japanese people 'forever renounce war as a sovereign right of the nation' and that 'land, sea and air forces, as well as other war potential, will never be maintained'. During the treaty negotiations in 1951–52, and despite its pacifist constitution, John Foster Dulles pressed Japan to undertake a program of rearmament as the price of restoring its sovereignty and terminating the American occupation. Reluctantly but eventually, Japan agreed to rearm with the coming into effect of the proposed peace and security treaties with the United States. The two treaties were signed in San Francisco on 8 September 1951. To fulfil its obligations, Japan created, with characteristic diplomatic euphemism and doublespeak, a series of para-military units that became known from 1954 onwards as the 'Self Defense Force'.

The debate about Japan's self-defense force and its pacifist constitution has persisted for more than sixty years. Washington has constantly urged the amendment of Article 9 of the constitution on the ground that it is an 'obstacle to strengthening the Japan–US alliance'. Secretary of State Colin Powell even insisted that if Japan hoped to become a permanent member of the United Nations Security Council, it would first have to get rid of its pacifist constitution. Others suggested that it would not become a 'normal' nation until it did so. But the resistance has been stalwart and in 2014 there was a proposal that the Japanese people be nominated for the Nobel Peace Prize for their preservation of Article 9. The remarkable irony is that, spurred by American exhortations and facilitated by its direct and indirect financial assistance, Japan's so-called Self Defense Force has become the world's fourth strongest military force, after those of China, Russia and the United States. Among other things, it possesses deadly fleets of submarines and attack helicopters. One might be excused for thinking that this is the very sort of 'war potential' that Article 9 prohibits.

South Korea's story is similar but different again. Its fragile national existence was less than two years old when the conflict erupted. Even more so than Taiwan and Japan, its military security was assured by Washington's decision to intervene in the conflict. Incongruously, more than sixty years later, South Korea's military fate remains almost as much in American hands as it was in 1950. The South Korean military, a monster force consisting of more than 600,000 active frontline personnel and 2.9 million reserves, remains under the wartime operational command and control of the United States. Desultory negotiations to return military sovereignty to South Korea have been put on hold and are not expected to resume until after 2020—unless the newly elected President Moon is able to revive and expedite the process. In the meantime, the US Eighth Army, which arrived in South Korea in 1950, has never left. And almost 30,000 American service personnel remain stationed across South Korea.

It is an open question whether the indefinite propping up of South Korea by the United States is in the long-term interests of stability in the region. The country was an American 'construct' at birth and in a practical sense remains dependent. Some have queried what might have happened if Dean Rusk had not drawn his pencil line across the map of Korea in 1945 or President Truman had not reacted so viscerally in June 1950. Simon Winchester is one who has speculated wistfully that the world might have been a safer place 'if the Soviets had been given free rein [in 1945] to invade all of Korea, and be done with it'. In that event, there would have been no Korean

War, 'merely a Leninist satrapy in the Far East that, most probably, would have withered and died, as did other Soviet satellite states'.

Instead, at the end of the war, a mutual defence treaty was agreed that gave the United States 'the [indefinite] right to dispose...land, air and sea forces' in South Korea and obliged each party to 'act to meet the common danger' in the event of an armed attack in the Pacific area in territories under their respective control. Over time, the South Korean arsenal arraigned against cities, towns and installations north of the 38th parallel has progressively increased in size and destructive power. So has that of North Korea. The Defense Ministry in Seoul proudly boasts of its 'Korea Massive Punishment and Retaliation' plan to employ ballistic missiles to reduce Pyongyang to ashes and remove it from the map. And the Pentagon has approved a top-secret military operational plan for the defence of South Korea, designated 'OPLAN 5027'. It is a pre-emptive strike plan. One wonders whether the incessant build-up of arms and weapons, not to mention the continuing presence on South Korean soil of United States military forces, can continue indefinitely.

Permanent Militarism

American militarism, not least in the Asia-Pacific region, has become a permanent phenomenon. It has its origin in the Korean conflict. When Japan surrendered at the end of World War II, the United States Army consisted of over eight million officers and men. Within a year, less than two million remained on active duty. A year later, that number was halved again. By 1950, the army's numbers were down to 600,000. The decision to intervene in Korea did not merely halt and reverse the process of demobilisation, it had a longer term effect. It unleashed the escalating and virtually unstoppable defence budgets that have so far characterised the American Century, facilitating—indeed encouraging—the relentless rise of militarism.

Since 1950, whether Korean War, cold war, Vietnam War, clandestine wars in Central and South America, war on terror, war on terrorists, war on drugs, war on tyranny or war on jihadists, the trajectory of increasing defence spending by the United States has continued almost unabated, spiralling upward, despite brief periodic reductions that have done nothing to alter the long-term trend. Massive defence spending—far exceeding that of any perceived adversary—has become the new normal. President Trump proposes to go further still.

And so a culture of militarism has become institutionalised. Data from the Stockholm International Peace Research Institute reveals that for the 2015 financial year, despite sequestration and cutbacks, the amount spent by United States on defence was approximately ten times that of Russia and greater than the combined total defence expenditure of Russia, China, Japan, the United Kingdom, France, Saudi Arabia and India. A Credit Suisse report reached a similar conclusion. In the modern era it has almost always been thus. In 2011, for example, the United States spent more on its military than the next thirteen nations combined. In that year, you had to add the total defence expenditures of Germany, Canada, Australia, South Korea, Brazil and Italy to that of the big seven countries already mentioned in order to approximate the level of defence expenditure of the United States. And in 2005, Andrew Bacevich—West Point graduate, Vietnam veteran and eminent military historian—made the alarming observation that 'by some calculations, the United States spends more on defense than all other nations in the world together'.

Such a level of defence expenditure is not sustainable. The cracks began to appear during the Reagan era, when America's cherished status as a creditor nation came to an end. President Reagan was not concerned, however, justifying more military spending by declaring that 'defense is not a budget item'. And for similar reasons, Vice President Cheney asserted during the Bush era that 'Deficits don't matter'. By the 2015 financial year, fifty-four per cent of all American federal discretionary spending was devoted to the military. Naturally, the Pentagon and the major corporations that manufacture and supply weapons, aircraft, ships, ammunition, missiles and electronic systems habitually seek more funding and ferociously resist any cutbacks. They represent the 'military-industrial complex' to which Dwight Eisenhower referred despairingly in his farewell presidential address—when he explained anxiously to the nation, less than eight years after the Korean armistice, that the 'conjunction of an immense military establishment and a large arms industry is new in the American experience'. He lamented the power of those who profit from, are sustained by and are committed to maintaining high levels of defence spending.

In old age, George Kennan once again put his finger on the pulse, when he prophesied that:

> Were the Soviet Union to sink tomorrow under the waters of the ocean, the American military-industrial complex would have to remain, substantially unchanged, until some other adversary could be invented. Anything else would be an unacceptable shock to the American economy.

He did not know that the Soviet Union would collapse a few short years after his prophesy, or that the cold war would be replaced by a global war on terror or terrorists or radical Islam or other perceived threats. Nor did he anticipate that almost any extension of Chinese or Russian territorial reach, or even military capacity, would be regarded as a threat to the national security or hegemony or credibility of the United States. But his point about 'inventing' some other adversary to avoid an unacceptable shock to the economy was well made. In 1991 General Colin Powell, when Chairman of the Joint Chiefs of Staff, came close to admitting as much when he commented wryly: 'Now that the Cold War is over, I'm running out of villains. I'm down to Castro and Kim Il-sung.'

The striking fact is that from the Korean conflict onwards, the United States defence industry and the military establishment have come together permanently in a coalescence of self-perpetuating mutual interest like never before. The institutionalisation of that relationship is what concerned Eisenhower. Its permanent conjunction was the feature that made it 'new in the American experience'. And it has never looked back. What was true then is even truer today. Early in his presidency,

Donald Trump declared that 'a strong military is more important than a balanced budget'. This is music to the ears of the defence and political elite in Washington—a 'self-selecting, self-perpetuating camarilla' that serves the interests of those who created the national security state and who benefit from its continued existence. Its members constitute an interlocking corporate, political and military directorate with a 'cast of mind that defines international reality as basically military'.

The irony is that the prodigious defence expenditure of the United States has produced a military capability that is superior but excessive; one that dwarfs any adversary but is at once 'massive and redundant'. The primary function of this superior American capability is 'global power projection', a notion that implies military activism without apparent limit, 'prowling around the globe—training, exercising, planning and posturing'. One might add 'intimidating', although naval and military commanders—perhaps suffering from myopia induced by institutional loyalty—prefer to say that they are keeping the peace, spreading democracy or preserving freedom. This is the supposed justification for the Pentagon's maintenance of so many foreign military bases, not to mention its carving up of the planet, even the universe, into separate territorial military commands. Military leaders speak openly, without a hint of recognition of the resentment that it causes, of 'full spectrum military dominance [of the world]'.

Of the earthly commands, Pacific Command is the oldest, the largest, the most territorially extravagant. From headquarters at Camp Smith in Hawaii, the Pacific commander directs operations stretching from the west coast of the United States to the western border of India and from Antarctica to the North Pole—a region comprising more than fifty per cent of the earth's surface and more than half its population. At his disposal are the colossal resources and firepower of separate subordinate commands known as the Pacific Fleet, US Army Pacific, US Pacific Air Forces, US Marine Forces Pacific, US Forces Japan, US Forces Korea, Special Operations Korea and Special Operations Pacific. Everywhere, this force projection is supplemented by other commands that operate without geographic restraint. The most important of these is Space and Strategic Command, to which huge sums are devoted for the secret development of weapons systems and blue-sky technologies that are the stuff of science-fiction novels beyond even the imagination of a modern-day Jules Verne, let alone the average citizen.

The most visible symbol of this military muscularity, constantly on parade, moving incessantly around the world's oceans, is the aircraft carrier. The carrier capacity of the United States Navy is prodigious. It has nineteen aircraft carriers, which is more than the rest of humanity combined. And ten of them are the Nimitz-class super carrier, the largest attack aircraft carrier in the world, which no other country has. Three more carriers in the 'Ford' class, technologically even further advanced, will soon be available. No ship is remotely comparable to the Nimitz- or Ford-class carriers. Each weighs in at a hundred thousand tons; is longer than three football fields; is capable of speeds in excess of thirty knots; and is powered by nuclear reactors that give it an essentially infinite radius of action. These super carriers move in strike groups with accompanying cruisers, destroyers, frigates, submarines and attack aircraft. The US Navy likes to refer to them as '4.5 acres of sovereign and mobile American territory'.

The comparison with other nations is revealing. France is the only other country with a nuclear-powered aircraft carrier. Russia has one conventionally powered aircraft carrier, as do Italy, Brazil, India and several other countries. China has one conventionally powered aircraft carrier and has launched, but not commissioned, a second. The United Kingdom will soon commission a conventionally powered Elizabeth-class carrier—and another is planned. And Japan has a number of helicopter-carrier ships. The comparison does not stop with aircraft carriers. The United States boasts more than 13,000 military aircraft while Russia and China, the next largest aerial powers, have only 3000–4000 aircraft each. And there are multiple American militaries. The Marine Corps, for example, has more attack aircraft than the entire British Royal Air Force. The United States Navy, Army and Air Force each has its own separate, even larger 'air force'. And the CIA is an army of its own. Its Special Activities Division and Special Operations Group are paramilitary units that undertake covert military operations all over the world. The latter operates on the basis of plausible deniability for everything it does and everywhere it goes.

It is little wonder that some commentators have concluded that Americans have been seduced by war; that they have come to value military power for its own sake, as if it were 'the truest measure of national greatness', as if the nation's strength and well-being should be defined 'in terms of military preparedness, military action, and the fostering...of military ideals'. Such an attitude idealises and sentimentalises the military experience and casts the ordinary soldier as an untarnished warrior. In reality, all junior officers know how much the enlisted men and women under their command are troubled, problem-ridden individuals, often socially and economically disadvantaged, whose education and employment prospects are problematic. Although they may no longer be Wellington's 'scum of the earth', a great deal of time is still spent getting these soldiers out of jail or attending to their personal and financial issues. It was ever thus. But like heroes from a Norman Rockwell painting, they are today taken to represent 'the apotheosis of all that is great and good about contemporary America'. In Donald Trump's world, they are our beloved military.

Paradoxically, in an earlier age, it was thought that only fascists and socialists celebrated war; that only they glorified the armed struggle; that only they depicted armies as expressions of national unity and collective purpose; that only they believed that 'power grows out of the barrel of a gun'. The civilised world regarded armed conflict as barbarism, brutality, ugliness and sheer waste, whose horror and futility were enshrined in the unfeigned verse of poets such as Sassoon and Owen and graphically depicted by writers such as Hemingway, Remarque and Graves. Now it is different, at least in the United States. No nation has more guns, weapons, ships and aircraft. No nation spends more on defence.

Few have dared to question the self-fulfilling phenomenon of American militarism. Not long after the Korean armistice, it was given the label 'military metaphysics'—a notion that translates into an unhealthy and unhelpful tendency to 'see international problems as military problems and to discount the likelihood of finding a solution except through military means'. It is a losing hand. But it has become the American way. It helps explain why, since 1950, the United States has instigated so many alarms, excursions and interventions; orchestrated so many coups; and undertaken so many wars. It is the major reason why there has been no resolution on the Korean peninsula; why the political division has been perpetuated; why the sorrow and resentment of Han is a uniquely Korean cultural trait.

CHAPTER 15

Dystopia

'The people that walked in darkness'

There is a sadness among the Korean people. It is their Han—a deep feeling of national grievance, a collective feeling of oppression and isolation, an unresolved resentment and a sense of helplessness. Both north and south are troubled. They are like brothers, estranged by forces beyond their control. Both say they want reunification. One is rich, angst-ridden and dependent on the United States; the other fiercely independent, raised in hardship and struggle, belligerent and delinquent. The two nations have diverged starkly, possibly permanently. No one can be sure where it will lead or what will happen. The tragedy is that their geographic and political division was foisted upon them by cold war perceptions that no longer apply—and were never really justified—and sustained by contemporary geopolitical strategic reasons that have nothing to do with the original rationale. The Korean peninsula is not—and never has been—the front line of the free world, as President Truman once thought it to be.

The Scars of Bitterness

For many Koreans—from north and south—it is 'an article of faith that the United States deserves the principal blame for the division of the peninsula'; that it was prepared to 'sacrifice Korean interests for the sake of its own emerging cold war strategic concerns'; that it was a 'self-interested interloper insensitive to the traumatic meaning of a divided

227

peninsula'; and that it is 'a false friend'. Kim Jong-pil, who served twice as South Korea's Prime Minister, made the point powerfully and pithily: 'American self-interest and convenience dictated our twin national disasters, the thirty-eighth parallel and the 1953 armistice line.'

For these Koreans, while the hated Japan was a colonial occupier, the United States was a destroyer. And unlike Japan, it physically divided the country. The scars of bitterness run especially deep in North Korea. For three years its people endured saturation bombing, crippling the country economically and leading to its short-term dependence on the Soviet Union and China. In contrast, the south's brutal but relatively brief anguish was over by late March 1951, when parity was once again restored to the 38th parallel. Virtually the whole population of the north that did not escape to China 'lived and worked in artificial underground caves...to escape the relentless attack of American planes', any one of which, from their perspective, may have been carrying an atomic bomb. These caverns housed schools, hospitals, barracks and small factories. The experience left North Koreans with a permanent siege mentality, a defensive, embattled, ultra-nationalistic spirit and a self-image based on pride at having survived an encounter with the most technologically advanced power in the world.

Their spirit is reinforced by a baffling state ideology in which notions of class struggle play no part, despite North Korea's early Soviet origins. The ideology, known as Juche, is closer to religious fundamentalism than Marxism-Leninism and has connotations of utopian autarky. Kim Il-sung devised it in the 1950s to emphasise and reward self-reliance, cooperative national struggle and categorical loyalty to the Workers' Party. Officially, the ideology is described as Kim's 'original, brilliant and revolutionary contribution to national and international thought'. In reality it helps promote the Kim family as the saviours of the Korean race and acts as the foundation for the cult of personality that surrounds the leader. It certainly helps explain North Korea's remarkable success in inculcating a spirit of communal effort.

The observations of Western visitors are revealing. A *New York Times* correspondent wrote that the 'best metaphor for North Korea is the medieval church'; another commentator said that it 'helps in understanding North Korea if you have lived in a fundamentalist Christian community'; another thought the country was like 'one big kibbutz'; and another said that North Korea is 'not so much a nation as a religion'. These are serious observations. Breaking down the North Korean ideology, as Professor Rüdiger Frank has stated, is 'much more challenging than some in Washington seem or want to believe'.

The siege mentality is daily exacerbated by the menacing presence of American troops just below the 38th parallel and the almost permanent deployment of naval ships and aircraft in the region. The Pyongyang regime knows—the whole world knows—that the United States has a stockpile of between 4000 and 7000 nuclear warheads; that over a thousand are actively deployed on ballistic missiles, submarines and at air bases; and that some are almost certainly targeted at Pyongyang. The country lives with a constant fear of invasion, subjugation and occupation—for which Pyongyang braces every spring when the United States and South Korea conduct their annual joint military exercises in the seas around the Korean peninsula.

The 2016 war games were the largest ever. And despite the Pentagon's insistence that they are only defensive, Pyongyang trembles every time. It knows that secret military planning for conflict with North Korea is constantly under review in Washington. And it is not persuaded by protestations that Washington does 'not seek an excuse to send our military north of the 38th parallel'. The current iteration of the United States military operation plan is OPLAN 5015. As one commentator from the James Martin Centre for Nonproliferation Studies in California quipped, 'We're practicing invading them. They are practicing nuking us.' The details of OPLAN 5015 are confidential but in 2009, when the ill health of Kim Jong-il became public knowledge, the United States Council on Foreign Relations published a disarmingly insensitive special report—only six years after the doomed invasion of Iraq—that included recommendations for a 'stabilization force' of 460,000 troops in the event of sudden change in North Korea, including collapse and armed insurgency.

Nuclear Never Surrender

In the face of such perceived threats, North Korea regards its nuclear program as 'an important deterrent to external aggression and a security guarantee for the regime's survival'. Nuclear weapons and ballistic missiles are its ultimate insurance. It is obvious that it will never surrender them in response to threats, coercion and sanctions. Pyongyang officials repeatedly state that nothing will stop their nuclear and missile development and that sanctions are not slowing down the process. There is every reason to believe them. The war has not ended. They feel threatened and have done so for nearly seven decades. And their conviction and sense of threat are real.

James Clapper, former United States Director of National Intelligence during the Obama presidency, could not have been clearer. He warned recently that the notion of getting North Korea to give up its nuclear capability is a 'lost cause' and a 'non-starter'. And General James F. Grant, a former director of intelligence for US Forces Korea, once explained that 'It [nuclear capacity] is their only current asset that makes them a serious player at the negotiating table. In their minds, it is the ultimate poison pill that will forestall military action against them.' In Grant's opinion, North Korea has four overall goals: 'regime and state survival and continuity, external respect and independence of action, controlling the nature and pace of internal change and the eventual peaceful unification of the Korean peninsula under terms acceptable to North Korea'. Invasion of the south is not one of them. Nor is a first strike on the United States or its armed forces. Kim Jong-un is neither irrational nor suicidal.

Pyongyang's resolve is only strengthened by its perception of American hypocrisy. While the United States professes to desire a world without nuclear weapons and demands a denuclearised Korean peninsula, it will not abide by the same rules. It abrogated the armistice treaty in 1957 by introducing nuclear weapons on the peninsula. It withdrew from the Anti-Ballistic Missile Treaty with Russia in 2001. And it recently opposed—and lobbied its allies to oppose—a groundbreaking United Nations resolution for multilateral negotiations designed to achieve a worldwide nuclear ban treaty. It complained that such a treaty would 'destroy the basis for US nuclear extended deterrence'. Quite so. But Washington only sees the world through its own lens and the resolution was passed anyway. Far from embracing negotiations for a worldwide nuclear ban treaty, President Trump has called for the United States to strengthen and expand its nuclear arsenal.

The hard fact is that as long as there is no peace treaty and the United States retains its military presence in South Korea, North Korea's apprehensions will not abate; the peninsula's social and political tensions will remain unresolved; and denuclearisation will remain an improbable aspiration. North Korea's nuclear capability is self-evidently a response to the American military presence, not the cause of it. Paradoxically, Washington has reversed the logic, portraying Pyongyang's nuclear capability as the justification for its indefinite military posture in South Korea and its continuing wartime operational control of the South's armed forces. As the geopolitical forecaster, George Friedman, has observed: 'There is a permanence to the current North Korean situation that many underestimate.'

Lost Opportunity

There was a time, not so long ago, when the permanence of the North Korean situation seemed less entrenched; a time of genuine hope and optimism, when Washington and Seoul were pursuing complementary conciliatory policies toward North Korea. In fact, in 1992 during a visit to Pyongyang, the Reverend Billy Graham came close to apologising on behalf of the United States. He declared that he shared 'the concerns of many Americans that my nation was one of those which had a part in those cold war decisions [to divide Korea], and I pray that the Korean people will soon be united peacefully'. Graham's prayer for reunification was followed in 1994 by the Clinton administration's historic agreement with Pyonyang—known as the Agreed Framework— to provide significant economic assistance and eventual diplomatic recognition in return for North Korea's pledge to freeze and eventually dismantle its nuclear weapons program.

By October 2000, despite frustrations, setbacks, obstructions, exasperations, deception and stalemate, incremental progress had been made. Kim Jong-il's second-in-command had visited Washington; a joint statement of commitment had been issued; Hyundai, the South Korean conglomerate, had been permitted to establish an industrial investment zone at Kaesong in North Korea; and Secretary of State Madeleine Albright and several presidential representatives, including former President Carter and former Defense Secretary Perry, had all made historic visits to Pyongyang. Clinton himself planned to visit, much to the chagrin of some of his advisors, but his term ended before it could be achieved.

At the same time, Kim Dae-jung, the South Korean President, lauded by his followers as the Nelson Mandela of Asia, was pursuing a parallel policy of engagement with North Korea. The objectives of his 'sunshine policy' were economic interaction between north and south, peaceful coexistence and flexible reciprocity. Kim Dae-jung took the long view and for his efforts was awarded the Nobel Peace Prize. He described the Korean peninsula's division since 1945 as 'a painful, brief anomaly compared with thirteen centuries of Korean unity'.

By 2000, the double-barrelled American and South Korean approach appeared to be bearing fruit. When athletes from North and South Korea marched together into the Olympic stadium in Sydney, they did so under the banner of a single white flag, although representing separate countries. And when the new Secretary of State Colin Powell first spoke on the subject of North Korea in March 2001, he told a press conference for the Swedish Foreign Minister: 'We do plan to engage with North Korea and to pick up where President Clinton and his administration left off.' But it never happened, and the opportunity to continue the engagement was lost. Powell was promptly and unceremoniously reversed by President George W. Bush and his inner circle of 'Vulcans'. He joked that he had 'got too far forward on his skis'.

That moment was pivotal. Since then, dark clouds have gathered and the times have changed. And distrust breeds distrust. Ironically, the end to meaningful dialogue with North Korea can be indirectly attributed to Billy Graham himself. For he was reputedly responsible for Bush the younger becoming a born-again Christian, who 'considered himself to be the agent of God placed on earth to combat evil'. As is well known, Bush saw foreign policy as an exercise in morality; commenced cabinet meetings by invoking the Lord's help with a prayer; and used his first executive order to establish the Office of Faith-Based Initiatives. It was his religious beliefs that led him to conclude that Kim Jong-il was evil, and that the United States government should no longer deal with North Korea—despite almost a decade of high-level peaceful engagement. That policy reversal was, according to Bush's most recent biographer, 'the first of a multitude of errors that came to haunt his presidency. Instead of bringing a denuclearized North Korea peacefully into the family of nations, as seemed within reach in 2001, the Bush administration isolated the government in Pyongyang, hoping for its collapse.'

There is now coercion not conversation, sanctions not trade, rhetoric not dialogue. The American policy of non-engagement has been carried to exceptional, some would say absurd, lengths. President Bush abandoned the innocuous working relationship between the United States and North Korean military forces to recover the remains of American soldiers missing or killed in action during the war. And within weeks of assuming office, President Trump refused to issue visas to allow even informal and unofficial talks to take place in New York between senior Pyongyang officials and private American experts. They later met in Norway anyway. The unstated premise of the policy of hostility and non-engagement toward North Korea is that if enough pressure is applied, the regime will succumb or collapse. But this is almost certainly wishful thinking. It has only exacerbated the atmosphere of threat and vulnerability in Pyongyang. The effective practical result has been to push North Korea into a corner, where successive leaders have regarded nuclear and ballistic missiles as essential instruments of survival.

Jimmy Carter was rankled by this military mindset among Pentagon and State Department officials, who insisted simplistically—

and still do—that North Korea is irrational, clownish and not worthy of engagement. It is probably a grave mistake. Carter thought it was 'an unrealistic approach that could well lead to war'. Nelson Mandela famously said: 'If you want to make peace with your enemy, you have to work with your enemy. Then he becomes your partner.' And Professor Rüdiger Frank, with his firsthand experience of the Soviet, East German and North Korean socialist systems, has argued repeatedly that:

> a much more effective and sustainable strategy to change
> North Korea would be to fund business relations and
> market activities—drivers of real social and values changes
> over the past decades. So far, the US is leaving this—and
> the information and soft power that comes with it—to the
> Chinese, which also happens to be its biggest strategic rival
> on the peninsula and in the region.

More recently, the respected British journalist Simon Jenkins put the point deftly: 'the most effective sanction on North Korea is economic, but in precisely the opposite way to "economic sanctions". It is the sanction of prosperity.'

Economic Reform

Piecemeal economic reform has actually been taking place in North Korea for the last thirty years, without American input. Some Chinese scholars believe it will continue, since economic reform seems to be 'the only path toward economic prosperity and political stability' and that it is 'historically inevitable'. Officially, however, 'reform' and 'opening' are considered to be dangerous imperialist concepts. At the historic Seventh Congress of the Workers' Party of Korea in May 2016, Kim Jong-un referred, in his inimitable way, to 'the filthy wind of bourgeois liberty and "reform" and "openness" blowing in our neighborhood'. But like some other political leaders in the world, he has a hardline support base to appease and is understandably reluctant to acknowledge any radical transformation of society. There is no denying, however, that the young

Kim has been quietly responsible for some important changes, despite considerable tensions and contradictions. He is even credited with the statement that 'food is more important than bullets'.

The first cautious overtures to economic reform in North Korea occurred as long ago as 1979, when the United Nations Development Program was invited to open an office in Pyongyang. Five years later, the country's first joint-venture law was introduced, resulting in a blossoming market for joint-ventured films and high-end department stores, among other things. Selig Harrison was astonished in 1987 to observe hundreds of citizens at one Pyongyang store 'filing through the aisles examining Gucci purses, gauzy Paris frocks, Savile Row suits and Japanese frozen foods'. And foreign investors began to show a tentative interest in the mineral resources of the mountainous northeast—especially magnesite, gold, zinc and rare earths. By the late 1990s, Kim Dae-jung—watching from the Blue House in Seoul—thought he could see the future. He said: 'there is a change going on in North Korea similar to what happened during the initial stages of the opening of China and the Soviet Union.' Perhaps, but not quite, not so extensive, and not yet.

After Kim Jong-il came to power in 1994, one senior Pyongyang representative demonstrated his enthusiasm, and perhaps his naiveté, by telling a Washington audience that 'we recognize that the world market has been unified into a single capitalist market' and that we are 'ready to plunge into it'. He repeated this refrain at Davos in 1997. That year, the International Monetary Fund was allowed, even encouraged, to send a fact-finding mission to Pyongyang, as was the World Bank. And the next year, Kim Jong-il introduced a new constitution, notionally guaranteeing the legitimate rights and interests of foreigners, encouraging joint ventures and business collaboration with foreign corporations and individuals, and relaxing limits on the ownership of private property. One article even pledged, somewhat improbably, to introduce cost accounting in economic management to 'ensure that such economic levers as cost, price and profits are properly used'.

But there were roadblocks. Japan vetoed North Korea's bid for membership of the Asian Development Bank. And when the application was renewed with South Korean support, the United States also vetoed it. The rebuff left a bad taste, made worse when the Bush administration would not allow North Korean observers to attend the annual meeting of the Asian Development Bank in Hawaii, despite more South Korean support. Kim Jong-il kept going. In the decade before his death in late 2011 he introduced an arc of modestly liberalising reforms, allowing limited private markets and a more independent operation of farms and businesses; announcing a Strategic 10 Year Plan; creating the National Development Bank and the Taepung International Investment Group; launching the country's first fully fledged Internet connection; and further developing the Rason economic trade zone near the border with China and Russia. And he kept visiting China—an unprecedented four times in 2010–11.

The youthful Kim Jong-un built on this heritage. An early object of his reform was the impoverished countryside, where the sight of oxen pulling wooden ploughs remains a common feature. Farmers, who had traditionally worked for a token payment and fixed, meagre rations on land belonging to state-managed farms, were permitted to register their households as 'work teams', allowing them to keep a larger portion of the harvest for themselves, giving them an investment in the land and providing them with an incentive to take better care of it. Serfs became sharecroppers; efficiency and harvests improved. This was followed by a broader, more intriguing initiative. According to a leaked policy document, the Central Committee agreed on 30 May 2014 to a 'significant reduction of state control of the economy and a dismantling of central planning'. The policy, which is not officially acknowledged, is said to mean that managers of state enterprises may purchase items on a free market, make deals with other enterprises or private businesses, hire and fire workers and pay them as much as they want.

Some Pyongyang watchers are excited. Bradley Babson, formerly of the World Bank, said in 2015 that: 'What is happening in the enterprise area is a development of major economic significance.' An embrace of capitalism it is not, but there are cautious and tentative similarities with the reforms instigated by Deng Xiaoping in China in the early 1980s. As always, progress remains hampered by ideological disagreements and conflicting economic interests within the ruling elite. Officials prefer to say they are trying out 'new management methods of our own style' but there is little doubt that they are 'dabbling'. Their dabbling includes relaxing some traditional controls and refraining from clamping down on the burgeoning capitalist-style private markets and small enterprises that have sprung up all over the country: food stalls, bicycle repair shops, truck deliveries, fishing enterprises, even small coal mines.

Sanctions, Elites and Dystopia

This unofficial grey economy now constitutes as much as thirty per cent of the North Korean economy. It is a natural human response to the hardships that have resulted from centralised government control, the economic contraction of the mid-1990s and increasing international sanctions. Sanctions have been North Korea's burden since the 1950s yet it has always proved resilient. Even taking into account the more extensive sanctions progressively imposed by the United Nations Security Council following Pyongyang's first nuclear test in 2006, the North Korean economy appears—to date—to have been growing. And since 2008, trade in Chinese yuan has been allowed, facilitating a surge in import and export transactions across the Yalu River, including many illicit transactions. Estimates from the Seoul-based Bank of Korea suggest moderate North Korean growth from 2011 to 2016. The trend for this period appears to have been gently upward. Some respected observers believe that the Bank of Korea is conservative and that real growth in North Korea in the period of Kim Jong-un's rule has so far been three to four per cent.

Outward signs of prosperity seemed everywhere apparent in the streets of Pyongyang in 2016—fashionable clothes, consumer goods, motor vehicles, buses, trams, bustling shops, well-tended public parks and smiling school children. At the border crossing at Dandong on the Yalu River, long queues of trucks laden with goods lined up day and night in both directions. And like the rest of the world, mobile telephones were ubiquitous. As elsewhere, their advance is relentless, reaching around three million subscribers in North Korea, and counting, in recent years.

China, however, is the key and the future is uncertain. Trade with China is the backbone of the North Korean economy. Although Pyongyang maintains trading relations with more countries than most Westerners realise, the lion's share is with China. Estimates of the amount of the China trade vary between seventy and ninety per cent of the national total. In recent years, coal has represented approximately one third of North Korea's exports to China. And until 2017, production steadily increased. In 2016, coal exports to China were 22.5 million tonnes, a substantial rise from the previous year. The coal trade flourished in spite of the United Nations sanctions because Beijing allowed exemptions for certain exports to ensure 'the people's well-being' and 'basic humanitarian needs'. But in February 2017, it responded to the latest nuclear test by announcing that it would temporarily stop all imports of coal from North Korea for the rest of the year. And in August, it agreed to more stringent, indefinite UN Security Council sanctions affecting the export of coal, iron, iron ore, lead and seafood. This will cause hardship, but it will not influence government policy.

Nor is it likely to precipitate the collapse of the Pyongyang regime, which depends for its survival on the support of the ruling elite rather than the general population. For the most part and with only rare exceptions, the members of the ruling elite constitute a relatively cohesive group. They are the beneficiaries of a class system based on political loyalty and family history known as *songbun*. Many are relatives and descendants of Kim Il-sung's original band of brothers—the men and women who accompanied him on his historic return to Korea from the Russian Far East in 1945. These people or their offspring now make up the 'core class'—the high-ranking military officers, Workers'

Party officials, senior bureaucrats, business leaders and diplomats who prosper because of family background and personal connections.

They support the regime because the regime supports them. Their rewards and inducements place them in a world apart from ordinary citizens, where they are insulated from economic hardship and the effects of sanctions. Their perquisites include subsidies, the right to travel and access to luxury goods. Most have housing and desirable jobs in Pyongyang, where only people with good *songbun* are allowed to live. Pyongyang is, in reality, a bubble of modern towers, state-of-the-art museums, science palaces, sporting venues and amusement parks. There is even a dolphinarium, an equestrian centre and a spectacular new water-world, not to mention a surprising number of coffee houses and nightclubs. The rich kids—the local Brat Pack—call it 'Pyonghattan'. In recent years, Kim Jong-un has enhanced their improbable lifestyle by constructing a beach resort on the east coast and a 'ridiculously luxe' ski resort in the mountains near Wonsan. The Masikryong Ski Resort was built in record time by 'soldier–builders' in 2013. With its luxury hotel, upscale restaurants, Heineken beer, European chocolates, Rossignol skis and Austrian Dopplemayr chairlifts, it is one of several signature projects for the young leader. At Pyeonchang, across the border in the same mountain range, South Korea has constructed its own facilities for the 2018 Winter Olympics.

The revenue source that funds these projects and supports the lifestyles of the North Korean elite is opaque. Since Kim Jong-un took power there has been a marked increase in the importation of luxury goods across the Chinese border. In the first quarter of 2017, the overall trade between China and North Korea grew by almost thirty-eight per cent. Illicit activities, some state-sanctioned, add another layer. Many of the ruling elite profit from these activities, which are conducted through a network of trading companies and production units coordinated by the mysterious operation known as 'Bureau 39' of the Workers' Party. Bureau 39 is responsible for 'acquiring the funds needed to support the senior leadership's lavish lifestyle and rewarding its supporters'.

Some of its activities are legitimate and include the sale of gold, pine, mushrooms and seafood. But it also participates in the trade in illicit goods such as counterfeit currency, cigarettes, fake pharmaceuticals and narcotics. And as sanctions have increased, it has become adept at harnessing the involvement of entrepreneurs and criminal networks. Viagra and crystal methamphetamine feature prominently in the illicit trade. The latter is known as *bingdu* in North Korea.

The arms trade is no longer the major force that it once was. Revenue from the sale of arms is said to have decreased by about ninety per cent from its peak levels a decade ago—a direct result of increased sanctions and more extensive scrutiny of shipping movements. There is, however, no shortage of African nations apparently willing or attempting to deal in arms with North Korea. Angola, Zimbabwe and Namibia have long been suspected of being established arms clients. And in May and June 2016, the national leaders of Chad, Gabon, Mali, Burundi, the Central African Republic, the Democratic Republic of Congo and the Republic of Equatorial Guinea, not to mention the former president of Mozambique—the country with an image of an AK-47 on its flag—were all visited by former Foreign Minister and top North Korean official Kim Yong-nam during an African sales and promotion tour. In August, there was another high-level delegation, led by Ri Yong-ho, North Korea's most senior diplomat.

Material inducements are not the only reason why the core class supports the leader and why the regime has never faced any major domestic opposition. Kim Jong-un, like his father and grandfather before him, has shown no compunction about eliminating any member of the ruling elite perceived to be a challenge to his authority. The Gang of Seven, for example, has disappeared from sight. They were the senior officials and close associates of Kim Jong-il who acted as pallbearers at his funeral in December 2011. Almost all of them have been executed, replaced or demoted, most notably Kim's uncle Jang Song-thaek, Vice Chairman of the National Defense Commission, and the elderly Vice Marshall Ri Yong-ho, the army Chief of Staff. The former was executed by firing squad and the latter is commonly believed to have suffered the same fate. More recently, Kim's half-brother, Kim Jong-nam, was apparently assassinated. The known list is probably not exhaustive.

For some troublesome relatives and members of the core class, there is the constant prospect of detention in a special prison for elites at Hyanghari, forty-eight kilometres from the Chinese border. Its conditions are less onerous than other prisons and notable detainees are said to have included Kim Jong-un's aunt, the wife of Jang Song-thaek, and Kim Il-sung's second wife, Kim Song-ae. Less fortunate political prisoners are considered to be ideologically irredeemable and are incarcerated for life in the notorious secret prison camps in the mountains of the far northeast region. A few years ago, their number was estimated to be between 80,000 and 120,000. Camp 15, which is spread over 370 square kilometres across several valleys in Yodok County, is an exception. Part of it is set aside as a 'revolutionizing zone' for members of the elite. The inmates there are held for less serious political wrongs and 'tend to come from privileged families with very good songbun'. They have a chance of being released after a few years—after hard work, participation in daily indoctrination sessions and often the payment of bribes. In an Orwellian touch, the department that administers the prison camps is known as the 'Farming Bureau'.

Endgame

There is nothing much to like about the North Korean regime. It is harsh, authoritarian, repressive and secretive, and its continuing economic structural problems are largely of its own making. Much of its retardation has been self-inflicted—a direct result of the huge and disproportionate expenditure on its military, its socialist economic principles and the greed, graft and moral obloquy of the ruling elite. But there has never been a popular uprising and the regime is likely to continue. As with Mark Twain's death, predictions of its imminent collapse are exaggerated. Such imaginings tend to be the preserve of enthusiasts in Seoul and the Pentagon; the same ones who insist that Kim Jong-un is irrational; the same ones who refuse to deal with

Pyongyang, hoping for collapse. More thoughtful analysts suggest that such simplification is dangerous.

The geopolitical reality is that North Korea is committed to being a nuclear state. It will miniaturise nuclear warheads on intercontinental ballistic missiles, if it has not already done so. A policy of hostility and non-engagement will not make it change course. Nor will sanctions. The only effect will be to maximise the fear, antagonism and pugnaciousness that have characterised North Korean policy for years. China's recent criticism was pointed. It counselled the United States that by not talking to Pyongyang 'you will only drive them in the wrong direction' and that a policy of non-engagement is 'only making things worse'. But while the Pentagon obsesses about Pyongyang's nuclear and missile capacity, Northeast Asia is changing around it and the ground is shifting. Slowly, deliberately, China is reforming the international system of rules written under US primacy.

Russia and China are gradually forming a military semi-alliance in the region. Both countries are united in their desire to check American expansion in the Asia-Pacific. Their navies have held regular joint exercises in the region since 2012—in the East China Sea, the Sea of Japan, the South China Sea and, in September 2017, the Sea of Okhotsk, near the Russian border with North Korea. The South China Sea naval drills commenced on the day following the fifteenth anniversary of 9/11. And earlier in the year, the Russian and Chinese Foreign Ministers had issued a joint statement objecting to American intrusion in the dispute between the Philippines and China over territorial claims in the South China Sea, on the ground that the United States was not a littoral state. A perception of American hypocrisy was once again an issue. The United States has not ratified the very treaty— the United Nations Convention on the Law of the Sea—to which it demands China adhere. Unlike almost all of the rest of the world, the US Congress has stuck to a Trump-like view, originating in the Reagan era, that the convention is a bad bargain and not in the defence interests of the United States.

Russian and Chinese cooperation in the region is economic as well as military. Russia is a founding member of the Asian Infrastructure Development Bank, which was initiated in 2013 in conjunction with President Xi Jinping's 'One Belt One Road' policy of opening economic and strategic corridors across Eurasia. Both Russia and China are devoting considerable resources to the collaborative economic development of the Russian Far East and the Chinese provinces of Heilongjiang and Jilin—territories adjoining the Korean peninsula. The area is a treasure trove of natural resources, including oil and natural gas. Its development is a key priority for Russia. China has a vital interest, not just in the investment potential but in the international trade corridors that will link its north-eastern industrial centres with Russian ports. The commercial opportunities for the region and its potential associated transport, infrastructure and logistics projects were enthusiastically outlined at the second Eastern Economic Forum at Vladivostok in 2016. Representatives from China, Russia, South Korea and Japan, as well as hundreds of influential business leaders from those countries attended the forum.

In his opening address, President Putin announced that Russia had 'begun a new historic period of developing the eastern territories, and it is planned for decades ahead'. His eagerness was matched by that of President Abe of Japan and former President Park of South Korea. There was common ground that the Russian Far East 'is literally at the epicentre of dynamic integration processes'. China's representative from Heilongjiang could hardly contain his excitement at the potential increase in Chinese goods that would transit through the ports of the Russian Maritime Province known as Primorye. Only President Park stated expressly what everyone recognised: 'North Korea leaves us with a break in the chain that makes it hard to realize in full the Far East's tremendous potential.' But, she added, 'when these links are joined together once more, the Far East will become a bridge of peace and prosperity linking Eurasia and the Asia-Pacific region'. Inevitably and eventually, that bridge of prosperity will allow oil and gas pipelines, as well as an extension of the Trans-Siberian Railway, to run the length of the Korean peninsula.

The inexorable pressure of commercial opportunity is weighing on the Korean peninsula. The surrounding countries, especially China, have a powerful economic interest in the resolution of conflict and the preservation of stability. But the interest of the United States is different. Its primary objective is the maintenance of its military and strategic hegemony in the region and in pushing back against the rise of China. The American popular and institutional fear of China is deep-rooted. President Trump's head of the National Trade Council is the author of a book entitled *Death by China*, whose melodramatic thesis is that China is the root of all evil in the United States. Another of his books, *Crouching Tiger: What China's Militarism Means*, is a 'call to arms against a menacing rival superpower...portrayed as acting out of the worst motives'. As a former *Financial Times* bureau chief in Beijing and Washington observed, the book ignores 'the impact of Washington's own policies'. He pointed out that 'more than 70 years after the end of the second world war, the US still has troops in Japan and South Korea'.

Others also recognise the significance of the presence of the troops. A former Special Assistant to President Reagan observed that there is 'much that [the US] could proffer as negotiable, starting with upcoming military maneuvers with Seoul and even the presence of American troops in the South'. The seven-decade-long deployment of US troops on the Korean peninsula is part of the problem. It is a living emblem of hostility, to which the Pentagon clings with rigid determination. China's perspective is the same. It thinks America's 'hostile policy is to blame for North Korea's weapons program'.

The American troops in South Korea have become part of the symbolism of Washington's global power projection; part of its broader strategic agenda to hold on—against the tide of history—to military hegemony in the Asia-Pacific region. That symbolism is directed as much to China as it is to North Korea, probably more so. Even the proposed THAAD missile defence system for South Korea is hostile to China. It will have no effect on North Korea's powerful artillery and short-range missiles but will enhance surveillance of the military situation in China's hinterland.

It is obvious that the 'only reason the North would consider striking the United States is because of Washington's military involvement in the peninsula'. China's recent joint proposal with Russia represents the way forward—a two-track path toward both denuclearisation and a peace mechanism. Washington appears to want the former without acknowledging the necessity of the latter. It seems determined to remain locked in its unresolved seventy-year-old war with North Korea, unable to see that a peace treaty, including the removal of its military forces from South Korea, is the price for denuclearisation.

Thomas L. Friedman, writing in the *New York Times*, has proffered the solution that Washington seems unwilling to recognise. The United States should 'offer to recognize the legitimacy of the North Korean regime'; it should 'open an embassy in Pyongyang, engage in economic trade and aid'; and it should put 'a very clear peace offer to the North Koreans' that 'if you fully denuclearize and end your missile program, we will offer you full peace, full diplomacy, full engagement, economic aid, and an end to the Korean War.' This is the only endgame.

The Trump administration is so far perpetuating the instability and the standoff. Its military mindset is reminiscent of the closed attitude that resulted in the tragic deadlock on the prisoner repatriation issue during the armistice negotiations in 1952–53. That impasse was only broken when the United States was taken out of the equation; when it was agreed to place non-repatriate prisoners in neutral hands. The United States made peace more difficult to achieve then. So it is today.

AFTERWORD

The Battle for Maryang San

'I have a rendezvous with Death, On some scarred slope of battered hill'

The battle for Maryang San was just one of the many futile infantry operations in Korea that took place during the two years of drawn-out armistice negotiations—while the war continued and the bombing of North Korea intensified. Its object, like so many similar operations during the grotesque standoff across the parallel, was to push the battle-line forward, to steal a few kilometres from the enemy—in the forlorn hope that by doing so, the bargaining position of the American negotiators at Panmunjom might be improved. In the case of Maryang San, it was a forlorn hope in more ways than one. The victory was pyrrhic and success was short lived. Only a month after the mountain was taken, the Chinese won it back. Like so much else about the war, it was unnecessary. In the final analysis, nothing was achieved, except death and bloodshed.

My father was a platoon commander at Maryang San. Korea was his first war and Maryang San his first battle. His Sword of Honour from Duntroon counted for little. He was just twenty-three years old and was fired with the enthusiasm of youth. Rudyard Kipling's immortal words were fixed in his brain: 'When you're wounded and left on Afghanistan's plains, and the women come out to cut up what remains, jest roll to your rifle and blow out your brains and go to your God like a soldier.' It was a code of honour for his generation of young infantry officers. He returned home with a Military Cross but rarely marched in the annual celebrations of death and battle and disliked the sentimentalisation of war. Looking back near the end of his life, in mellow old age, he told me that it was difficult to reconcile the fact that he and his men had gone out deliberately, knowingly, expecting to kill other human beings. At the time, however, it was different.

He remembered vividly that autumn morning across the border in North Korea. It was October 1951, high above the Imjin River, on the slopes of a striking, conical-shaped mountain named Maryang San, marked 'Hill 317' on the military maps. The mountain rises above the surrounding massif and commands a sweeping view of the broad river looping in a south-westerly direction on its journey to the Yellow Sea. General Van Fleet, who had replaced Ridgway as Eighth Army Commander in April following MacArthur's dismissal, regarded Maryang San as a prize target. If the Chinese were pushed off it, they would have to retreat to the next line of hills two to three kilometres to the northwest, where they would lose their oversight of the Imjin River.

There had been two previous attempts to take Maryang San— straight-line, daylight frontal assaults by American battalions with mechanised support. Both had been rebuffed with heavy casualties. The third attempt was given to the Australians. It was to be the second of a two-phase assault by a brigade consisting of two British infantry battalions and one Australian battalion. The plan worried the two British battalion commanders, one of whom complained that there would be a thousand casualties. In fact, so bitter was he that he later plotted and achieved his brigadier's downfall. Hassett, the Australian battalion commander, was also troubled. When he consulted the Americans, he was told, 'You won't get Maryang San but perhaps you might get Kowang San.' Captain Shelton recalled that 'Hill 317 was much deeper into Chinese held territory and the Chinese were expected to fight very hard to hold [it]'.

The operation was to be an old-fashioned infantry battalion attack, advancing on foot, carrying packs, small arms, grenades and trenching tools—twelve infantry platoons in four 'rifle' companies operating in tandem, covering, complementing and supporting each other, at speed, in a collective strike. There has not been one since. Hassett planned a surprise assault from the east, approaching the left flank of the Chinese defenders along the ridgelines and spurs that snaked down to the Imjin River. The Chinese knew an attack was imminent because they had been shelled all night, but they did not expect an approach from the river.

On the first day, C Company waited in reserve. All the long day, its new officers attempted to follow the course of battle, peering through binoculars, listening to the cackle of the radio, hearing of the casualties. For these young men, not yet blooded by the white heat of conflict, eager to perform yet uncertain how they would fare, it was an anxious time. Then in mid-afternoon the orders came—to pass through D Company, take the final knoll and secure the summit before dusk, running where possible, in fighting order, and leaving behind heavy packs, sleeping rolls, anything inessential. Time was of the essence if momentum and surprise were to be maintained.

At the fire ground, the detritus of battle was strewn across the hillside and the pungent, acrid smell of cordite permeated the air and infiltrated the lungs. There was a brief moment of exhilaration as the exhausted D Company men urged on the fresh legs, but as the adrenalin-charged soldiers of Pembroke's platoon scrambled on hands and knees up the sheer eastern side of the summit, they saw the enemy withdrawing on the reverse side, seeking to avoid contact. They had been beaten for pace and would not be a threat today. The real battle for Maryang San was just beginning.

At first light on 6 October, after a miserable night without blanket rolls or ration packs, Pembroke took his best men forward in two sections to secure a wooded knoll in the distance, about 400 metres northwest of 317. The knoll, known as 'Sierra', was more than halfway to another feature known as the 'Hinge', to which the main body of Chinese had fallen back. In thick fog, not knowing what was ahead, the men crouched, then crawled. The odd man out was Lance Corporal Yeo, a late-night reinforcement who had begged to be included. Pembroke had misgivings but stipulated that he stay by his shoulder. Yeo joined his platoon commander, his platoon sergeant and the signaller (Barlow) in the small platoon HQ section. It was a bad omen.

As they approached the knoll, they all went to ground, waiting for the signal. The men were tense, rifles ready, holding their four-second fuse grenades with pin removed, striker lever depressed. The ensuing grenade attack was devastating. The Chinese soldiers were huddled together, cooking their breakfast, their vulnerability increased by their mutual proximity. Most suffered multiple, irregularly shaped wounds caused by the asymmetrical shape and size of the shrapnel, increasing blood loss and maximising organ damage. Nineteen enemy soldiers lay dead. Many more were badly wounded. And seven shocked and bewildered Chinese soldiers were taken prisoner. They were fortunate. The priority was to clear the site, to consolidate defences, to dig in and reorganise, to clear away the bodies of the dead Chinese soldiers—who were pushed roughly over the side into the gullies and re-entrants—and to prepare for a counter-attack. The two under-strength sections dug in furiously. It was just as well.

Probing counter-attacks came all day, accompanied by constant mortar fire and shelling. Chinese soldiers returned, crawling through the scrub in small parties, firing their burp guns, lobbing grenades, unsettling the platoon's precarious position. Sergeant Newell kept among the men, soothing them, issuing ammunition and rations, checking on casualties. And Pembroke moved from pit to pit, issuing instructions, aligning defences, adjusting lines of fire, and at one stage, suffering a near miss when he was knocked down and temporarily concussed by the blast from an exploding shell. Toward dusk, reinforcements arrived and the platoon's numbers were boosted. Defences were strengthened for the night.

In the morning, B Company moved through to attack the Hinge; 9 Platoon remained and held Sierra. Troops, ammunition, porters and stretcher-bearers passed through. The successful attack on the Hinge took the immediate pressure off Sierra. But although the sniping diminished, the shelling and mortar bombs intensified, becoming increasingly accurate as the Chinese found their range and attempted to interdict the supply route from 317 through Sierra to the Hinge. Toward dusk the battle faded away. The worst seemed to be over. Some men privately, perhaps foolishly, congratulated themselves on having come through. What followed was a night of Sturm und Drang.

Pembroke was in his weapon pit, hoping for a quiet night. He glanced at his watch. It was eight o'clock. Suddenly, in an enormous arc to the north, the sky lit up with a series of unrelenting flashes— brighter, wider, more intense than any the Australians had ever seen. Time seemed to stand still as the defenceless men in their pits waited, listening to the whine of artillery shells, hoping against hope. Seconds later the first explosions occurred. The area from 317 to Sierra to the Hinge was saturated by an immense concentration of artillery shells. It was the largest Chinese barrage of the war to date. The ground heaved as shells thudded and burst. Dirt and rocks were thrown high. The land became pockmarked with craters. Trees were obliterated. Movement was impossible.

For one relentless, unforgiving hour, the Australian infantrymen huddled in their weapon pits, heads down beneath the blast wind and pitiless shrapnel. They could do nothing. Pembroke understood for the first time the 'monstrous anger of the guns' and the 'shrill, demented choir of wailing shells'. Some men prayed, while for others—

Dullness best solves
The tease and doubt of shelling
And Chance's strange arithmetic
Comes simpler than the reckoning of their shilling.

When the guns ceased their firing and the barrage came to an end, the Chinese counter-attacked. In the darkness and confusion, with the rapid rattle of stuttering rifles constantly in the air, the Chinese were fast moving, difficult to get in one's sights. There was no front and they came from all directions. Three times they attacked with superior numbers. After each attack, they withdrew, then renewed their shelling with artillery and mortar, and then attacked again. Eventually, after a fight that went on all night, the shelling stopped before dawn. An uneasy silence reigned. It was 8 October. With the first rays of pale light, Chinese stretcher parties noiselessly appeared. For three hours they quietly attended to their wounded and recovered their dead. No orders were given to the Australians, nothing needed to be said. Their battle for Maryang San was over; they were spent and their job was done. They handed over control of 317 to the King's Own Scottish Borderers and withdrew.

The worst moments of those few days and nights have long since been pushed to the far recesses of memory. They are recalled only with reluctance; never fully revealed; best left in the deliberate, protective haze of old age. They are the stuff of all wars—like the fate of poor Lance Corporal Yeo, who died only hours after joining 9 Platoon, just as the signal to release grenades was given, when a Chinese sentry emerged from hiding, firing his submachine gun from the hip. The first burst shattered Yeo's cranium, removing the top of his skull and spattering his brains on his platoon commander's shoulder. Pembroke and Sergeant Newell reacted instantly, instinctively, shooting the sentry at point blank range, but Yeo was already dead. Then, after the grenade attack, there was the Chinese soldier, just a youth, mortally wounded and barely alive, looking up with terrified eyes. The response to the soldier's enquiry, 'What will I do with him, sir?' was obvious. The boy's death was swift but he would have died anyway, and more slowly.

So much worse was the instant death of the three soldiers who received a direct hit on their weapon pit from a Chinese shell. They were eviscerated and pulverised, no bodily parts intact. In the momentary silence, brave Barlow's voice could be heard on the radio informing Company HQ, 'This is niner, niner, niner.' That single event shattered platoon morale more than anything else. The men's confidence sagged and Pembroke's nerve was tested. Later in the night, when jagged nerves were rawer still, there was confrontation of a different sort. Pembroke reacted with indignation and rage, threatening to shoot two soldiers from another company who were fleeing the battlefield, seeking to escape the cauldron on the Hinge. But then he paused, turned the men around at the point of his gun and sent them back into the harrowing darkness.

Most galling and in some respects, most poignant of all, was the Chinese counter-attack four weeks later on the night of 4 November. As the Australians watched from distant hills, the British were overrun, a great many were killed, more were captured, a Victoria Cross was earned and Maryang San was surrendered. It remained in Chinese hands for the rest of the war. If you know what you are looking for, you can just glimpse it in the distance, north of the border, as you travel along Reunification Highway from Pyongyang to Kaesong.

Postscript

Few people, and even fewer Americans, know the true story of the Korean War; few understand the reasons for North Korean hostility toward the United States; and few acknowledge any historical responsibility for the current impasse. Not so long ago, over five days of trekking and bonhomie in Tasmania's Central Highlands, a distinguished American candidly responded to me: 'We do not know that narrative in our country'. This is a significant part of the problem. For if you do not know the history, you cannot see the future. And when ignorance is coupled with Presidential derision, bullying and threats, the tensions are prone to tragic escalation.

Since completing this book in draft and coming to the United States, the temperature has risen further—fuelled by more North Korean nuclear and missile testing, more extensive sanctions and President Trump's unfortunate speech to the United Nations General Assembly on 19 September 2017. His threat to 'totally destroy' North Korea—presumably by bombing, burning and killing a nation of twenty-five million men, women and children—was itself, arguably, a contravention of the United Nations Charter. And the use of ridicule as a rhetorical device—'Little Rocket Man'—was a failure of leadership, to which the North Korean Foreign Minister aptly quipped, 'I feel sorry for his aides'.

If the threat were carried into effect, it would constitute an unprecedented crime against humanity. Neither nations nor civilians are legitimate primary targets of military hostility. Most civilised states, although not the United States, have ratified the 1977 Protocol to the Geneva Conventions that prohibits the excessive, indiscriminate or disproportionate use of force affecting the civilian population. The President's behaviour calls to mind that of his predecessor President Truman, in the dark days of December 1950, when some thought that restraint of the United States was more important than restraint of China.

North Korea will not denuclearise solely in response to military threats and economic sanctions. The underlying problem is not the existence of its nuclear capability but the hostile relationship that has engendered it. Ever since the 1953 armistice, Washington has treated North Korea as a pariah and has historically set its face against a peace treaty. And in 1957, it unilaterally abrogated the armistice by introducing nuclear weapons on to the peninsula. The harmonisation of the relationship requires a long-term strategy of transforming relations. Denuclearisation may occur if there is a guarantee of North Korea's security and the removal of the US military threat. That means there must be a peace treaty to end the unfinished war, including a non-aggression pact; and Washington should consider withdrawing its military forces from the Korean peninsula.

Voltaire said that history should be written as philosophy—as an account of human culture and civilisation, not of kings and conquests, but as an insight into the nature of mankind. The history of the Korean peninsula since its division in 1945 is a sad testament to the ignorance and intransigence of some men and women. But it is a passing nightmare.

1 November 2017

Epigraphs

'Tyger, tyger burning bright, In the forests of the night'
'The Tyger'
William Blake, 1794

'Therefore a curse consumes the earth'
Isaiah 24:6

'Our inheritance is turned over to strangers'
Lamentations 5:2

'If hopes were dupes, fears may be liars'
'Say Not the Struggle Nought Availeth'
Arthur Hugh Clough, 1869

'The agony of separation is the human agony'
'To the Living'
May Sarton, 1945

'And in their greed they will exploit you with false words'
2 Peter 2:3

'Where there is strife, there is pride'
Proverbs 13:10

'The horsemen and the footmen are pouring in amain'
'Horatius'
Thomas Babington Macaulay, 1842

'I hate war as only a soldier who has lived it can'
Address before the Canadian Club
Dwight D. Eisenhower, 1946

'The trumpet shall sound'
Handel's *Messiah*, 1741

'For behold, darkness shall cover the earth'
Handel's *Messiah*, 1741

'Since by man came death'
Handel's *Messiah*, 1741

'Behold, I tell you a mystery'
Handel's *Messiah*, 1741

'Behold, and see if there be any sorrow'
Handel's *Messiah*, 1741

'All we like sheep have gone astray'
Handel's *Messiah*, 1741

'The people that walked in darkness'
Handel's *Messiah*, 1741

*'I have a rendezvous with Death, On some
scarred slope of battered hill'*
'I Have a Rendezvous with Death'
Alan Seeger, 1917

Notes

These notes and links are accessible online at
michaelpembroke.com/books/korea

Abbreviations

ABC	Australian Broadcasting Corporation
CCP	Chinese Communist Party
CINCFE	Commander-in-Chief Far East
CINCUNC	Commander-in-Chief United Nations Command
COS	UK Joint Chiefs of Staff Committee
CRO	Commonwealth Relations Office
CMC	Chinese Military Commission
DA	Department of the Army
DIS	Daily Intelligence Summary
FEC	Far East Command
FO	Foreign Office
FRUS	Foreign Relations of the United States
HSTL	Harry S. Truman Library
ICJ	International Court of Justice
JCS	US Joint Chiefs of Staff
NSC	US National Security Council
PIR	Periodic Intelligence Report
UKHC	United Kingdom High Commission

Archives

Franklin D. Roosevelt Library & Museum, New York

Foreign Relations of United States, Office of the Historian

Harry S. Truman Library & Museum, Missouri

Imperial War Museum, London

Library of Congress, Washington

National Security Archive, George Washington University

Needham Research Institute, East Asian History of Science Library, Cambridge

National Archives, London

US Department of State Archives

Introduction

xvi daily death rate for American servicemen 'America's Wars', US Department of Veteran Affairs: https://www.va.gov/opa/publications/factsheets/fs_americas_wars.pdf, accessed 15/8/2017

xvi attempting to snuff out a small war Andrew Bacevich, *Washington Rules: America's Path to Permanent War*, Metropolitan Books, 2010, p. 108

xvi the most disgraceful Russell Spurr, *Enter the Dragon: China's Undeclared War Against the US in Korea 1950–1951*, Newmarket Press, 1988, p. xxxii

xvi the most infamous Jonathan Pollack, 'The Korean War and Sino-American Relations' in Harry Harding and Yuan Ming (eds.), *Sino-American Relations 1945–1955: A Joint Assessment of a Critical Decade*, Delaware Scholarly Resources, 1989, p. 224

xvi one of the worst military disasters David McCullough, *Truman*, Simon & Schuster, 2010, p. 984

xvii rightful place among the nations Shu Guang Zhang, *Mao's Military Romanticism: China and the Korean War 1950–1953*, University Press of Kansas, 1995, p. 252

xviii rebuffed communism in Asia Henry Kissinger, *Diplomacy*, Simon & Schuster, 1994, p. 480

xviii strange new world…anyone, anywhere Geoffrey Wheatcroft, *The New York Times*, 10 February 2011: https://mobile.nytimes.

com/2011/02/11/opinion/11iht-edwheatcroft11.html, accessed
15/8/2017

xviii How different world history Alistair Horne, *Hubris: The Tragedy of War in the Twentieth Century*, Hachette, 2015, p. xxix

CHAPTER 1 This Accursed Land

4   without comparison with that of Japan Ralph Cory, 'Some Notes on Father Gregorio de Cespedes, Korea's First European Visitor', *Royal Asiatic Society-Korea Branch*, 1937, vol. 27, p. 44: http://www.raskb.com/transactions/VOL27/KORS0749D_VOL27.pdf, accessed 22/8/2017

4   Kingdom is very dangerous The Journal of Hendrick Hamel: http://www.hendrick-hamel.henny-savenije.pe.kr/holland5.htm, accessed 26/7/2017

5   a white stallion galloping Stewart Lone and Gavan McCormack, *Korea: Since 1850*, Longman Australia, 1994, p. ix

5   misty ages of the past James Scarth Gale, *History of the Korean People*, Seoul Computer Press, 1972, p. 93

7   untold amount of misery and suffering George Paik, *The History of Protestant Missions in Korea 1832–1910*, Yonsei University Press, 1970, p. 18

CHAPTER 2 Missionaries and Gunboats

9   stifling all feelings Paik, p. 35

10   as pilots of the gunboat Paik, p. 43

10   reputedly 8000 Bruce Cumings, *Korea's Place in the Sun: A Modern History*, W.W. Norton & Company, 1997, p. 96

10   twenty-four heads in one fell swoop Marguerite Harrison, *Asia Reborn*, Harper & Brothers Publishers, 1918, p. 354

11   yet it was a terrible year Gale, p. 309

11   illegally and clandestinely exhuming...perfect burlesque
Wilson Strand, 'Satanic Devils in the Hermit Kingdom', *Royal Asiatic Society-Korea Branch*, 2002, vol. 77, p. 152: http://www.raskb.com/transactions/VOL77/KORS0749D_VOL77.pdf, accessed 22/8/2017

12   **Little War with the Heathen** *The New York Herald*, 24 July 1871:
     https://www.newspapers.com/newspage/21554251/, accessed
     22/8/2017; Cumings (1977), p. 97

13   **the last of the exclusive countries** Frederick Drake, *The Empire
     of the Seas: A Biography of Rear Admiral Robert Wilson Shufeldt, USN,*
     University of Hawaii Press, 1984, p. 298

15   **annex ten Korean acres** Cumings (1997), p. 114

17   **approval of the Japanese cabinet** Michael Finch, *Min Yong-hwan:
     A Political Biography,* University of Hawaii Press, 2002, p. 74

17   **crouched, pale and trembling** George Lensen, *Balance of Intrigue:
     International Rivalry in Korea & Manchuria 1884–1899,* University Press
     Florida, 1982, vol. 1, pp. 583–84

18   **the British government would maintain** Finch, p. 152

19   **monopolistic privilege over the peninsula** Djun Kil Kim, *The
     History of Korea,* Greenwood Publishing Group, 2005, p. 119

20   **sacrificing his body** Finch, p. 173

21   **over 7000 dead, almost 16,000 wounded** CNN, 28 February
     2011: http://ireport.cnn.com/docs/DOC-563446, accessed
     3/4/2017

CHAPTER 3 A Fateful Division

26   **no member of SWNCC had any idea** Dean Rusk, *As I Saw It,*
     W.W. Norton, 1990, pp. 123–24

26   **Operation August Storm** David Glantz, 'August Storm: Soviet
     Tactical and Operational Combat in Manchuria 1945', *Combat
     Studies Institute,* June 1983: http://usacac.army.mil/cac2/cgsc/carl/
     download/csipubs/LP8_AugustStormSovietTacticalAndOperationalC
     ombatInManchuria_1945.pdf, accessed 4/4/2017

26   **raised it with Stalin** *FRUS*, 1945, 6:1098 (1945)

27   **suddenly became of interest** Sheila Miyoshi Jager, *Brothers at War:
     The Unending Conflict in Korea,* W.W. Norton & Company, 2013, p. 18

27   **would want all of Manchuria, Korea** *The Entry of the Soviet Union
     into the War against Japan: Military Plans,* 1941–45, p. 51: https://babel.
     hathitrust.org/cgi/pt?id=mdp.39015002987595;view=1up;seq=61,
     accessed 8/8/2017

27 **Russians to deal with the Japs** *FRUS*, 1945, 1:905 (18 June 1945)⸳

28 **Truman anxious to have Korea occupied promptly** Robert Donovan, *Tumultuous Years: The Presidency of Harry S. Truman 1949– 1953*, University of Missouri Press, 1982, p. 90

28 **higher than that trodden by the crowd** Cardozo J., *Meinhard v Salmon* 249 N.Y. 458 (1928) at 464

28 **astonishing in its origin** Gregory Henderson, Richard Lebow and John Stoessinger, *Divided Nations in a Divided World*, David McKay Company, 1974, p. 43

29 **toward the Military Government** *FRUS*, 1947, 6:611 (25 February 1947)

30 **as an enemy of the United States** Max Hastings, *The Korean War*, Pan Books, 1988, p. 17

30 **puppet show** Jager, p. 31

30 **Our misunderstanding of local feelings** Interview with Lieutenant Ferris Miller, USN, 12 October 1985 in Hastings, p. 19

31 **common reference point of opposition** Anthony Farrar-Hockley, *The British Part in the Korean War: A Distant Obligation*, HMSO Publications, 1990, vol. 1, p. 6

32 **American propensity** Hastings, p. 23

32 **preference for charismatic individuals** Michael Burleigh, *Small Wars, Faraway Places: The Genesis of the Modern World 1945–1965*, Pan Books, 2014, p. 21

32 **every eccentric schemer** Bruce Cumings, *The Origins of the Korean War: Liberation and the Emergence of Separate Regimes 1945–1947*, Princeton University Press, 1981, vol. 1, p. 188

32 **haunted and irritated Foggy Bottom** Bruce Cumings, *The Korean War: A History*, Modern Library, 2011, p. 106

32 **essentially [a] demagogue** 'Prospects for Survival of the Republic of Korea', CIA, 1948, p. 9: https://www.cia.gov/library/readingroom/docs/DOC_0000258357.pdf, accessed 8/8/2017; also Cumings (1997), p. 215

33 **conspired against established State Department policy** Cumings, (1981) p. 189

33 **a measure of corruption** Hastings, p. 23

34 **Real Power is apparently in the hands** Australian Mission in Japan, Departmental Despatch no. 29, 11 November 1947; Lone and McCormack, p. 101

34 **dangerous fascist, or lunatic** Bruce Cumings, *The Origins of the Korean War: The Roaring of the Cataract 1947–1950*, Princeton University Press, 1990, vol. 2, p. 227

35 **willing tools of a tyranny** Hastings, p. 32

35 **The defeat of Russian troops** Radio Address of Stalin, 6 September 1945: http://www.marx2mao.com/Stalin/GPW46. html#s37, accessed 29/6/2017

36 **the translators...powerful ambassadors** Lim Un (pseud.), *The Founding of a Dynasty in North Korea: An Authentic Biography of Kim Il-sung*, Jiyu-sha, 1982, p. 144

36 **A more reliable estimate** Farrar-Hockley, p. 20

37 **core institutions of the pro-Soviet regime** Jager, p. 22

37 **give instructions to the troops** Jager, p. 20

37 **shoot on sight** Cumings (1981), p. 389

37 **placed enormous emphasis** Jager, p. 25

39 **almost every adult northern Korean** Allan Millett, 'The Korean People: Missing in Action in the Misunderstood War, 1945–1954' in William Stueck (ed.), *The Korean War in World History*, The University Press of Kentucky, 2004, p. 30

CHAPTER 4 Two States Emerge

41 **keen, ruthless and incisive** Farrar-Hockley, p. 9

41 **I am unable to fit trusteeship** *FRUS*, 1945, 6:1130 (20 November 1945)

41 **stepped out of bounds of his authority...independence they wanted** Jager, p. 42

42 **policemen and their rightist allies** Jager, p. 44

43 **attainment of the national independence**, United Nations, General Assembly Resolution, 14 November 1947, p. 17: https://documents-dds-ny.un.org/doc/RESOLUTION/GEN/NR0/038/19/IMG/NR003819.pdf?OpenElement, accessed 26/6/2017

44 **be confined to Southern Korea** Letter Truman to Mackenzie King, 5 January 1948 in Farrar-Hockley, pp. 16–17

44 **tenacious of independence** Kumara Menon, *Many Worlds: An Autobiography*, Oxford University Press, 1965, p. 254

44 **formation of a separate government...as national** Kumara Menon, *Report to the Interim Committee of the General Assembly*; Bong-youn Choy, *A History of the Korean Reunification Movement: its issues and prospects*, Research Committee on Korean Reunification, Institute of International Studies, 1984, p. 52

45 **introduced a resolution** Menon, p. 257

45 **such parts of Korea as are accessible** Direction dated 26 February 1948 from the Interim Committee to the Commission; Martin Hart-Landsberg, *Korea: Division, Reunification, and US Foreign Policy*, Monthly Review Press, 1998, p. 86; Lone and McCormack, p. 102

45 **sustained United States pressure** Australian Delegation, United Nations, to Department External Affairs, 24 February 1948: http:// dfat.gov.au/about-us/publications/historical-documents/Pages/ volume-16/139-australian-delegation-united-nations-to-department-of-external-affairs.aspx, accessed 26/6/2017; Lone and McCormack, p. 101

46 **general appeasement of Soviet Russia** *FRUS*, 1948, 6:1126 (22 February 1948)

46 **a majority of the public** Choy, p. 56; Hart-Landsberg, p. 86

46 **Their joint declaration** Andrei Lankov, *From Stalin to Kim Il-sung: The Formation of North Korea 1945–1960*, Hurst & Company, 2002, pp. 45–46

47 **bricks in the wall** Hastings, p. 35

47 **officially sponsored violence** Lone and McCormack, p. 102

47 **Rhee's police goons** Burleigh, p. 73

47 **far from satisfied** *FRUS*, 1948, 6:1215 (4 June 1948)

47 **a valid expression of the free will** *FRUS*, 1949, 7:2:971 (22 March 1949)

47 **the government as now constituted** Telegrams Canberra to Tokyo, 3 and 4 August 1948; Lone and McCormack, p. 102

47 **the difficulty of blessing** Letter from HM Consul-General, Seoul, to FO, 20 July 1948; Farrar-Hockley, p. 21

48 **both foolish and improper** FO Minute, Japan and Pacific Department to United Nations, Political and Legal Adviser, 28 June 1948; Farrar-Hockley, p. 21

48 **pettifogging obstruction** Seoul to FO, 26 July 1948; Farrar-Hockley, p. 22

48 **having effective control** United Nations, General Assembly Resolution, 12 December 1948, p. 25: https://documents-dds-ny. un.org/doc/RESOLUTION/GEN/NR0/043/66/IMG/NR004366. pdf?OpenElement, accessed 26/6/2017

48 **a cohesive, peaceful** Jager, p. 51

48 **an apparent similarity** Cumings (1997), p. 226

49 **now recognised as such** for the British legal position see *re Al-Fin Corporation's Patent* [1970] Ch 160 at 180

50 **moment of major battles...stoppage of American aid** Cumings (1997), pp. 248–52

CHAPTER 5 Power Play

55 **Russian Foreign Ministry report** Soviet Foreign Ministry *Report on the Question of a United Government in Korea*, 10 December 1945, Wilson Center: https://digitalarchive.wilsoncenter.org/ document/122108.pdf?v=88abb9bc6ff03ff75534e7fa142a34f2, accessed 27/6/2017; Kathryn Weathersby, 'Soviet Aims in Korea and the Origins of the Korean War 1945–1950: New Evidence from Russian Archives', *Working Paper No. 8*, Cold War International History Project, Woodrow Wilson International Center, 1993, p. 11

55-6 The ideals of the United States Weathersby (1993), p. 16

56 **broken by our side...will be understood** Conversation between Stalin and Kim Il-sung, 7 March 1949; Kathryn Weathersby, 'Should We Fear This? Stalin and the Danger of War with America', *Working Paper No. 39*, Cold War International History Project, Woodrow Wilson International Center, 2002, p. 4

57   **to give freedom of action** Telegram from Stalin to Shtykov, 17
      April 1949; Weathersby (2002), p. 4

57   **induce the adversary to launch** Telegram from Stalin to Shtykov,
      30 October 1949; Weathersby (2002), p. 8

57   **no less than forty-eight telegrams** Selig Harrison, *Korean
      Endgame: A Strategy for Reunification and US Disengagement*, Princeton
      University Press, 2002, p. xiv

57   **elite attack divisions** Report on Kim Il-sung's visit to the USSR,
      30 March-25 April 1950; Weathersby (2002), p. 10

58   **China is no longer busy** Report on Kim Il-sung's visit to the
      USSR, 30 March–25 April 1950; Weathersby (2002), p. 9

58   **If you should get kicked in the teeth** Jager, p. 62; Weathersby
      (2002), pp. 11–12

58   **If we let Korea down** Meeting in the President's Office, 27
      June 1950, HSTL: https://www.trumanlibrary.org/whistlestop/
      study_collections/korea/large/documents/pdfs/ki-2-40.pdf, accessed
      7/8/2017; Lloyd Gardner (ed.), *The Korean War*, The New York Times
      Company, 1972, p. 7

58   **All the prior policies** Clay Blair, *The Forgotten War: America in Korea
      1950–1953*, Times Books, 1987, p. 72

59   **earth-shattering significance** Andrew Bacevich, *The Limits of
      Power: The End of American Exceptionalism*, Black Inc., 2008, p. 111

59   **We overreacted to Stalin** Robert Beisner, *Dean Acheson: A Life in the
      Cold War*, Oxford University Press, 2006, p. 243

59   **half of the country had been destroyed** *Kennan on the Cold War:
      An Interview on CNN*, May and June 1996: http://www.johndclare.net/
      cold_war7_Kennan_interview.htm, accessed 28/4/2017

59   **better form of organisation of society** Robert Dallek, *The Lost
      Peace: Leadership in a Time of Horror and Hope 1945–1953*, Harper, 2010,
      p. 183

59   **virtues of the Soviet system** Dallek, p. 185

60   **already a mighty power** Dallek, p. 184

60   **no position to fight a new war** *Kennan on the Cold War*: An
      Interview on CNN, May and June 1996: http://www.johndclare.net/
      cold_war7_Kennan_interview.htm, accessed 28/4/2017

60   **did not intend to conquer** Sir Richard Evans, ABC Radio
National, 24 July 2015: http://www.abc.net.au/radionational/
programs/sundayextra/our-nazi-obsession-from-fear-of-conquest-to-
holocaust-horror/6642758, accessed 28/4/2017

60   **Kremlin's neurotic view** Telegram from George Kennan to
George Marshall ('Long Telegram'), 22 February 1946, HSTL:
https://www.trumanlibrary.org/whistlestop/study_collections/
coldwar/documents/pdf/6-6.pdf, accessed 27/6/2017

60   **fears, paranoia and isolation** David Halberstam, *The Coldest
Winter: America and the Korean War,* Pan Books, 2007, p. 197

60   **effort to achieve without war** Henry Lieberman, *The New York
Times*, 1 January 1950: http://www.nytimes.com/1950/01/01/
archives/gigantic-questions-for-maoand-for-us-too-what-does-
communism.html, accessed 29/6/2017

60   **delayed declaration of war** Dallek, p. 185

61   **committed fanatically to the belief** Telegram from George
Kennan to George Marshall ('Long Telegram'), 22 February 1946,
HSTL: https://www.trumanlibrary.org/whistlestop/study_collections/
coldwar/documents/pdf/6-6.pdf, accessed 27/6/2017

61   **adroit and vigilant application** 'X' George Kennan, 'The
Sources of Soviet Conduct', *Foreign Affairs,* July 1947: https://www.
foreignaffairs.com/articles/russian-federation/1947-07-01/sources-
soviet-conduct, accessed 27/6/2017

61   **My thoughts about containment** Kennan on the Cold War: An
Interview on CNN, May and June 1996: http://www.johndclare.net/
cold_war7_Kennan_interview.htm, accessed 28/4/2017

61   **absurd to suppose** Kennan on the Cold War: An Interview on
CNN, May and June 1996: http://www.johndclare.net/cold_war7_
Kennan_interview.htm, accessed 28/4/2017

61   **serious and inexcusable error** Kennan on the Cold War: An
Interview on CNN, May and June 1996: http://www.johndclare.net/
cold_war7_Kennan_interview.htm, accessed 28/4/2017

61   **Stalin saw anti-capitalist talk** Dallek, p. 186

62   **several thousand armed men** Address of the President to
Congress: Recommending Assistance to Greece and Turkey,

12 March 1947, HSTL: https://www.trumanlibrary.org/
whistlestop/study_collections/doctrine/large/documents/index.
php?documentdate=1947-03-12&documentid=5-9&pagenumber=1,
accessed 27/6/2017

62 **apocalyptic...grandiose and sweeping** Dallek, p. 232

62 **trying to take over the world** Robert Blum, *Drawing the Line:
The Origin of the American Containment Policy in East Asia*, Norton,
1982, p. 13; Rosemary Foot, *The Wrong War: American Policy and the
Dimensions of the Korean Conflict 1950–1953*, Cornell University Press,
1985, p. 32

63 **establishment of imperial control by Moscow** Dean Acheson,
Letter of Transmittal, 30 July 1950: https://archive.org/stream/VanS
lykeLymanTheChinaWhitePaper1949/Van%20Slyke,%20Lyman%20
-%20The%20China%20White%20Paper%201949_djvu.txt, accessed
30/6/2017; Dallek, p. 286

63 **work of advocacy** John Gaddis and Paul Nitze, 'NSC 68 and the
Soviet Threat Reconsidered', *International Security*, Spring 1980, vol. 4,
no. 4, p. 168; Wilson Miscamble, *George F. Kennan and the Makings of
American Foreign Policy 1947–1950*, Princeton University Press, 1992,
p. 309

63 **NSC 68** *A Report to the National Security Council*, 14 April 1950, HSTL:
https://www.trumanlibrary.org/whistlestop/study_collections/
coldwar/documents/pdf/10-1.pdf, accessed 28/4/2017

63 **inflated Moscow's capabilities** Beisner, p. 243

63 **bludgeon the mass mind** Beisner, p. 238

63 **dramatization and magnification** Dean Acheson, *Present at
the Creation: My Years in the State Department*, Norton, 1969, pp. 374–
75

64 **militarise American foreign policy** Halberstam, p. 194

64 **worst advised military commander...supply officer**
Halberstam, p. 235; Douglas Macdonald, *Adventures in Chaos: American
Intervention for Reform in the Third World*, Harvard University Press, 1992,
p. 110

66 **God, the man is great** *Time* magazine, 10 July 1950; Halberstam,
p. 104

66　**something like a war** Halberstam, p. 240; Jeff Blackwell, 'The
China Lobby: Influences on US-China Foreign Policy in the Post-
War Period 1949–1954', *The Forum: Journal of History*, vol. 2, iss.
1, art. 9: http://digitalcommons.calpoly.edu/cgi/viewcontent.
cgi?article=1026&context=forum, accessed 21/8/2017

66　**Part of him wanted** Halberstam, p. 243

66　**remove her as a further threat** Douglas MacArthur, *Reminiscences:
General of the Army*, McGraw-Hill, 1964, p. 378

66　**I pray nightly that they will** Matthew Ridgway, *The Korean* War,
Doubleday, 1967, p. 38; Foot (1985), p. 85

66　**The epitaph for America's China policy** Simei Qing, *From Allies
to Enemies: Visions of Modernity, Identity, and US-China Diplomacy 1945–
1960*, Harvard University Press, 2007, p. 141

66　**deep bitterness and frustration** Hastings, p. 40

67　**US would militarily intervene** Shu Guang Zhang, *Mao's Military
Romanticism: China and the Korean War 1950–1953*, University Press of
Kansas, 1995, p. 54

67　**justifiably complained that** Zhang, p. 33

68　**continue to support** Qing, p. 62

68　**Marshall was appalled** Qing, p. 83

68　**our national defence will be consolidated** Mao Zedong,
Speech at the Chinese People's Political Consultative Conference,
21 September 1949: https://www.marxists.org/reference/archive/
mao/selected-works/volume-5/mswv5_01.htm, accessed 28/6/2017;
Zhang, p. 51

68　**a nation subject to insult and humiliation** Mao Zedong,
Speech at the Chinese People's Political Consultative Conference,
21 September 1949: https://www.marxists.org/reference/
archive/mao/selected-works/volume-5/mswv5_01.htm, accessed
28/6/2017

68　**spectrum of ideologies…stand up to imperialism** Qing, p. 32

68　**ally with an enemy's enemy** Zhang, p. 38

68　**unusual grace** Zhang, p. 39

69　**abiding hatred of the Soviet Union** Adam Ulam, *Stalin: The Man
and his Era*, Tauris Parke Paperbacks, 2007, p. 695; Chen Jian, *China's*

Road to the Korean War: The Making of the Sino-American Confrontation, Columbia University Press, 1994, p. 204

69   If the Chinese comrades do not agree Cable from Vyshinsky to Mao Zedong, Relaying Stalin's Stance on Permission for North Korea to attack South Korea, 14 May 1950, Wilson Center: http://digitalarchive.wilsoncenter.org/document/115976.pdf?v= 1f040b5d715c0862b689f19df2a1b007, accessed 29/6/2017; Qing, p. 152

69   manoeuvred Mao into a position William Stueck, *Rethinking the Korean War: A New Diplomatic and Strategic History,* Princeton University Press, 2002, p. 103

69   if Americans take part in combat activities Telegram from Roschchin to Stalin, 16 May 1950; Weathersby (2002), pp. 12–13

70   China might deploy Qing, p. 153

71   China's bedrock national interest Harrison, p. 310

CHAPTER 6 American Hubris

72   withdraw their armed forces to the 38th parallel United Nations, Security Council Resolution *82*, 25 June 1950, p. 4: https://documents-dds-ny.un.org/doc/RESOLUTION/GEN/ NR0/064/95/IMG/NR006495.pdf?OpenElement, accessed 29/6/2017

72   repel the armed attack United Nations, Security Council Resolution *83*, 27 June 1950, p. 5: https://documents-dds-ny.un.org/ doc/RESOLUTION/GEN/NR0/064/95/IMG/NR006495. pdf?OpenElement, accessed 29/6/2017

72   obliterated the 38th parallel *FRUS,* 1950, 7:373 (13 July 1950)

73   back across the line *FRUS,* 1950, 7:373 (13 July 1950)

73   all legal and moral right *FRUS,* 1950, 7:461 (24 July 1950)

73   emotional moralistic attitudes *FRUS,* 1950, 7:624 (21 August 1950)

74   rules made for lesser men Hastings, p. 62

74   ensure the people of Korea an opportunity Special Message to the Congress Reporting on the Situation in Korea, 19 July 1950, HSTL: https://trumanlibrary.org/publicpapers/index.php/index. php?pid=822&st=&st1=, accessed 12/5/2017

74   **march up to a surveyor's line** Acheson, p. 451

75   **free, independent and united** Radio and Television Report
to the American People on the situation in Korea, 1 September
1950, HSTL: https://trumanlibrary.org/publicpapers/index.
php?pid=861&st=&st1, accessed 30/6/2017

75   **secret recommendation (NSC 81/1)** *NSC 81: United States Courses
of Action With Respect to Korea*, 1 September 1950, HSTL: https://
www.trumanlibrary.org/whistlestop/study_collections/koreanwar/
documents/index.php?pagenumber=1&documentdate=&documentid
=ki-17-1, accessed 30/6/2017

75   **destroy the North Korean forces** *FRUS*, 1950, 7:793 (27
September 1950)

75   **major Soviet or Chinese communist forces** *FRUS*, 1950, 7:781
(26 September 1950)

76   **they will become aggressors** Commonwealth of
Australia, *Parliamentary Debates*, 27 September 1950, no.
19, p. 3: http://parlinfo.aph.gov.au/parlInfo/genpdf/
hansard80/hansardr80/1950-09-27/0117/hansard_frag.
pdf;fileType=application%2Fpdf, accessed 30/6/2017; Robert
O'Neill, *Australia in the Korean War 1950–53: Strategy and Diplomacy*, The
Australian War Memorial and the Australian Government Publishing
Service, 1981, vol. 1, p. 123

76   **For his eyes only...unhampered tactically and strategically...
militarily necessary to do so** *FRUS*, 1950, 7:826 (29 September
1950); Farrar-Hockley, p. 209

76   **let action determine the matter** JCS to CINCFE, 1 October
1950; Joseph Goulden, *Korea: The Untold Story of the War*, Times Books,
1982, p. 239

76   **decided to avoid the issue** Goulden, p. 238

76   **I regard all of Korea open** CINCFE to DA for JCS, 1 October
1950; Goulden, p. 239

76   **a fait accompli dictated by MacArthur** UKHC India to CRO,
3 October 1950; Farrar-Hockley, p. 216

77   **long running international minuet** Farrar-Hockley, p. 221

77 **Have any instructions been issued** FO cable to Washington, 3 October 1950; Farrar-Hockley, p. 220

77 **immediately unleash his air force** FO, 3 October 1950; Foot (1985), p. 85

77 **situation was somewhat confused** COS 162nd Meeting, 5 October 1950; Farrar-Hockley, p. 224

77 **questioned the wisdom of a crossing** Memorandum Air Marshal Lord Tedder to General Omar Bradley, 5 October 1950; Goulden, p. 243

78 **all appropriate steps be taken** *FRUS*, 1950, 7:904 (7 October 1950)

78 **wondrously loose** Goulden, p. 243

78 **ambiguous to an absurd degree** Blair, p. 328

79 **appears to be in such wide terms** O'Neill (1981), p. 120

79 **General MacArthur at once stripped** Acheson, p. 455

79 **the state of the world guaranteed** Noam Chomsky, *Hegemony or Survival: America's Quest for Global Dominance*, Penguin Group, 2004, p. 29

79 **instrument of ideological propaganda** Paul Johnson, *Modern Times: A History of the World from the 1920s to the 1990s*, Phoenix Giant, 1996, p. 450

80 **transformed the nature of the Korean war** O'Neill (1981), p. 126

80 **action by forces under your control offers a reasonable chance of success** *FRUS*, 1950, 7:915 (9 October 1950)

80 **in order not to bring into question** *FRUS*, 1950, 7:893 (6 October 1950); Farrar-Hockley, p. 225

80 **despite his press conference assurances** William Manchester, *American Caesar: Douglas MacArthur 1880–1964*, Hutchinson Group Australia, 1978, p. 585

80 **the one most critical decision** Walter Millis, *Arms and the State: Civil Military Elements in National Policy*, Twentieth Century Fund, University of Michigan, 1958, p. 278; Manchester, p. 585

80–1 **The wisdom and morality** O'Neill (1981), p. 117

81 **a bold, even arrogant man** Stueck (2002), p. 115

81 **well-blazed Japanese invasion routes** Beisner, p. 415

81 **barely a working state** Beisner, p. 415

81 **arrogance, condescension and naiveté** Stueck (2002), p. 101

81 **China will always stand** James Schnabel, *Policy and Direction: The First Year,* Center of Military History, United States Army, 1992, p. 197

82 **American army on her Manchurian flank** UKHC India to CRO, 27 September 1950; Farrar-Hockley, p. 211

82 **any decision or even suggestion** UKHC India to CRO, 27 September 1950; Farrar-Hockley, p. 211

82 **absolutely will not tolerate foreign aggression** Allen Whiting, *China Crosses the Yalu,* The Macmillan Company, 1960, p. 108

82 **The US troops are going to cross** *FRUS,* 1950, 7:839 (3 October 1950)

82 **So America has knowingly elected for war** Kavalam Madhava Panikkar, *In Two Chinas: Memoirs of a Diplomat,* Allen & Unwin, 1955, p. 111

83 **the mere vaporings of a panicky Panikkar** Walter Isaacson and Evan Thomas, *The Wise Men: Six Friends and the World They Made,* Simon & Schuster Paperbacks, 1986, p. 533; Halberstam, p. 337

83 **an emergence of war mania** Zhang, p. 56

84 **any change of battleground** Chai Chengwen, *Banmendian Tanpan: The Panmunjom Negotiations,* PLA Press, Beijing, 1989, pp. 39–40; Zhang, p. 71

84 **politically justified but also militarily advantageous** Telegram Deng Hua to the CMC, 31 August 1950; Zhang, p. 76

84 **know yourself and know your enemy** Sun Tzu (translated by Jonathan Clements), *The Art of War,* Constable, 2012, p. 54

84 **notes of the meeting** Minutes of the 13th Army Corps Command Meeting, 13 August 1950; Zhang, p. 76

85 **penetration, circling and disintegration** Zhang, p. 77

85 **We have decided to send troops** Donggil Kim, 'China's Intervention in the Korean War Revisited', *Diplomatic History,* 2016, vol. 40, iss. 5, p. 9

86 **wait there year after year** Zhang, p. 81

86 **If its troops are poised** Appu Soman, *Double-Edged Sword: Nuclear Diplomacy in Unequal Conflicts: The United States and China 1950–1958*, Praeger, 2000, p. 69

86 **China formally decided to enter the war** Mao Zedong, Order to the Chinese People's Volunteers, 8 October 1950: https://www.marxists.org/reference/archive/mao/selected-works/volume-5/mswv5_10.htm, accessed 3/7/2017; Sergei Goncharov, John Lewis and Xue Litai, *Uncertain Partners: Stalin, Mao, and the Korean War*, Stanford University Press, 1993, p. 184

86 **cabled Kim Il-sung** Telegram Mao to Kim Il-sung, 8 October 1950; Zhang, p. 82

86 **not yet ready to assist** Xiong Huayuan, 'Zhou Enlai's Secret Visit to the Soviet Union Right Before China's Entry in the War to Resist US Aggression and Aid Korea,' *Dang de Wenxian*, 1994, vol. 3, pp. 83–86; Zhang, p. 83; Jian, pp. 198–200

87 **decision on the 13th Army Group's entry** Telegram Mao to Peng Dehuai, 12 October 1950; Zhang, p. 83

87 **we won't be afraid** Telegram Mao to Zhou Enlai, 13 October 1950; Zhang, p. 84; Jian, pp. 202–23

87 **buried his head in his hands** Jung Chang and Jon Halliday, *Mao: The Unknown Story*, Jonathan Cape, 2005, p. 379

87 **deeply moved** Zhang, p. 84; Goncharov, Lewis and Litai, p. 195

87 **relented somewhat** Goncharov, Lewis and Litai, p. 195; Jian, p. 208

CHAPTER 7 China Crosses the Yalu

88 **averaged nearly 24 miles a day** Roy Appleman, *United States Army in the Korean War: South to the Naktong, North to the Yalu*, Centre for Military History Publications, 1992, p. 750

90 **shot down one of the Mustangs** Robert O'Neill, *Australia in the Korean War 1950–53: Combat Operations*, The Australian War Memorial and the Australian Government Publishing Service, 1985, vol. 2, p. 318

90 **concentrated in force in Manchuria** Appleman (1992), p. 751

90 **the gate of hell** Halberstam, p. 363

91   **They were an army of ghosts** Andrew Salmon, *Scorched Earth, Black Snow: Britain and Australia in the Korean War 1950,* Aurum Press, 2011, p. 242

92   **best examples of antiquity** Appleman (1992), p. 770

92   **success of this simple discipline** Farrar-Hockley, p. 275

92   **check the enemy's offensive** David Tsui, *China's Military Intervention in Korea: Its Origins and Objectives,* Trafford Publishing, 2015, p. 161

93   **Mao telegraphed Peng** Tsui, p. 162

94   **seated astride a massive cowboy saddle** Hastings, p. 147

95   **strangest sight I have ever seen** Appleman (1992), p. 690

96   **almost like a track meet** Halberstam, p. 26

98   **There was just mass hysteria** Hastings, p. 150

99   **Primary Conclusions of Battle Experience** Appleman (1992), p. 720

100 **would be the greatest slaughter** Memorandum, Substance of Statements Made at Wake Island Conference, 15 October 1950, HSTL: https://www.trumanlibrary.org/whistlestop/study_collections/achesonmemos/view.php?documentVersion=both&documentid=67-6_18&documentYear=1950&pagenumber=19, accessed 4/7/2017

100 **failed to put out adequate security** Appleman (1992), p. 764

101 **simpering and reverential** Halberstam, p. 373

101 **an insular organisation** Oral History Interview with Paul Nitze, 17 June 1975, HSTL: https://www.trumanlibrary.org/oralhist/nitzeph1.htm#oh2, accessed 4/7/2017

101 **dream-world of self-worship** Stueck (2002), p. 113

101 **Army chief of staff in Washington estimated** H. A. DeWeerd, *Strategic Surprise in the Korean War,* The Rand Corporation, June 1962, p. 22: http://www.dtic.mil/dtic/tr/fulltext/u2/612431.pdf, accessed 4/7/2017

102 **all ideology and almost never any facts** Frank Wisner, Head of CIA's Directorate of Plans in Halberstam, p. 374

102 **certitude after certitude** Halberstam, p. 379

102 **pulled along by the power of the command above** Halberstam, p. 382

102 **the saddest thing** Halberstam, p. 382

102 **The conduct of the drive to the Yalu** Hastings, p. 153

103 **We cannot sit idly by** *FRUS*, 1950, 7:852 (2 October 1950); Goncharov, Lewis and Litai, p. 179

103 **if US forces crossed the 38th parallel** FEC DIS, 7 October 1950; Appleman (1992), p. 759

103 **total of 24 divisions are disposed** Appleman (1992), p. 759

103 **415,000 were Chinese communist** Appleman (1992), p. 762

103 **unconfirmed and thereby unaccepted** FEC DIS, 9 November 1950; Goulden, p. 287

104 **thousands of Chinese in the area** Halberstam, p. 18

104 **when General Paik looked** Goulden, p. 289; Appleman (1992), p. 677

104 **incorporated into North Korean units** Goulden, p. 288

105 **integral CCF units have been committed** X Corps PIR, 30 October 1950; Appleman (1992), p. 755

105 **indications so far** Schnabel (1992), p. 240; Goulden, p. 297

105 **one of the most glaring failures** Justin Haynes, *Intelligence Failure in Korea: Major General Charles A. Willoughby's Role in the United Nations Command's Defeat in November 1950*, Pickle Partners Publishing, 2015, p. 10

105 **Part of the reason** Oral History Interview with Paul H. Nitze, 5 August 1975, HSTL: https://www.trumanlibrary.org/oralhist/nitzeph3.htm#oh4, accessed 16/8/2017

CHAPTER 8 American Calamity

107 **all but destroyed** Roy Appleman, *Disaster in Korea: The Chinese Confront MacArthur*, Texas A&M University Press, 1989, p. 3

107 **cut to pieces** Appleman (1989), p. 3

107 **MacArthur's wildly inaccurate estimate** Appleman (1989), p. 27

107 **most successful mass infiltration** Salmon, p. 246

107 **showdown with Communism** O'Neill (1981), p. 136

107 **dreams of the conquest of Asia** Reginald Thompson, *Cry Korea*, White Lion Publishers, 1974, p. 87

107 **Genghis Khan in reverse** Thompson, p. 87

108 installation, factory, city and village Robert Futrell, *The United States Air Force In Korea: 1950–1953*, Office of Air Force History, 1983, p. 221; Blair, pp. 392–93

108 a phantom which cast no shadow S.L.A. Marshall, *The River and the Gauntlet: Defeat of the Eighth Army by the Chinese Communist Forces, November 1950, in the Battle of the Chongchon River, Korea*, Greenwood Press, 1970, p. 1

108 nine back to support one forward Thompson, p. 147

108 needed almost thirty kilograms Hastings, p. 162

108 only fifty tons of supplies per day Hastings, p. 162

108 bag of millet meal Thompson, p. 147

109 seventeen transport aircraft Appleman (1989), p. 37

109 turkey, cranberry sauce Jager, p. 129; *The New York Times*, 21 November 1950: http://www.nytimes.com/1950/11/21/archives/armys-holiday-menu-turkey-n-fixings-promised-to-men-for.html, accessed 5/7/2017

109 the stricken refugees Thompson, p. 231

109 a full turkey dinner Antony Beevor, *Ardennes 1944*, Penguin Books, 2015, p. 78

110 There are some indications FEC DIS, 25 November 1950; Appleman (1989), p. 41

110 alarm and despondency Thompson, p. 236

110 home for Christmas Thompson, p. 235

110 end of war offensive CINCUNC communiqué 12, 24 November 1950; Thompson, p. 236

112 Every man for himself! Hastings, p. 165

112 disorder, ineptness, breakdown Appleman (1989), p. 161

112 only a few hundred yards Goulden, p. 338

112 general withdrawal was being openly discussed Major General Basil Coad, *Report on the Operations of the 27th British Infantry Brigade between 29 August 1950 and 31 March 1951*, Imperial War Museum, London

113 licked their wounds Thompson, p. 259

114 death ride Hastings, p. 168

114 every small arms weapon Appleman (1989), p. 296

115 **most hideous ordeal** Salmon, p. 294

115 **Over 4,000 men** Appleman (1989), p. 337

115 **every one of their pieces** Appleman (1989), p. 336

115 **six weeks later** Appleman (1989), p. 450; Col. Emerson C. Itschner, 'Engineers in Operation BUG-OUT', *The Military Engineer*, 43:294 (July–August 1951), p. 255

116 **American lack of determination...handicap to battle** Lt. Gen. Sir Robert Mansergh in Hastings, p. 207

116 **not a single vehicle, artillery piece** Roy Appleman, *East of Chosin: Entrapment and Breakout in Korea 1950*, Texas A&M University Press, 1987, p. 300

116 **no other story of the Korean War** Appleman (1987), p. 3

117 **scared of being shot** Appleman (1987), p. 69

117 **an entirely new war** Goulden, p. 406; Appleman (1987), p. 169; *The New York Times*, 29 November 1950: http://www.nytimes.com/1950/11/29/archives/marthur-calls-aides-hints-he-needs-new-un-orders-needs-new-orders.html, accessed 5/7/2017

119 **begged me to shoot them** Donald Knox and Alfred Coppel, *The Korean War: Pusan to Chosin: An Oral History*, Harcourt Brace Jovanovich, 1985, vol. 1, p. 552; Robert Neer, *Napalm: An American Biography*, Harvard University Press, 2013, p. 101

119 **thud of impacting rounds** Appleman (1987), p. 241

119 **huddled and crouched around the trucks** Appleman (1987), p. 237

119 **reluctance, the surly unwillingness** Appleman (1987), p. 316

119 **the wounded screaming in anguish** Appleman (1987), p. 228

119 **shot them dead** Interview with Capt. Edward Stamford, 28 and 29 October 1980 in Appleman (1987), p. 240

120 **everyone for himself** Thomas Ricks, *The Generals: American Military Command from World War II to Today*, The Penguin Press, 2012, p. 146

120 **seemed like the world gone mad** Ricks, p. 147

120 **no resistance left in the column** Appleman (1987), p. 322

120 **disorganised mob, hysterical with fright** Appleman (1987), p. 288

120 **nearly all the officers** Appleman (1987), p. 315

121 **I believe a winter campaign** Letter Major General Oliver
Smith to Marine Commandant General Cates, November 1950 in
Halberstam, p. 434

122 **1500 of them in all** Goulden, p. 367

122 **dazed air of men** Marguerite Higgins, *War in Korea: The Report of a
Woman Combat Correspondent*, Doubleday, 1951, p. 182

122 **10,000 troops and more** Goulden, p. 372

122 **worst ordeal in Marine history** Goulden, p. 378

CHAPTER 9 Indignation & Attrition

127 **few buildings [will be] left** *Combat Bulletin No. 106: U.N. Forces
Consolidate Below 38th Parallel*, 20 December 1950–20 January 1951:
https://www.youtube.com/watch?v=G2p9qs2mU_s, accessed
6/7/2017

127 **razing of villages** Harrison, 2002, p. 9

127 **a nation put to the torch** Salmon, p. 309

128 **burned a rations dump** Knox and Coppel, p. 659; Jager, p. 145

128 **blackened monuments of barbarism** Rebecca Felton, *Country
Life in Georgia: In the Days of My Youth*, University of North Carolina,
p. 228: http://docsouth.unc.edu/fpn/felton/felton.html, accessed
25/5/2017

128 **100 tons of British ammunition** Appleman (1989), p. 385

129 **a terrible sense of shame** Halberstam, p. 485

129 **soldiers are soldiers** Salmon, p. 403

129 **man with a violin** Richard Goldstein, *The New York Times*,
20 October 2001: http://www.nytimes.com/2001/10/20/us/
leonard-larue-rescuer-in-the-korean-war-dies-at-87.html, accessed
23/5/2017

129 **most spectacular, most terrible** Salmon, p. 405

130 **cost the price of a Cadillac** Anthony Sobieski, *Fire For Effect!
Artillery Forward Observers in Korea*, Author House, 2005, p. 32

130 **unquestionably a major failure** Letter from George Kennan
to Dean Acheson, 4 December 1950, HSTL: https://www.
trumanlibrary.org/whistlestop/study_collections/achesonmemos/

view.php?documentVersion=both&documentid=68-2_15&document
Year=1950&pagenumber=2, accessed 25/5/2017

130 **fight the Chinese to a standstill** Acheson, pp. 476–77

130 **stay and fight as long as possible** George Kennan, *Memoirs: 1950–1963,* Hutchinson, 1972, vol. 2, p. 33; Beisner, p. 418

130 **Proclamation of National Emergency** Harry S. Truman, Proclamation 2914–Proclaiming the Existence of a National Emergency, 16 December 1950: http://www.presidency.ucsb.edu/ws/?pid=13684, accessed 6/7/2017

131 **power, position and prestige** Dean Acheson, 'Remarks before the American Society of International Law', 25 April 1963, 57 American Society of International Law Proceedings, 1963, p. 14

131 **most nations shared the British view** Goulden, p. 421

131 **less important than restraint of the United States** Richard Stebbins, *The United States in World Affairs 1950,* Harper & Row, 1951, p. 415

132 **list of retardation targets** Foot (1985), p. 114

132 **attack on a platoon of United States troops** *FRUS,* 1950, 7:1330 (3 December 1950)

132 **repay the Chinese for their deeds** *FRUS,* 1950, 7:1335 (3 December 1950)

132 **security of the United States** Memorandum for the President, 18 January 1951; Foot (1985), p. 120

132 **could try to void China** *FRUS,* 1950, 7:1327 (3 December 1950)

132 **using Taiwan as a base** *FRUS,* 1950, 6:163 (30 November 1950)

133 **fighting the second team** *FRUS,* 1950, 7:1326 (3 December 1950)

133 **retained considerable appeal** Richard Stebbins, *The United States in World Affairs 1951,* Harper & Row, 1952, pp. 85–86

133 **a supreme effort** *FRUS,* 1951, 4:1:910

133 **Every command post I visited** Ridgway, pp. 86–87

133 **toughening of the soul** Goulden, p. 438

134 **time was right for talking** Foot (1985), p. 170

134 **Some day I hope to meet you** Letter from Harry S. Truman to Paul Hume, 6 December 1950, HSTL: https://www.trumanlibrary.org/trivia/letter.htm, accessed 6/7/2017

134 despite initial opposition Rosemary Foot, 'Anglo-American Relations in the Korean Crisis: The British Effort to Avert an Expanded War, December 1950–January 1951', in *Diplomatic History*, Winter 1986, vol. 10, no. 1, p. 53

135 UN failure to recognise China as an aggressor *FRUS*, 1951, 7:1:27–28 (1951)

135 derailed by an unauthorised *FRUS*, 1951, 7:265–66 (24 March 1951); Foot (1985), p. 134

135 save Asia from the engulfment *FRUS*, 1950, 7:1631 (30 December 1950)

135 into every community Gardner (1972), p. 22

136 no publicity be given *FRUS*, 1951, 7:1:730 (25 July 1951)

136 strong efforts to deflate *FRUS*, 1951, 6:1:36 (17 May 1951)

136 baser concern with showing Asia Foot (1985), p. 243

136–37 get peace or hit harder *FRUS*, 1951, 7:448 (23 May 1951)

137 favoured bombing Manchuria *FRUS*, 1951, 1:90 (5 June 1951)

137 all the help they needed to attack Foot (1985), p. 156

137 Taiwan would never be allowed *FRUS*, 1951, 7:448 (23 May 1951)

137 A colonial Russian government Dean Rusk, 'Chinese-American Friendship', *Department of State Bulletin*, 28 May 1951, p. 847: https://babel.hathitrust.org/cgi/pt?id=uiuo.ark:/13960/t8jd6fh7v;view=1up;seq=332;size=125, accessed 6/7/2017

137 Even Truman was troubled *FRUS*, 1951, 7:2:1672 (21 May 1951)

137 espoused by General MacArthur FO Weekly Political Summary, 19–25 May 1951; Foot (1985), p. 140

137 show of force *FRUS*, 1951, 7:2:1608 (25 March 1951)

137 increase the problems of control *FRUS*, 1951, 7:2:1674 (22 May 1951)

137–38 involvement with guerrilla warfare *FRUS*, 1951, 7:2:1598–1605 (21 March 1951)

138 immediate preparations *FRUS*, 1951, 7:1:296 (5 April 1951)

138 without further reference *FRUS*, 1951, 7:1:386 (28 April 1951)

138 minimising allied dissension *FRUS*, 1951, 7:1:399 (2 May 1951)

138 further widening of Ridgway's authority *FRUS*, 1951, 7:1:1107–08 (3 November 1951)

138 significant strategic opportunity *FRUS,* 1951, 7:1:1390 (20 December 1951)

139 that Moscow, St Petersburg, Mukden Longhand Note of President Harry S. Truman, 27 January 1952, HSTL: https://www. trumanlibrary.org/whistlestop/study_collections/trumanpapers/psf/ longhand/index.php?documentid=hst-psf_naid735292-01&docum entYear=1952&documentVersion=both&pagenumber=1, accessed 6/7/2017

139 war by tantrum James Reston, *The New York Times,* 9 April 1974: http://www.nytimes.com/1974/04/09/archives/nixon-aides-scores-coverage-of-war-speech-writer-is-critical-of.html, accessed 8/8/2017

139 disturbed at the thought James Schnabel and Robert Watson, *History of the Joint Chiefs of Staff: The Joint Chiefs of Staff and National Policy 1951–1953, The Korean War,* vol. 3, part 2, p. 147: http://www. dtic.mil/doctrine/doctrine/history/jcs_nationalp3b.pdf, accessed 25/5/2017

140 power blackout in North Korea Foot (1985), p. 178

140 no more surprises John Gittings, 'Talks, Bombs and Germs: Another Look at the Korean War', *Journal of Contemporary Asia,* 1 January 1975, vol. 5, iss. 2, p. 214

140 snafu FO, 24 June-17 July 1952; Foot (1985), p. 179

140 for fear that the allies would raise objections FO, 24 June–17 July 1952; Foot (1985), p. 179

141 for all the great and sincere efforts Hastings, pp. 285–86

141 peak number of American ground forces Jager, p. 482

142 weeks, even months, without glimpsing Hastings, p. 312

142 flak seldom troubled them Hastings, p. 318; Callum MacDonald, *Korea: The War Before Vietnam,* The Free Press, 1986, p. 229

CHAPTER 10 The Bombing Campaign

143 long, leisurely and merciless Blaine Harden, *The Washington Post,* 24 March 2015: https://www.washingtonpost.com/opinions/ the-us-war-crime-north-korea-wont-forget/2015/03/20/fb525694-ce80-11e4-8c54-ffb5ba6f2f69_story.html?utm_term=.86c9dfd1b148, accessed 1/6/2017

143 **father of overkill** Bacevich (2010), p. 36

143 **back to the Stone Age** Curtis LeMay and MacKinlay Kantor, *Mission with LeMay: My Story*, Doubleday, 1965, p. 565

143 **one of the most terrible things** David Gallen, *The Quotable Truman*, Carroll & Graf, 1994, p. 162

144 **smell the flesh burning** Neer, p. 81; ABC Radio National *Radio Eye: Tokyo's Burning*, 1995: http://www.abc.net.au/radionational/programs/radioeye/2008-05-24/3276076, accessed 5/6/2017

144 **weren't even in the same league** Bacevich (2010), p. 44

144 **Over a period of three years** Richard Kohn and Joseph Harahan (eds.), *Strategic Air Warfare: An Interview with Generals Curtis E. LeMay, Leon W. Johnson, David A. Burchinal, and Jack J. Catton*, Office of Air Force History, 1988, p. 88

144 **no innocent civilians** Michael Sherry, *The Rise of American Air Power: The Creation of Armageddon*, Yale University Press, 1987, p. 287

144 **abstract form of violence** Gardner (1972), p. 129

144 **we killed off over a million** Kohn and Harahan p. 88; Neer, p. 100

144 **tried as a war criminal** Colonel Alfred Hurley and Major Robert Ehrhart (eds.), *Air Power and Warfare: The Proceedings of the 8th Military History Symposium, United States Air Force Academy*, Office of Air Force History, 1979, p. 200; A. C. Grayling, *Among the Dead Cities: Is the Targeting of Civilians in War Ever Justified?* Bloomsbury, 2007, p. 171

144 **wanton destruction of cities** Article 6, *Agreement for the Prosecution and Punishment of the Major War Criminals of the European Axis, and Charter of the International Military Tribunal*, 8 August 1945: https://ihl-databases.icrc.org/applic/ihl/ihl.nsf/Article.xsp?action=openDocument&documentId=AB2411F0665BE7C9C12563CD00519BF5, accessed 29/8/2017

144 **inhumane acts** Article 6, *Agreement for the Prosecution and Punishment of the Major War Criminals of the European Axis, and Charter of the International Military Tribunal*, 8 August 1945: https://ihl-databases.icrc.org/applic/ihl/ihl.nsf/Article.xsp?action=openDocument&d

ocumentId=AB2411F0665BE7C9C12563CD00519BF5, accessed
29/8/2017

145 instrument of enforcement Grayling, p. 230

145 concrete and direct military advantage Article 51, *Protocol Additional to the Geneva Conventions of 12 August 1949, and Relating to the Protection of Victims of International Armed Conflicts (Protocol 1)*, 8 June 1977: https://ihl-databases.icrc.org/applic/ihl/ihl.nsf/Article.xsp? action=openDocument&documentId=4BEBD9920AE0AEAEC125 63CD0051DC9E, accessed 29/8/2017

145 not indiscriminate Futrell, p. 41; Neer, p. 96

145 We did it all later anyhow US Senate, *Military Situation in the Far East: Hearings before the Committee on Armed Services and Committee on Foreign Relations*, Eighty-Second Congress, (MacArthur Hearings), June 1951, part 4, p. 3110: https://babel.hathitrust.org/cgi/pt?id=uc1.$b643208; view=1up;seq=556, accessed 10/7/2017

145 Joint Chiefs would generally disapprove Futrell, p. 194

146 When China intervened Neer, p. 96

146 destroy every means of communication Futrell, p. 221; Blair, p. 393

146 O'Donnell's testimony at MacArthur hearings MacArthur Hearings, June 1951, part 4, p. 3110: https://babel.hathitrust.org/ cgi/pt?id=uc1.$b643208;view=1up;seq=556, accessed 10/7/2017

146 more forceful action Foot (1985), p. 177; Futrell, p. 448

146 scheduled for destruction O'Neill (1985), p. 390

147 as a strategic target Charles Young, *Name, Rank and Serial Number: Exploiting Korean War POWs at Home and Abroad*, Oxford University Press, 2014, p. 77

147 undermining the morale *FRUS*, 1952–1954, 15:1:469–70 (1 September 1952)

147 all major factories were on the periphery *US Strategic Bombing Survey: The Effects of the Atomic Bombings of Hiroshima and Nagasaki*, 19 June 1946, HSTL: https://www.trumanlibrary.org/ whistlestop/study_collections/bomb/large/documents/index. php?documentid=65&pagenumber=1, accessed 14/7/2017; Gar Alperovitz, *The Decision to Use the Atomic Bomb*, Vintage Books, 1996,

p. 523; Ralph Raico 'Harry Truman and the Atomic Bomb', *Mises Institute*, 24 November 2010: https://mises.org/library/harry-truman-and-atomic-bomb, accessed 21/8/2017

147 **systematically bombed town by town** Young, p. 77

147 **never seen such devastation** MacArthur Hearings, May 1951, part 1, p. 82: https://babel.hathitrust.org/cgi/pt?q1=almost%20 destroyed%20that%20nation;id=umn.31951d02097857x;view=1up;se q=92;start=1;sz=10;page=search;num=82, accessed 10/7/2017

147 **every brick standing on top of another** Robin Anderson, *A Century of Media, A Century of War*, Peter Lang Publishing 2006, p. 41; *Korea: The Unknown War* (1988), DVD, London, Thames Television; extracts from the DVD can be viewed at https://www.youtube.com/watch?v=ba3dgDUtE9A, accessed 15/8/2017

147 **everywhere we marched** Young, p. 77

148 **virtually no structures remained** Young, p. 77

148 **most unpopular affair** Cabinet Meeting Minutes, 12 September 1952, HSTL: https://www.truman1.org/whistlestop/study_collections/mjc/index.php?documentVersion=original&documentid=hst-mjc_naid2839578-02, accessed 10/7/2017

148 **the relentless bombing** Ian Irvine, *The Independent*, 30 September 2006: http://www.independent.co.uk/news/people/profiles/george-blake-i-spy-a-british-traitor-418245.html, accessed 10/7/2017

149 **strafing at low level** Gittings, p. 213

149 **blowing up all over** Gittings, p. 213

149 **almost no buildings were left** Harrison, p. 9

149 **fetish for credibility** Jeffrey Goldberg, 'The Obama Doctrine: How He's Shaped the World', *The Atlantic*, April 2016, vol. 317, no. 3, p. 74

149 **no immediate publicity** Foot (1985), p. 178

149 **removal of all restrictions** *FRUS*, 1952–1954, 15:1:528 (23 September 1952)

149 **against appropriate targets** JCS Records, Omar Bradley, 9 October 1952; Foot (1985), p. 184

149 **all set for a big offensive** John Munro and Alex Inglis (eds.), *Mike: The Memoirs of the Rt. Hon. Lester B. Pearson 1948–1957*,

University of Toronto Press, 2015, vol. 2, p. 327; Foot (1985),
p. 186

149 stop fooling around Richard Haynes, *The Awesome Power: Harry S.
Truman as Commander in Chief,* Louisiana State University Press, 1974,
p. 237; Foot (1985), p. 189

150 Never in the history of our Nation Congressman Gordon
McDonough in Foot (1985), p. 190

150 losing 600 million to Communism Address of Senator Nixon
to the American People: The 'Checkers Speech', 23 September
1952: http://www.presidency.ucsb.edu/ws/?pid=24485, accessed
17/8/2017

150 described as a trap Foot (1985), p. 193

150 favoured repudiation *FRUS*, 1952–1954, 15:1:894 (8 April 1953)

150 Buildings, crops and irrigation John Gittings, 'The War before
Vietnam' in Gavan McCormack and Mark Selden (eds.), *Korea, North
and South: The Deepening Crisis,* Monthly Review Press, 1978, p. 68;
Gavan McCormack, *Cold War Hot War: An Australian Perspective on the
Korean War,* Hale & Iremonger, 1983, p. 126

150 wiped out rice paddies Harrison, p. 9

151 almost completely destroyed David Rees, *Korea: The Limited War,*
Penguin Books, 1970, p. 381

151 the resultant floodwaters O'Neill (1985), p. 397

151 cause famine in North Korea Rees, p. 381

151 never really became conscious Harden: https://www.
washingtonpost.com/opinions/the-us-war-crime-north-korea-wont-
forget/2015/03/20/fb525694-ce80-11e4-8c54-ffb5ba6f2f69_story.
html?utm_term=.86c9dfd1b148, accessed 1/6/2017

151 cooking oil Neer, p. 93

152 hell bombs Neer, p. 92

152 Burn 'em out, cook 'em, fry 'em John Ford, *This is Korea!*
1951: https://www.youtube.com/watch?v=pn_dLez1g9k, accessed
5/6/2017

152 Napalm, the No. 1 Weapon *New York Tribune*, 15 October 1950;
Neer, p. 93

152 a small company of scientists Vannevar Bush, *Pieces of the Action,* Morrow, 1970, p. 31

153 large burning globs of sticky gel Louis Fieser, *The Scientific Method: A Personal Account of Unusual Projects in War and in Peace,* Reinhold Publishing, 1964, p. 12

154 James Bond's Q Branch Neer, p. 42

154 adheres to every solid body Pliny the Elder, 'Of Maltha', *The Natural History:* http://www.perseus.tufts.edu/hopper/text?doc=Perse us%3Atext%3A1999.02.0137%3Abook%3D2%3Achapter%3D108, accessed 13/7/2017

154 A shattered structure Neer, p. 17

154 large targets...suffered more damage per ton 'Fundamentals of Aerospace Weapons Systems', Air Force ROTC Air University, Government Printing Office, 1961, p. 133; Neer, p. 17

155 corpse bolt upright René Cutforth, *Korean Reporter,* A. Wingate, 1952, p. 174

155 kept the exact postures George Barrett, *The New York Times,* 9 February 1951: https://query.nytimes.com/search/sitesearch/?act ion=click&contentCollection&region=TopBar&WT.nav=searchWid get&module=SearchSubmit&pgtype=Homepage#/george+barrett/ from19510209to19510209/, accessed 13/7/2017

155 stinking of the vomit Walter Karig, *Battle Report: The War in Korea,* Council on Books in Wartime, 1960, vol. 6, p. 111; Alan Levine, *Stalin's Last War: Korea and the Approach to World War III,* McFarland & Company, 2005, p. 70

155 I do not like this napalm bombing Churchill Memorandum, 22 August in Michael Dockrill, 'The Foreign Office, Anglo-American relations and the Korean Truce Negotiations July 1951–1953' in James Cotton and Ian Neary (eds.), *The Korean War in History,* Manchester University Press, 1989, p. 108

155 sensationalised reporting Acheson to Pusan Embassy, 17 February 1951 in Cumings (2011), p. 30

156 harm Anglo-American relations Dockrill, pp. 107–08

156 burned the skin to a crisp Knox and Coppel, p. 552; Neer, p. 101

156 like a surgical glove Salmon, p. 123

156 **a slaughter such as I have never heard of** MacArthur
Hearings, May 1951, part 1, p. 82: https://babel.hathitrust.org/cgi/
pt?q1=almost%20destroyed%20that%20nation;id=umn.31951d02097
857x;view=1up;seq=92;start=1;sz=10;page=search;num=82, accessed
26/7/2017

157 **average good day** Neer, p. 99

157 **only 17.2 percent** B. C. Koh, 'The War's Impact on the Korean
Peninsula', *The Journal of American-East Asian Relations*, Spring 1993,
vol. 2, no. 1, p. 59

157 **air bombing was so devastating** State Department, Bureau of
Far Eastern Affairs, 10 October 1953 in Rosemary Foot, *A Substitute
for Victory: The Politics of Peacemaking at the Korean Armistice Talks*, Cornell
University Press, 1990, p. 208

157 **two to four million...most of it non-combatants** Mark
Selden, 'A Forgotten Holocaust: US Bombing Strategy, the
Destruction of Japanese Cities & the American Way of War from
World War II to Iraq', *The Asia-Pacific Journal*, Japan Focus, May
2007, vol. 5, p. 17

157 **about three million Koreans** Koh, pp. 57–58

157 **declined by 1.3 million** Koh, p. 68

158 **massive retaliation** Emmet Hughes, *The Ordeal of Power: A Political
Memoir of the Eisenhower Years*, Atheneum, 1963, p. 163

158 **our clear superiority** Hughes, p. 105

CHAPTER 11 Nuclear Near Miss

159 **the most revolutionary force...no possibility of control**
Einstein letter, 22 January 1947, Einstein Archives: https://fas.org/
sgp/eprint/einstein.html, accessed 31/5/2017

159 **disastrous illusion** *Albert Einstein Warns of Dangers in Nuclear Arms
Race*, 2 December 1950, NBC Learn: https://archives.nbclearn.com/
portal/site/k-12/flatview?cuecard=39895, accessed 31/5/2017

160 **tremendously pepped up** *FRUS*, 1945, 2:1361 (18 July 1945)

160 **a changed man** Edward Boorstein and Regula Boorstein,
Counterrevolution: US Foreign Policy, International Publishers, 1990,
p. 47

160 It was natural Peter Townsend, *The Postman of Nagasaki*, Penguin Books, 1985, p. 54

160 exterminating civilian populations *History of The Strategic Arms Competition: 1945–1972*, Office of the Secretary of Defense, Historical Office, March 1981, part 1, p. 65: https://archive.org/stream/Histor yoftheStrategicArmsCompetition19451972Part1/History%20of%20 the%20Strategic%20Arms%20Competition%201945-1972%20 Part%201#page/n83/mode/2up/search/exterminating+civilian+pop ulations, accessed 4/8/2017

160 take out *FRUS*, 1950, 7:159–60 (25 June 1950); Roger Dingman, 'Atomic Diplomacy during the Korean War', *International Security*, Winter 1988–89, vol. 13, iss. 3, p. 55

161 let the world know…determination to prevail Curtis LeMay, Diary, 8 July 1950; Dingman, pp. 57–59

161 Russian target materials LeMay, Diary, 8 July 1950; Dingman, pp. 57–59

161 demonstrate America's resolve Dingman, p. 59

161 wide consequences…unfriendly act Dingman, p. 58

162 the probable costs *FRUS*, 1950, 7:1098–100 (8 November 1950)

162 one of the worst blunders Blair, p. 522

163 military commander in the field The President's News Conference, 30 November 1950, HSTL: https://trumanlibrary.org/ publicpapers/index.php?pid=985, accessed 17/7/2017

163 Some diplomatists were so convinced Farrar-Hockley, p. 356

163 America had to be restrained FO, 2 December 1950; Foot (1986), p. 45

163 fears and doubts of all Foot (1986), p. 46

164 get Truman's finger off *The New York Times*, 1 December 1950: http://www.nytimes.com/1950/12/01/archives/britons-dismayed-by-trumans-talk-misgivings-are-acute-over-us.html, accessed 17/7/2017; Dingman, p. 66

164 to share command and control *FRUS*, 1950, 7:1431–32 (7 December 1950)

164 he desired commander's discretion…a list of retardation targets Cumings (1997), p. 290

164 frighten our allies to death…a wasting asset NSC meeting minutes, 25 January 1951 in Dingman, p. 69

164 cut them off…Sweeten up my B-29 force General Bolte to General Collins, 13 July 1950 in Cumings (1990), p. 749

164 dropped 30 or so atomic bombs…plan was a cinch *The New York Times*, 9 April 1964: http://www.nytimes.com/1964/04/09/texts-of-accounts-by-lucas-and-considine-on-interviews-with-macarthur-in-1954.html, accessed 31/5/2017

165 Enemy planes parked wingtip Dingman, p. 72

165 expel the US from Korea *FRUS*, 1951, 7:1:426 (10 May 1951)

165 just one phase of this battle MacArthur Hearings, May 1951, part 2, p. 731: https://babel.hathitrust.org/cgi/pt?id=uc1.$b643206;view=1up;seq=17, accessed 17/7/2017

166 contact persons capable *FRUS*, 1951, 7:2:1476–1503 (6–7 January and 12–13 January 1951); Dingman, p. 76

166 lay waste their cities *FRUS*, 1951, 7:2:1476–1503 (6–7 January and 12–13 January 1951)

166 Americans can bomb us Kavalam Panikkar, *In Two Chinas: Memoirs of a Diplomat*, George Allen & Unwin, 1955, p. 108

166 timely identification Cumings (1990), p. 752

166 the atomic blast would go Daniel Calingaert, 'Nuclear Weapons and the Korean War', *Journal of Strategic Studies*, June 1988, vol. 11, no. 2, p. 184

166 a ground to ground vehicle Foot (1985), p. 260

167 Moscow, St Petersburg *Diary entry of Harry S Truman*, 27 January 1952, HSTL: https://www.trumanlibrary.org/whistlestop/study_collections/mjc/index.php?documentVersion=both&documentid=hst-mjc_naid2839562-03&pagenumber=1, accessed 31/5/2017

167 tactical use of atomic weapons JCS, 3 April 1952 in Foot (1985), p. 177

167 nuclear weapons would be essential Bevin Alexander, *Korea: The First War We Lost*, Revised ed., Hippocrene Books, 1998, p. 468; Foot (1985), p. 201

168 A Policy of Boldness John Dulles, 'A Policy of Boldness', *Life*, Time Inc., 19 May 1952, vol. 32, no. 20, pp. 146–63

168 **moral problem...break down this distinction** *FRUS*, 1952–1954, 15:1:770 (11 February 1953)

168 **in complete agreement** *FRUS*, 1952–1954, 15:1:827 (31 March 1953)

168 **voiding the armistice** Foot (1985), p. 211

169 **achieve a substantial victory** *FRUS*, 1952–1954, 15:1:826 (31 March 1953)

169 **misguided self-righteousness** Foot (1985), p. 210

169 **necessary to expand the war** *FRUS*, 1952–1954, 15:1:805–06 (6 March 1953)

169 **stronger rather than a lesser** *FRUS*, 1952–1954, 15:1:1068 (21 May 1953)

169 **most likely to achieve the objective** *FRUS*, 1952–1954, 15:1:1067 (20 May 1953)

CHAPTER 12 Secrets and Lies

170 **starting an atomic war is totally unthinkable** Harry S. Truman's Farewell Address, 15 January 1953, HSTL: https://www.trumanlibrary.org/publicpapers/index.php?pid=2059, accessed 27/7/2017

170 **invalid reasoning of the Russians** Letter from Thomas Murray to Harry S. Truman, 16 January 1953, HSTL: https://trumanlibrary.org/whistlestop/study_collections/bomb/large/documents/index.php?documentdate=1953-01-16&documentid=2-6&pagenumber=1, accessed 7/6/2017

170 **worse than gas or biological warfare** Letter from Harry S. Truman to Thomas Murray, 19 January 1953, HSTL: https://trumanlibrary.org/whistlestop/study_collections/bomb/large/documents/index.php?documentdate=1953-01-19&documentid=28&pagenumber=1, accessed 7/6/2017

170 **bacteriological methods of warfare** *Protocol for the Prohibition of the Use of Asphyxiating, Poisonous or Other Gases, and of Bacteriological Methods of Warfare*, 17 June 1925: https://ihl-databases.icrc.org/applic/ihl/ihl.nsf/Article.xsp?action=openDocument&documentId=58A096110540867AC12563CD005187B9, accessed 24/8/2017

170 second only to the Manhattan Project Stephen Endicott and
Edward Hagerman, *The United States and Biological Warfare,* Indiana
University Press, 1998, p. 31

171 over 3800 military personnel David Franz, Cheryl Parrott
and Ernest Takafuji, 'The US Biological Warfare and Biological
Defense Programs', *Medical Aspects of Chemical and Biological
Warfare,* Office of The Surgeon General at TMM Publications,
1997, p. 427

171 special consultant on biological warfare Henry Stimson
and Paul McNutt to Franklin Roosevelt, 12 May 1944, Franklin D.
Roosevelt Library: http://www.fdrlibrary.marist.edu/_resources/
images/psf/psf000318.pdf, accessed 7/6/2017

172 more extensive than those of Dr Josef Mengele Christopher
Reed, 'The United States and the Japanese Mengele: Payoffs and
Amnesty for Unit 731', *The Asia-Pacific Journal,* August 2006, vol. 4,
iss. 8, p. 2: http://apjjf.org/-Christopher-Reed/2177/article.html,
accessed 29/8/2017

172 hundreds of thousands...as many as ten thousand Amy
Smithson, *Germ Gambits: The Bioweapons Dilemma, Iraq and Beyond,*
Stanford University Press, 2011, p. 232

173 Evidence gathered in this investigation...was a pittance Dr
Edwin Hill, 'Summary Report on Biological Weapons Investigations',
12 December 1947 in Sheldon Harris, *Factories of Death: Japanese
Biological Warfare 1932–1945 and the American Cover-up,* Routledge, 2002,
p. 66; and John Powell, 'Japan's Germ Warfare: The US Cover-up of
a War Crime', *Bulletin of Concerned Asian Scholars,* October-December
1980, vol. 12, no. 4, p. 10

173 utmost secrecy is essential Sheldon Harris, *Factories of Death:
Japanese Biological Warfare 1932–1945 and the American Cover-up,*
Routledge, 2002, p. 208

173 be held in intelligence channels Jeanne Guillemin, *Biological
Weapons: From the Invention of State-Sponsored Programs to Contemporary
Bioterrorism,* Columbia University Press, 2005, p. 79

173 for the benefit of the United States Letter from General
Willoughby to Chief of Staff, Far East Command, 17 July 1947, in

Reed, p. 5: http://apjjf.org/-Christopher-Reed/2177/article.html, accessed 29/8/2017

173 **bitter experience for me** Reed, p. 3: http://apjjf.org/-Christopher-Reed/2177/article.html, accessed 29/8/2017

174 **no useful distinction...not enough is being done** *Report of the Committee on Chemical, Biological and Radiological Warfare and Recommendations*, 30 June 1950, US Department of Energy, Office of History and Heritage Records: https://www.osti.gov/opennet/servlets/purl/16006024.pdf, accessed 7/6/2017

174 **The biological warfare allowance** Endicott and Hagerman (1998), p. 48

174 **Fort Detrick was expanded** Franz, Parrott and Takafuji, p. 429

174 **large-scale realistic trials** *Memorandum by the Joint Advanced Study Committee for the Joint Chiefs of Staff on Biological Warfare, JCS 1837/26*, 21 September 1951, Library of Congress, Washington

174–75 **actual readiness be achieved** Secretary of Defense Directive, 21 December 1951: http://nsarchive.gwu.edu/radiation/dir/mstreet/commeet/meet4/brief4.gfr/tab_1/br4l1b.txt, accessed 27/7/2017

175 **a strong offensive BW...be prepared to employ whenever** *Joint Chiefs of Staff, 'Decision on JCS 1837/26'*, 25 February 1952, Library of Congress, Washington

175 **enthusiastic** Simon Winchester, *Bomb, Book and Compass: Joseph Needham and the Great Secrets of China*, Penguin Group, 2008, p. 209

175 **9500 documents had been restored** Scott Shane, *The New York Times*, 21 February 2006: http://www.nytimes.com/2006/02/21/politics/us-reclassifies-many-documents-in-secret-review.html, accessed 27/7/2017

175 **a secret government program** *The Washington Post*, 27 February 2006: http://www.washingtonpost.com/wp-dyn/content/article/2006/02/26/AR2006022601087.html, accessed 27/7/2017

175 **to cover up embarrassments** Shane: http://www.nytimes.com/2006/02/21/politics/us-reclassifies-many-documents-in-secret-review.html, accessed 27/7/2017

176 intelligence staff told him Winchester, p. 210

176 false areas of exposure...false plague regions Kathryn
Weathersby, 'New Evidence on the Korean War: Deceiving the
Deceivers: Moscow, Beijing, Pyongyang, and the Allegations of
Bacteriological Weapons Use in Korea', *Bulletin 11*, Cold War
International History Project, Woodrow Wilson International Center,
Winter 1998, pp. 176–85, esp. p. 180

177 joint field trials Smithson (2011), p. 231–32, in Endicott and
Hagerman, p. 76

177 arthropod dissemination...a more effective vehicle Endicott
and Hagerman, pp. 74–77

177 devising means and mechanisms Department of Defense,
Committee on Biological Warfare, *1951 Program Guidance Report*, 5
December 1950; Stephen Endicott and Edward Hagerman, 'United
States Biological Warfare during the Korean War: Rhetoric and
Reality', York University, June 2002: http://www.yorku.ca/sendicot/
ReplytoColCrane.htm, accessed 27/7/2014

178 biological bomb HQ Air Force Materiel Command, Weapons of
the US Air Force: A Selective Listing, 1960–2000, Historical Study
No. 14, Wright-Patterson Air Force Base, Ohio, 2000; Endicott and
Hagerman, (2002): http://www.yorku.ca/sendicot/ReplytoColCrane.
htm, accessed 27/7/2014

179 to escape injury and fatalities Endicott and Hagerman (1998),
appendix 4

179 only one moral obligation Lieutenant General (retired) Jimmy
Doolittle, April 1952 in Conrad Crane, 'Chemical and Biological
Warfare during the Korean War: Rhetoric and Reality', *Asian
Perspectives*, 2001, vol. 25, no. 3, pp. 74–75

179–80 burn barrel Endicott and Hagerman (1998), p. 172

180 Far East Command ordered Far East Command, Command
Report, July–Sept 1956 in Paul Cassell, 'Establishing Violations
of International Law: Yellow Rain and the Treaties Regulating
Chemical and Biological Warfare', *Stanford Law Review*, January
1983, vol. 35, iss. 2, p. 271; Endicott and Hagerman (1998),
p. 172

180 Deception in Biological Warfare field *Memoranda to the Joint Chiefs of Staff, US Army and Chief of Naval Operations,* 1 February 1952, Library of Congress, Washington; Endicott and Hagerman, (2002_: http://www.yorku.ca/sendicot/ReplytoColCrane.htm, accessed 27/7/2014

180 the United States did not intend...impossible Endicott and Hagerman, (2002): http://www.yorku.ca/sendicot/ReplytoColCrane. htm, accessed 27/7/2017

180 some of which were destroyed...to kill someone US Senate, 'Unauthorised Storage of Toxic Agents', *Hearings before the Select Committee to Study Governmental Operations with Respect to Intelligence Activities of the United States Senate,* Ninety-Fourth Congress, 16 September 1975, Washington, vol. 1, pp. 22–23: https://www.intelligence.senate.gov/sites/default/files/94intelligence_activities_I.pdf, accessed 27/7/2017

180 floating laboratories Young, p. 113

181 may face charges of treason Attorney General Herbert Brownell's Press Release, 15 August 1953, in Jeffrey Lockwood, *Six-Legged Soldiers: Using Insects as Weapons of War,* Oxford University Press, 2009, p. 184

181 those who collaborated Lockwood, p. 184

181 effete and indulgent society Jager, p. 294

181 concern about the credibility Meeting of POW Working Group, Operations Coordinating Board, 13 November 1953 in Endicott and Hagerman (1998), p. 167

182 Let me tell you something Zhu Chun interview in Endicott and Hagerman (1998), p. 158

182 The lady doth protest too much William Shakespeare, *Hamlet,* Act 3, Scene 2

182 most articulate defender Crane, p. 78

182 large-scale field experiments Harrison, p. 9

183 gentle and somewhat mystical Tom Buchanan, 'The Courage of Galileo: Joseph Needham and the "Germ Warfare" Allegations in the Korean War', *History,* October 2001, vol. 86, iss. 284, pp. 507–08

CHAPTER 13 Propaganda Prisoners

184 cross the 38th Parallel [again] Foot (1985), p. 240

185 the language of machismo Foot (1985), p. 241

185 compromise with the Communists Barton Bernstein, 'The Struggle over the Korean Armistice: Prisoners of Repatriation?' in Bruce Cumings, *Child of Conflict: The Korean American Relationship 1943–53*, University of Washington Press, 1983, p. 268

186 firm and clear commitment Foot (1990), p. 17

186 treacherous savages *FRUS*, 1951, 7:1:788 (7 August 1951)

186 common criminals Foot (1990), p. 11

186 quality of talking animals *FRUS*, 1952–1954, 15:1:513 (15 September 1952)

186 sons of bitches Foot (1990), p. 11

186 if only they were bombed enough Alexander, p. 468

186 arrive at parallel advantages Foot (1990), p. 17

187 would accomplish the military purposes MacArthur Hearings, June 1951, part 3, p. 1782: https://babel.hathitrust.org/cgi/pt?id=uc1.$b643207;view=1up;seq=132, accessed 18/7/2017

187 would fulfil the main purposes Alexander, p. 426; Foot (1990), p. 45

187 tremendous victory for the United Nations MacArthur Hearings, May 1951, part 1, p. 454: https://babel.hathitrust.org/cgi/pt?id=uc1.$b643205;view=1up;seq=464, accessed 18/7/2017

187 statement by Jacob Malik *FRUS*, 1951, 7:1:560 (27 June 1951); Foot (1990), p. 37

187 appeasement peace Foot (1990), p. 38

187 somewhat more than an even military result Foot (1990), p. 46

188 everything possible to deflate *FRUS*, 1951, 6:1:33–63 (17 May 1951)

188 minimum negotiating position *FRUS*, 1951, 7:1:739–45 (27 July 1951)

188 strong sense of guilt Foot (1990), p. 47

188 as contemporaries recognised Bernstein, p. 269

188 for two hours and eleven minutes *FRUS*, 1951, 7:1: 807 (11 August 1951)

188–89 a display of US power Foot (1990), p. 59

189 purple adjectives *FRUS*, 1951, 7:1:931 (22 September 1951)

189 resisting making concessions *FRUS*, 1951, 7:1:960 (26 September 1951)

189 decided not to follow our views *FRUS*, 1951, 7:1:960 (26 September 1951)

189 more steel and less silk *FRUS*, 1951, 7:1:1129 (13 November 1951)

190 attacked all structures Young, p. 25

190 not necessitated by combat conditions Mark Elliott, 'The United States and Forced Repatriation of Soviet Citizens, 1944–47', *Political Science Quarterly,* June 1973, vol. 88, no. 2, p. 259

191 growing reluctance Elliott, p. 272

191 distressing cases *Report on the Work of the Conference of Government Experts for the Study of the Conventions for the Protection of War Victims,* 14–26 April 1947, p. 245: https://www.loc.gov/rr/frd/Military_Law/pdf/RC_report-1947.pdf, accessed 19/7/2017; J. A. C. Gutteridge, 'The Repatriation of Prisoners of War', *International and Comparative Law Quarterly,* April 1953, vol. 2, p. 211

192 Austria proposed an amendment *Final Record of Diplomatic Conference of Geneva of 1949, Section A: Minutes of Plenary Meetings* (Final Record, Geneva 1949), April and May 1949, vol. 2, p. 324: https://www.loc.gov/rr/frd/Military_Law/pdf/Dipl-Conf-1949-Final_Vol-2-A.pdf, accessed 19/7/2017

192 might not be able to express himself Final Record, Geneva 1949: https://www.loc.gov/rr/frd/Military_Law/pdf/Dipl-Conf-1949-Final_Vol-2-A.pdf, accessed 19/7/2017

192 an un-coerced, unintimidated, informed choice Foot (1990), p. 125

193 systematic physical torture was not employed Young, p. 49

193 four times greater Hastings, p. 379

193 for whose services Hastings, p. 385

193 least impressive manpower Hastings, p. 381

193 Gambling, drink and local whores Hastings, p. 381

193 we ended up with the scum...waiting for trouble Hastings, pp. 379–80

194 below even the American dregs Young, p. 34

194 shall be directed toward their exploitation *FRUS*, 1950, 7:718 (9 September 1950)

194 vigorous propagandists Young, p. 39

194 Each compound seethes with intrigue 'The Enemy: Beggars' Island', *Time* magazine, 28 January 1952, vol. 59, iss. 4

195 psy-warriors could not have realised Young, p. 36

196 severely punished, sentenced to slave labour Foot (1990), p. 87

196 Australian Ambassador was forthright *FRUS*, 1952–1954, 15:1:171 (26 April 1952)

196 debatable whether any prisoner...intensive re-education Foot (1990), p. 100

196 savoured the [expected] propaganda victory Bernstein, p. 282

197 strict observance Letter from Dean Acheson to George Marshall, 27 August 1951, HSTL: https://www.trumanlibrary.org/ whistlestop/study_collections/korea/large/documents/pdfs/kp-4-7. pdf#zoom=100, accessed 15/6/2017

197 State Department officers also warned *FRUS*, 1952–1954: 15:1:38–39 (4 February 1952)

197 the president's tendency Foot (1990), p. 89

197 not an equitable basis *FRUS*, 1951, 7:1:1073 (29 October 1951)

197 Are they murdered Longhand note of Harry S. Truman, 18 May 1952, HSTL: https://www.trumanlibrary.org/whistlestop/ study_collections/trumanpapers/psf/longhand/index.php?document Version=both&documentid=hst-psf_naid735312-01&pagenumber=1, accessed 15/6/2017

198 would undermine the whole basis Bernstein, pp. 278–79

198 Well, we have rationalised *FRUS*, 1952–1954, 15:1:494 (8 September 1952)

198 would be repugnant...seriously jeopardise *FRUS*, 1952–1954, 15:1:44 (8 February 1952)

199 approximately 125,000 Americans Walter Hermes, *Truce Tent and Fighting Front*, United States Department of the Army, Office of Military History, 1966, p. 501

199 American ambassador labelled 'Gestapos' Oral History Interview with John Muccio Special Representative of the President to Korea 1948–49, 18 February 1971, HSTL: https://www. trumanlibrary.org/oralhist/muccio2.htm, accessed 15/8/2017

199 remain in the POW camp indefinitely *FRUS*, 1952–1954, 15:1:99 (14 March 1952)

199 Down with communist dogs Young, p. 42

199 if not outright assistance *FRUS*, 1952–1954, 15:1:99 (14 March 1952); Foot (1990), p. 112

199 shooting them for relatively trivial Foot (1990), p. 110

199 British and Australian observers Foot (1990), p. 110

199–200 I couldn't get over how cruel Hastings, p. 329

200 prisoners who throw or attempt Foot (1990), pp. 120–21

200 the results of the screening Foot (1990), p. 116

200 step into dreamland Young, p. 77

200 organised murders *FRUS*, 1952–1954, 15:1:360 (28 June 1952)

200 A 20 May memorandum...some doubt Sargeant to Acheson, 20 May 1952; Foot (1990), p. 126

200 firecrackers under the table Foot (1990), p. 126

200 short supply of human rights, maintenance of dignity Foot (1990), p. 109

200 the actual objects of [US] concern Stelle to Nitze, 24 January 1952 in Foot (1990), p. 125

201 refusal of some 80,000 Foot (1990), p. 127

201 both *The Economist* and *The Times* Foot (1990), p. 134

201 struggled to block other nations Bernstein, p. 301

201 seduced America's allies...the conspirators Acheson to Truman, 25 October 1952; Bernstein, p. 302

201 divisions among us Acheson, 22 November 1952; Bernstein, p. 303

202 Zhou En-lai proposed *FRUS*, 1952–1954, 15:1:920 (20 April 1953)

202 outside the control of the detaining power *FRUS*, 1952–1954, 15:1:920 (20 April 1953)

202 protecting them...propaganda victories Young, p. 96

203 less than one-sixth Young, p. 101

203 the commission concluded Final Report of the Neutral Nations
Repatriation Commission; Young, p. 101

203 would have seen their families Young, p. 102

CHAPTER 14 New World Order

207 If we have to use force Interview US Secretary of State
Madeleine Albright on the NBC Today Show, 19 February 1998:
https://1997-2001.state.gov/www/statements/1998/980219a.html,
accessed 19/6/2017

207 Korea's legacy is practically incalculable Lloyd Gardner,
'Korean Borderlands—Imaginary Frontiers of the Cold War' in
Stueck (2004), p. 142

207–8 We honor no treaties Gore Vidal, *Perpetual War for Perpetual Peace:
How We Got to Be So Hated*, Public Affairs, 2002, p. 158

209 to exert upon the world Henry Luce, 'The American Century',
Life magazine, 17 February 1941, vol. 10, no. 7, p. 63

209 Korea saved us Dean Acheson, Princeton Seminars, 9 July 1953 in
Gardner (2004), p. 142; Beisner, p. 377

209 perpetual war for perpetual peace Vidal, 2002

209–10 underwriting about 80 percent Michael Nojeim and David
Kilroy, *Days of Decision: Turning Points in US Foreign Policy*, Potomac
Books Inc., 2011, p. 74

210 Where our own security Robert McNamara and Brian
VanDeMark, *In Retrospect: The Tragedy and Lessons of Vietnam*, Time
Books, 1995, p. 323

210 By 1952, the number of personnel Goulden, p. 475

210 a rogue elephant Bacevich (2010), p. 124

210 reach into every corner James Srodes, *Allen Dulles: Master of Spies*,
Regnery Publishing, 1999, p. 439

211 Operation TP-Stole Goulden, pp. 462–75

212 a personal, secret, unaccountable Chalmers Johnson, *Nemesis:
The Last Days of the American Republic*, Metropolitan Books, 2006,
p. 93

212 an order of Knights Templar Bacevich (2010), p. 39

212 prized zeal rather than balance Bacevich (2010), p. 39

212 significant steps towards *Nicaragua v United States of America*,
ICJ Reports 1986, p. 14 at [169]

**212 However the regime in Nicaragua...some particular
ideology or political system** *Nicaragua v United States of America*, ICJ
Reports 1986, p. 14 at [263]

213 the well-wisher to the freedom of all 'John Quincy Adams on
US Foreign Policy (1821)', *The Future of Freedom Foundation*: https://
www.fff.org/explore-freedom/article/john-quincy-adams-foreign-
policy-1821/, accessed 19/7/2017

213 unexcelled by any other position...safety moat William
Manchester, *American Caesar: Douglas MacArthur 1880–1964*, Hutchinson
Group Australia, 1978, p. 35

214 Philippines are ours forever Senator Albert Beveridge, 'In
Support of an American Empire', 9 January 1900: https://www.
mtholyoke.edu/acad/intrel/ajb72.htm, accessed 20/6/2017; Wendy
Wolff (ed.), *The Senate 1789–1989, Classic Speeches 1830–1993*, US
Government Printing Office, 1994, vol. 3, p. 493

214 opposed to having the eagle Mark Twain, *New York Herald*, 15
October 1900: https://www.loc.gov/rr/hispanic/1898/twain.html,
accessed 20/6/2017

214 'Christianize' the heathens Interview with President William
McKinley in *The Christian Advocate*, 22 January 1903, p. 17

214 The strategic boundaries of the US *FRUS*, 1948, 6:699 (5 March
1948)

214 to prevent the rise of any other *US Force Posture Strategy
in the Asia Pacific Region: An Independent Assessment*, Centre for
Strategic and International Studies, August 2012, p. 13: https://
csis-prod.s3.amazonaws.com/s3fs-public/legacy_files/files/
publication/120814_FINAL_PACOM_optimized.pdf, accessed
20/6/2017

215 US affiliated encampments James Fallows, *The Atlantic*,
December 2016: https://www.theatlantic.com/magazine/
archive/2016/12/chinas-great-leap-backward/505817/, accessed
28/7/2017

215 **The American bases in the Asia-Pacific** David Vine, *Base Nation: How US Military Bases Abroad Harm America and the World*, Metropolitan Books, 2015, pp. 6–7

215 **Okinawa, the poorest prefecture** Vine, pp. 255–57

215 **Tiny Guam** Vine, pp. 84–86

216 **just measure of Pacific lebensraum** Simon Winchester, *Pacific: The Ocean of the Future*, William Collins, 2015, p. 423

216 **withdraw to its natural sphere** Marvin Ott, 'Southeast Asian Security: A Regional Perspective', *Asian Perspectives on the Challenges of China*, Papers from the Asia-Pacific Symposium 7–8 March 2000, National Defense University Press, Washington, 2001, p. 42

216 **a long-term overstretch...financially unsustainable** Peter Hartcher, *Sydney Morning Herald*, 29 November 2016: http://www.smh.com.au/comment/chinas-warning-for-australia-dont-side-against-us-with-donald-trump-20161128-gsyyrq.html, accessed 19/7/2017

216 **absolute material and strategic equality** Interview with Henry Kissinger in Jeffrey Goldberg, *The Atlantic*, December 2016: https://www.theatlantic.com/magazine/archive/2016/12/the-lessons-of-henry-kissinger/505868/, accessed 19/7/2017

216 **firm goals, set dates** Winchester, (2015) p. 415

217 **no special military significance** 'China: US Policy Since 1945', *Congressional Quarterly*, 1980, p. 88; Cheng-yi Lin, 'The Legacy of the Korean War: Impact on US-Taiwan Relations', *Journal of Northeast Asian Studies*, Winter 1992, vol. 11, iss. 4

217 **force or other forms of coercion** Section 2(b)(6), *Taiwan Relations Act*, 10 April 1979

217 **Grace of Heaven...one huge [American] supply depot** Michael Schaller, 'The Korean War: The Economic and Strategic Impact on Japan, 1950–1953' in Stueck (2004), p. 148

218 **forever renounce war** Article 9, *The Constitution of Japan*, 3 May 1947

218 **obstacle to strengthening** Sayuri Umeda, 'Japan: Article 9 of the Constitution', *The Law Library of Congress*, February 2006,

p. 32: https://www.loc.gov/law/help/JapanArticle9.pdf, accessed 19/7/2017

218 Colin Powell even insisted...a 'normal' nation Johnson, p. 199

219 Soviets had been given free rein Winchester, (2015) p. 156

220 the [indefinite] right to dispose Article 4, *Mutual Defense Treaty Between the United States and the Republic of Korea*, 1 October 1953

220 act to meet the common danger Article 3, *Mutual Defense Treaty Between the United States and the Republic of Korea*, 1 October 1953

220 down to 600,000 Bacevich (2010), p. 125

221 Data from the Stockholm International Peace Research Institute *SIPRI*, 5 April 2016: https://www.sipri.org/media/press-release/2016/world-military-spending-resumes-upward-course-says-sipri, accessed 31/7/2017

221 Credit Suisse report reached a similar conclusion Sky Gould and Jeremy Bender, *Business Insider*, 1 September 2015: https://www.businessinsider.com.au/the-us-defense-budget-is-massive-2015-8?r=US&IR=T, accessed 19/7/2017

221 by some calculations Andrew Bacevich, *The New American Militarism: How Americans Are Seduced by War*, Oxford University Press, 2013, p. 17

221 defense is not a budget item Bacevich (2008), p. 40

221 Deficits don't matter Andrew Yarrow, *Forgive Us Our Debts: The Intergenerational Dangers of Fiscal Irresponsibility*, Yale University Press, 2008, p. 59

221 By the 2015 financial year 'Fighting for a US Federal Budget that Works for All Americans', *National Priorities Project*: https://www.nationalpriorities.org/budget-basics/federal-budget-101/spending/, accessed 19/7/2017

221 military-industrial complex Dwight D. Eisenhower, Farewell Speech, 17 January 1961: https://archive.org/details/dde_1961_0117, accessed 19/7/2017

222 Were the Soviet Union to sink George Kennan, Foreword in Norman Cousins, *The Pathology of Power*, Norton, 1987

222 I'm running out of villains Jim Wolfe, 'Powell Sees Opportunity for US to Reduce Military Strength', *Defense News*, 8 April 1991; Harrison, p. 187

223 strong military is more important Alex Johnson, *NBC News*, 26 January 2017: http://www.nbcnews.com/news/us-news/president-trump-says-military-more-important-balanced-budget-n712836, accessed 4/8/2017

223 self-selecting, self-perpetuating Bacevich (2008), p. 81

223 cast of mind that defines Bacevich (2008), p. 82

223 massive and redundant Bacevich (2013), p. 17

223 prowling around the globe Bacevich (2013), p. 17

223 full spectrum military dominance Bacevich (2008), p. 130

225 truest measure of national greatness Bacevich (2013), p. 2

225 the scum of the earth Philip Henry, 5th Earl Stanhope, in *Notes of Conversations with the Duke of Wellington 1831–1851*, 4 November 1831, Pickle Partners Publishing, 2011 (originally published in 1870)

225 the apotheosis of all that is great Bacevich (2013), p. 23

225 power grows out of the barrel of a gun Mao Zedong, Speech addressing the Problems of War and Strategy, 6 November 1938: https://www.marxists.org/reference/archive/mao/selected-works/volume-2/mswv2_12.htm#p2, accessed 19/7/2017

225 military metaphysics C. Wright Mills, *The Power Elite*, Oxford University Press, 2000, p. 222 (originally published 1956)

226 international problems as military problems Bacevich (2013), p. 2

CHAPTER 15 Dystopia

227 an article of faith...self-interested interloper Harrison, p. 103

228 American self-interest and convenience Choong-Nam Kim, 'The Management of the ROK-US Relations in the Post-Cold War Era', *The Journal of East Asian Affairs*, Spring/Summer 2003, vol. 17, iss. 1, p. 90

228 artificial underground caves Harrison, p. 8

228 original, brilliant and revolutionary contribution Don Oberdorfer, *The Two Koreas: A Contemporary History*, Perseus Books, 2001, p. 19

228–29 best metaphor Nicholas Kristof, *The New York Times*, 20 August 1989: http://www.nytimes.com/1989/08/20/magazine/great-leader-to-dear-leader.html?pagewanted=all, accessed 25/7/2017

229 helps in understanding Harrison, p. 18

229 one big kibbutz Bernard Krisher, 'Report from North Korea', *Gekkan Asahi*, September 1991, p. 15; Harrison, p. 16

229 not so much a nation as a religion Kristof: http://www.nytimes.com/1989/08/20/magazine/great-leader-to-dear-leader.html?pagewanted=all, accessed 25/7/2017

229 much more challenging Rüdiger Frank, 'Between Wishful Thinking and Realism: Hopes for a Pyongyang Spring', *38 North*, 29 September 2016: http://www.38north.org/2016/09/rfrank092916/, accessed 24/7/2017

229 not seek an excuse Rex Tillerson, Remarks at the Press Briefing Room, 1 August 2017, US Department of State: https://www.state.gov/secretary/remarks/2017/08/272979.htm, accessed 7/8/2017

229 We're practicing invading them Jeffrey Lewis, 'North Korea Is Practicing for Nuclear War', *Foreign Policy*, 9 March 2017: http://foreignpolicy.com/2017/03/09/north-korea-is-practicing-for-nuclear-war/, accessed 24/7/2017

230 an important deterrent Dursun Peksen, 'Authoritarian Regimes and Economic Sanction Effectiveness: The Case of North Korea', *Korea Economic Institute of America*, 23 June 2016: http://www.keia.org/sites/default/files/publications/kei_aps_north_korea_sanctions.pdf, accessed 24/7/2017

230 'lost cause' and a 'non-starter' David Brunnstrom, *Reuters*, 26 October 2016: http://www.reuters.com/article/us-northkorea-nuclear-clapper-idUSKCN12P2L7, accessed 24/7/2017

230 their only current asset General Grant, 11 April 2000 in Harrison, p. 132

231 destroy the basis *United States Mission Non-Paper: Defense Impacts of Potential United Nations General Assembly Nuclear Weapons Ban Treaty*, Annexure 2, 17 October 2016: http://www.icanw.org/wp-content/uploads/2016/10/NATO_OCT2016.pdf, accessed 24/7/2017

231 **There is a permanence** George Friedman, 'The Dark Night: North Korean Strategy', *Mauldin Economics*, 21 March 2016: http://www.mauldineconomics.com/this-week-in-geopolitics/the-dark-night-north-korean-strategy, accessed 24/7/2017

231 **the concerns of many Americans** Dr Billy Graham, 31 March 1992 in Harrison, p. 108

232 **a painful, brief anomaly** Kim Dae Jung, 'The Once and Future Korea', *Foreign Policy*, Spring 1992, no. 86, p. 45

232 **We do plan to engage** Colin Powell, Press Conference, 6 March 2001, US Department of State: https://2001-2009.state.gov/ secretary/former/powell/remarks/2001/1116.htm; Jean Edward Smith, *Bush*, Simon & Schuster, 2016, p. 187

232 **got too far forward on his skis** Alan Sipress and Steven Mufson, *The Washington Post*, 26 August 2001: https://www.washingtonpost. com/archive/politics/2001/08/26/powell-takes-the-middle-ground/8999cf69-6d90-413e-8850-18bbc49f42c2/?utm_term=. fec73d6616f3, accessed 25/7/2017

233 **agent of God placed on earth** Smith, p. 233

233 **first of a multitude of errors** Smith, p. 188

233 **unrealistic approach** Harrison, p. 217

234 **If you want to make peace** Maureen Biwi, *Nelson Mandela's Quotes and Tributes*, AA Global Sourcing Ltd, 2013, p. 24

234 **much more effective** Rüdiger Frank, 29 September 2016: http://www.38north.org/2016/09/rfrank092916/, accessed 24/7/2017

234 **the most effective sanction on North Korea** Simon Jenkins, *The Guardian*, 6 July 2017: https://www.theguardian.com/ commentisfree/2017/jul/05/china-trump-kim-jong-un-north-korea-beijing, accessed 27/7/2017

234 **the only path toward economic prosperity** Nathan Beauchamp-Mustafaga, 'Prospects for Economic Reform in North Korea', *China Perspectives*, 2012, no. 4, p. 71

234 **the filthy wind of bourgeois liberty** Rüdiger Frank, 'The 7th Party Congress in North Korea: A Return to a New Normal', *38 North*, 20 May 2016: http://www.38north.org/2016/05/rfrank052016/, accessed 24/7/2017

235 food is more important than bullets 'Kim Jong-un: Food More Important Than Bullets', 27 October 2010: http://www.china.org. cn/world/2010-10/27/content_21212218.htm, accessed 24/7/2017; Beauchamp-Mustafaga, p. 71

235 filing through the aisles Harrison, p. 30

235 change going on in North Korea 'President Says DPRK Taking First Steps Toward Openness', *Korea Herald*, 1 October 1998: http:// nautilus.org/napsnet/napsnet-daily-report/napsnet-daily-report-01-october-1998/, accessed 25/7/2017

235 we recognize that the world market Kim Jong U, 'North Korea's External Economic Policy', Conference Paper, 22–23 April 1996, in Harrison, p. 34

235 ensure that such economic levers Article 33, *Constitution of the Democratic People's Republic of Korea*, 1998: http://www.asianlii.org/kp/ legis/const/1998/3.html, accessed 25/7/2017

236 significant reduction of state control Andrei Lankov, *The New York Times*, 21 January 2015: https://www.nytimes. com/2015/01/22/opinion/north-korea-dabbles-in-reform.html, accessed 24/7/2017

236–37 What is happening in the enterprise area Eric Talmadge, *The Guardian*, 5 March 2015: https://www.theguardian.com/ world/2015/mar/05/north-korea-economic-reforms-show-signs-paying-off, accessed 24/7/2017

237 new management methods Talmadge: https://www.theguardian. com/world/2015/mar/05/north-korea-economic-reforms-show-signs-paying-off, accessed 24/7/2017

237 Estimates from the Seoul-based Bank of Korea Andrei Lankov, *NK News*, 6 February 2017: https://www.nknews.org/2017/02/the-limits-of-north-koreas-meagre-economic-growth/, accessed 27/7/2017

237 Some respected observers Lankov, 6 February 2017: https:// www.nknews.org/2017/02/the-limits-of-north-koreas-meagre-economic-growth/, accessed 27/7/2017

239 ridiculously luxe ski resorts *New York Post*, 17 March 2016: http://nypost.com/2016/03/17/north-korea-has-a-ridiculously-luxe-ski-resort/, accessed 31/7/2017

239 grew by almost 38 percent Jane Perlez and Yufan Huang, *The New York Times*, 13 April 2017: https://www.nytimes.com/2017/04/13/world/asia/china-north-korea-trade-coal-nuclear.html, accessed 27/7/2017

239 acquiring the funds needed Mark Weissman and Linus Hagstrom, 'Sanctions Reconsidered: The Path Forward with North Korea', *The Washington Quarterly*, Fall 2016, vol. 39, iss. 3, p. 71

240 African nations apparently willing Salem Solomon, *VOA News*, 22 March 2017: https://www.voanews.com/a/sanctioned-and-shunned-north-korea-finds-arms-deals-in-africa/3777262.html, accessed 27/7/2017

240 Kim Yong-nam Ha-young Choi, *NK News*, May 2016: https://www.nknews.org/2016/05/top-north-korean-official-meets-african-leaders/, accessed 7/8/2017

240 North Korea's most senior diplomat Elizabeth Shim, *UPI*, 15 August 2016: https://www.upi.com/Top_News/World-News/2016/08/15/KCNA-North-Korea-delegation-met-with-Democratic-Republic-of-Congo-officials/1551471313274/, accessed 7/8/2017

241 between 80,000 and 120,000 *Report of the Commission of Inquiry on Human Rights in the Democratic People's Republic of Korea* (Commission Report) A/HRC/25/CRP.1, 7 February 2014, p. 226

242 tend to come from privileged families Commission Report, p. 223

242 you will only drive them…only making things worse Fu Ying, Munich Security Conference, 18 February 2017: https://www.youtube.com/watch?v=WXmaseU6h5Q, accessed 24/7/2017

243 begun a new historic period…literally at the epicentre Vladimir Putin, Eastern Economic Forum, 3 September 2016: http://en.kremlin.ru/events/president/news/52808, accessed 25/7/2017

243 North Korea leaves us with a break…bridge of peace and prosperity Park Geun-hye, Eastern Economic Forum, 3 September 2016: http://en.kremlin.ru/events/president/news/52808, accessed 25/7/2017

244 impact of Washington's own policies Richard McGregor, *Financial Times*, 7 February 2016: https://www.ft.com/content/ b30b0be0-cb61-11e5-be0b-b7ece4e953a0, accessed 24/7/2017

244 former Special Assistant to President Reagan Doug Bandow, *The National Interest*, 24 February 2017: http://nationalinterest.org/ feature/how-america-can-avoid-second-korea-war-19571, accessed 25/7/2017

244 America's hostile policy is to blame Bandow: http:// nationalinterest.org/feature/how-america-can-avoid-second-korea-war-19571, accessed 25/7/2017

245 only reason the north Bandow: http://nationalinterest.org/ feature/how-america-can-avoid-second-korea-war-19571, accessed 25/7/2017

245 joint proposal Joint statement by the Russian and Chinese foreign ministries on the Korean Peninsula's problems, 4 July 2014: http://www.mid.ru/en/foreign_policy/news/-/asset_ publisher/cKNonkJE02Bw/content/id/2807662, accessed 17/8/2017

245 offer to recognize...end to the Korean War Thomas Friedman, *The New York Times*, 10 August 2017: https://www.nytimes. com/2017/08/10/opinion/trump-north-korea-strategy.html, accessed 15/8/2017; Friedman interview on CNN, 11 August 2017: https:// www.newsbusters.org/blogs/nb/brad-wilmouth/2017/08/11/ friedman-us-should-offer-peace-treaty-full-relations-north-korea; accessed 15/8/2017

Afterword

246–47 Rudyard Kipling's immortal words Rudyard Kipling, 'The Young British Soldier', 1892

247 later plotted and achieved Michael Scott, *Scapegoats: Thirteen Victims of Military Injustice*, Elliot and Thompson, 2013; pp. 185–208

247 You won't get Maryang San John Essex-Clark, DSM, *Hassett: Australian Leader*, Australian Military History Publications, 2005, p. 15

247 Captain Shelton recalled Maurie Pears and Fred Kirkland, *Korea Remembered*, Doctrine Wing, Combined Arms Training and Development Centre, 1998, pp. 270–71

250 monstrous anger of the guns Wilfred Owen, 'Anthem for Doomed Youth', 1917

250 shrill demented choir Wilfred Owen, 'Anthem for Doomed Youth', 1917

250 Dullness best solves Wilfred Owen, 'Insensibility', 1918

Notes on Sources

These notes are intended to assist those interested readers who wish to probe further. I have grouped them by reference to the principal topics addressed in the narrative, but they are a beginning not an end.

The Demilitarised Zone
The leading environmental historians on the strange and unintended ecological experiment that has occurred inside the demilitarised zone, are Lisa Brady from Boise State University, Peter Coates from Bristol University and Julia Adeney Thomas of Notre Dame. Their extensive writings on the subject are easily located. Readers may also like to consult the DMZ Forum, whose mission is to support the conservation of the unique biological and cultural resources of the demilitarised zone.

Geography and Climate
In addition to the many scientific and meteorological disquisitions, a condensed layman's guide to North Korea's extreme winter weather and the effect of the Siberian 'High' can be found in William Dando's *Food and Famine in the 21st Century* (2012). A more comprehensive survey is contained in *North Korea: Geographical Analysis* (2003) published by the United States Military Academy, West Point.

The Pre-modern History
The history and anthropology of Korea before 1860 is attractively summarised for the popular reader in Chapter 1, 'The Virtues', in

Bruce Cumings *Korea's Place in the Sun* (1997). A more detailed account can be found in Cumings' earlier work *The Origins of the Korean War*, vol. 1 (1981). James Scarth Gale's *History of the Korean People*, originally published in 1927, is a classic but excessively romantic history that combines myth, legend and poetry.

The Missionaries

The remarkable story of the intrepid Jesuits who went to China, Japan and Korea is neatly condensed, with many useful notes, in the paper 'Jesuits in Korea: Influence without Presence' by Franklin D. Rausch. The later history of the Protestant missions in Korea is explained in George Paik's *The History of Protestant Missions in Korea 1832–1910*, first published in 1927. And a comprehensive modern account of both can be found in James Grayson's *Korea—A Religious History* (2013).

The Gunboats

An accessible account of the opening of Korea to Western trade and influence after 1860, the accompanying international rivalries and the brutal Japanese assassination of Queen Min, appears in Cumings' *Korea's Place in the Sun*, Chapter 2, 'The Interests, 1860–1904'. Michael Finch's *Min Yong-hwan: A Political Biography* (2002) puts these events into the context of the short ardent life of Prince Min.

The Division of Korea

Dean Rusk's autobiographical reminiscences in *As I saw It* (1990) provide an invaluable insight from someone who actually drew the line. Sheila Miyoshi Jager's monumental work *Brothers at War* (2013) provides an important modern commentary. And Cumings is once again comprehensive in his *Origins*, Vol.1. David Glantz's article 'August Storm: Soviet Tactical and Operational Combat in Manchuria' explains the awesome power and speed with which the Soviet Army moved into North Korea.

The Military Occupations

Sheila Miyoshi Jager and Cumings are again significant on this issue; as is Alan Millett, especially in his *The War for Korea 1945–1950* (2005) and Kathryn Weathersby in her paper 'Soviet Aims in Korea and the Origins of the Korean War, 1945–1950'. I enjoyed the accounts by two of the leading British writers on the subject—the former war correspondent Sir Max Hastings and the former general Sir Anthony Farrar-Hockley. Hastings' classic work *The Korean War* (1987) is essential reading and Farrar-Hockley's official history *The British Part in the Korean War* (1990) is replete with detailed and useful information.

Emergence of Separate States

On the failure of the United Nations process, the role of the United States in that failure and the emergence of two separate republics, Farrar-Hockley is perceptive, Sheila Miyoshi Jager is excellent and Cumings' *Origins,* vol. 1, is comprehensive. A different, less critical perspective is provided in the numerous writings of the respected American historians William Stueck and Allan Millett; a pithy, critical account appears in *Korea: Since 1850* (1993) by Stewart Lone and Gavan McCormack and in *Cold War, Hot War* (1983) by Gavan McCormack; and a scholarly account by the Korean-born historian Bong-youn Choy is set out in his *A History of the Korean Reunification Movement,* 1984.

Russia and China Intervention

The leading American scholar on the Soviet decision to support Kim-il Sung's reunification attempt is Kathryn Weathersby. Her extensive writings drawn from Russian archives are readily found in the *Bulletins* and *Working Papers* of the Cold War International History Project, Woodrow Wilson Center for Scholars. Of the accounts focussing on China's position, some of the best are: Jian, *China's Road to the Korean War* (1994); Zhang, *Mao's Military Romanticism* (1995); and Tsui, *China's Military Intervention in Korea* (2015). William Stueck addresses both the Russian and Chinese involvement in his *Rethinking the Korean War.*

Crossing the 38th Parallel

Washington's diplomatic dissembling over the decision to cross the 38th parallel is laid bare with many additional references to the British position by Farrar-Hockley. Both Hastings and Rosemary Foot in *The Wrong War* (1985) are also informative on this issue. Walter Millis in *Arms and the State* (1958) criticises the decision but other American writers and historians—including David Halberstam, *The Coldest Winter (2008)*; Joseph Goulden, *Korea: The Untold Story of the War* (1982); Bevin Alexander, *Korea: The First War We Lost* (1986), Clay Blair, *The Forgotten War* (1987); and William Stueck—deal less fully with the issue.

China Crosses the Yalu

S.L.A. Marshall's *The River and the Gauntlet: Defeat of the Eighth Army by the Chinese Communist Forces* (1953) is a classic exposition of the retreat of the American-led forces in late 1950, superbly told by a former infantry operations analyst with the Eighth Army. The entry of the Peoples' Volunteers into North Korea is vividly portrayed by the former British foreign correspondent Russell Spurr in *Enter the Dragon* (1988). Roy Appleman demonstrates a professional soldier's respect for the feats of the Chinese forces in his trilogy—*South to the Naktong, North to the Yalu* (1962), *East of Chosin* (1987) and *Disaster in Korea* (1989). And Halberstam, Hastings and Farrar-Hockley provide insightful detail. The best Chinese military account is Zhang, *Mao's Military Romanticism*.

The Conduct of the War

Of the many American battlefield histories of the war, the volumes of Appleman's trilogy are compulsory reading. So are Halberstam, Goulden and Alexander. Clay Blair's account is sweeping; Hastings is acerbic; and Farrar-Hockley's official history contains valuable detail, albeit from a British perspective; as does Andrew Salmon's *Scorched Earth, Black Snow* (2011). The contemporaneous account by the war correspondent Reginald Thompson in *Cry Korea* (1954) is moving. And James Schnabel's *Policy and Direction: The First Year* (1972) is useful but generally uncritical.

Bombing and Napalm

The chronicle of the bombing campaign as it was increasingly used for urban area bombardments and as a means of influencing the armistice negotiations, is told by Rosemary Foot in *The Wrong War* (1985) and in *A Substitute for Victory: The Politics of Peacemaking at the Korean Armistice Talks* (1990), as well as by Callum MacDonald in *Korea: The War Before Vietnam* (1986). Futrell's official history *The United States Air Force in Korea, 1950–53* (1983) is core reading but avoids controversy. John Gittings' paper 'Talks, Bombs and Germs: Another Look at the Korean War' (1975) is jam-packed with useful information; while Robert Neer's *Napalm* (2013) tells the frightening story of napalm with much scholarly detail.

Nuclear Weapons

Roger Dingman's comprehensive article 'Atomic Diplomacy during the Korean War' (1988) is an indispensable resource on this topic. So are Rosemary Foot's papers 'Anglo-American Relations in the Korean Crisis: The British Effort to Avert an Expanded War' (1986) and 'Nuclear Coercion and the Ending of the Korean Conflict' (1988). Another valuable contribution is Daniel Calingaert's article 'Nuclear Weapons and the Korean War' (1988).

Biological Warfare

The issue of the use of biological weapons by the US Air Force in Korea is controversial, but no one has investigated it more thoroughly than the Canadian scholars Stephen Endicott and Edward Hagerman. Their book *The United States and Biological Warfare* (1998) is meticulous, albeit passionate; as is their 2002 paper 'Rhetoric and Reality—Reply to Colonel Crane'. The contrary views of Crane in the journal *Asian Perspectives* and Kathryn Weathersby writing for the Cold War International History Project are important contributions. Readers might also like to consult *Germ Gambits* (2016) by Amy Smithson, a leading scholar in the general field of biological warfare.

Armistice Negotiations and POWs

The tragic deadlock over the repatriation of prisoners is revealed in painstaking detail in Rosemary Foot's *A Substitute for Victory: The Politics of Peacemaking at the Korean Armistice Talks* (1990). Hermes provides a solid reconstruction of the negotiations in his official account *Truce Tent and Fighting Front* (1988) and Hastings is characteristically trenchant. The plight of the exploited prisoners who were used and abused for propaganda purposes is well told by Charles Young in *Name, Rank and Serial Number: Exploiting Korean War POWs at Home and Abroad* (2014).

New World Order

Noam Chomsky, Andrew Bacevich and Chalmers Johnson are all well-respected intellectuals who have written extensively about American imperialism, militarism and overreach. Their popular and troubling books are readily obtainable. Simon Winchester provides an entertaining account of Chinese naval ambitions in the Asia-Pacific region in his book *Pacific: The Ocean of the Future* (2015) and David Vine's alarming revelations in *Base Nation* (2015) explain the staggering worldwide reach of the United States military.

Dystopia—North Korea

Few commentators have a deeper understanding of North Korea, its history, motivations, capabilities and intentions than the Russian scholars Andrei Lankov, from Kookmin University, Seoul, and Leonid Petrov, from the Australian National University, and the former East German Rüdiger Frank, now a professor at the University of Vienna. The readily accessible writings of these internationally renowned experts display a positive pragmatism and native insight absent in the mainstream media.

Battle for Maryang San

For those who seek more detail about the Battle of Maryang San, the most authoritative military histories are Volume 2 of O'Neill's official history, *Australia in the Korean War 1950–53: Combat Operations* (1985),

Bob Breen's *The Battle of Maryang San* (1994) and Essex-Clark's *Hassett: Australian Leader* (2005). An intriguing insight into a controversial aspect of the British role in that battle is contained in Chapter 9 of *Scapegoats: Thirteen Victims of Military Injustice* (2013) by Michael Scott.

Film and Television

Easily the best film representation of the Korean War in English is the television documentary *Korea: The Unknown War* (1988), Thames Television/PBS (six one-hour episodes). The British version is the original, but PBS censored the American version, cutting out footage of the bombing of Pyongyang by the United States Air Force. Richard Lentz's *Korean War Filmography* (2003) lists over ninety feature film productions in English. It is a megaguide to the celluloid.

Politics, Controversy and Historiography

A final word must be said about balance and objectivity. Readers should be aware that with a few notable exceptions, most American commentators and historians are sensitive to criticism of their country's role in the Korean conflict and do not grapple with it. This is exemplified by the respected historian Allan Millett, who once amusingly dismissed certain significant writers—Sir Max Hastings, Rosemary Foot, Callum MacDonald and David Rees—as 'British revisionists' who continue 'the British tradition of special criticism of American policy'. He added that Gavan McCormack 'gives the anti-US account an Australian twist'. And he treated the minority of critical American writers—Cumings, Goulden, Alexander and I.F. Stone—with the same disdain. No doubt his attitude to Halberstam would have been similar if his book had been published at the time of his remarks. The problem is cultural and readers should draw their own conclusions.

International Treaties

These international treaties are accessible at
michaelpembroke.com/books/korea

Protocol for the Prohibition of the Use of Asphyxiating, Poisonous or Other Gases, and of Bacteriological Methods of Warfare, 17 June 1925
https://ihl-databases.icrc.org/ihl/INTRO/280?OpenDocument
> Not ratified by the US until 10 April 1975, subject to reservation
> https://ihl-databases.icrc.org/applic/ihl/ihl.nsf/Notification.xsp
> ?action=openDocument&documentId=EFD4B7E2E4A4232BC1
> 256402003F7670

Protocol Additional to the Geneva Conventions of 12 August 1949, and Relating to the Protection of Victims of International Armed Conflicts (Protocol 1), 8 June 1977
https://ihl-databases.icrc.org/applic/ihl/ihl.nsf/Treaty.xsp?action=o
penDocument&documentId=D9E6B6264D7723C3C12563CD002D6
CE4
> Not ratified by the US
> https://ihl-databases.icrc.org/applic/ihl/ihl.nsf/States.xsp?xp_
> viewStates=XPages_NORMStatesSign&xp_treatySelected=470

Protocol on Prohibitions or Restrictions on the Use of Incendiary Weapons (Protocol III), 10 October 1980
https://ihl-databases.icrc.org/ihl/INTRO/515
> Not ratified by the US until 21 January 2009, subject to reservation
> https://ihl-databases.icrc.org/applic/ihl/ihl.nsf/Notification.xsp?action=openDocument&documentId=3AB9E36D37F951ECC1257558003E6A3F

Convention III relative to the Treatment of Prisoners of War, 12 August 1949
https://ihl-databases.icrc.org/applic/ihl/ihl.nsf/Treaty.xsp?action=openDocument&documentId=77CB9983BE01D004C12563CD002D6B3E
> Not ratified by the US until 2 August 1955, subject to reservations made on 2 August 1955, 31 December 1974 and 4 March 1975
> https://ihl-databases.icrc.org/applic/ihl/ihl.nsf/Notification.xsp?action=openDocument&documentId=D6B53F5B5D14F35AC1256402003F9920

United Nations Convention on the Law of the Sea, 10 December 1982
https://treaties.un.org/doc/Publication/UNTS/Volume%201833/volume-1833-A-31363-English.pdf
> Not ratified by the US
> http://www.un.org/depts/los/reference_files/status2010.pdf, (p. 8)

Anti-Ballistic Missile Treaty, 26 May 1972
https://fas.org/nuke/control/abmt/text/abm3.htm
> Withdrawal by the US on 13 June 2002
> https://www.armscontrol.org/act/2002_07-08/abmjul_aug02

Japan

Treaty of Peace with Japan, 8 September 1951
https://treaties.un.org/doc/publication/unts/volume%20136/
volume-136-i-1832-english.pdf

Security Treaty Between the United States and Japan, 8 September 1951
http://avalon.law.yale.edu/20th_century/japan001.asp

Treaty of Mutual Cooperation and Security Between Japan and the United States of America, 19 January 1960
http://www.mofa.go.jp/region/n-america/us/q&a/ref/1.html

Taiwan

Mutual Defense Treaty Between the United States and the Republic of China and Taiwan, 2 December 1954
http://avalon.law.yale.edu/20th_century/chin001.asp#art1

South Korea

Mutual Defense Treaty Between the United States and the Republic of Korea;
1 October 1953
http://avalon.law.yale.edu/20th_century/kor001.asp

ANZUS

Security Treaty between Australia, New Zealand, and the United States of America, 1 September 1951
http://www.austlii.edu.au/au/other/dfat/treaties/1952/2.html

Korea Timeline

668	Kingdom of Silla
918	Kingdom of Koryŏ
1271	Yuan dynasty (Kublai Khan)
1392	Chosŏn dynasty (until 1897)
1592	Japanese invasion by Toyotomi Hideyoshi
1627–37	Manchu invasions
1801–66	Catholic persecutions
1866	The *General Sherman* destroyed in Pyongyang
1876	Korea's first foreign treaty (Japan)
1882	Korea's first treaty with the United States
1885	Treaty of Tianjin between China and Japan
1894–5	First Sino-Japanese War
1895	Assassination of Queen Min
1897	King Kojong proclaimed as Emperor
1902	Anglo-Japanese Alliance
1904–5	Russo-Japanese War
1905	Japan-Korea Protectorate Treaty
1910	Japanese annexation of Korea
1945	Japanese surrender
1945–8	American and Russian military occupations
1948	Republics of South and North Korea proclaimed
16.12.49	Mao Zedong visits Moscow
14.2.50	Sino-Soviet Treaty of Friendship
30.3.50	Kim Il-sung visits Moscow

25.6.50	North Korean invasion
25.6.50	First UN Security Council resolution for 'withdrawal' to 38th parallel
27.6.50	President Truman orders Seventh Fleet to 'neutralise' Taiwan Strait; Second UN Security Council resolution to 'repel' and 'restore'
7.7.50	General MacArthur appointed commander of UN Command forces
15.9.50	Inchon landing
27.9.50	Joint Chiefs authorise (secretly) MacArthur to advance north of 38th parallel
29.9.50	MacArthur told to 'feel unhampered tactically and strategically to proceed north of 38th parallel'
30.9.50	UN Command forces commence to cross 38th parallel
3.10.50	Zhou Enlai issues warning that China 'cannot sit idly by and remain indifferent'
7.10.50	UN General Assembly recommends that 'all appropriate steps be taken to ensure conditions of stability throughout Korea'
8.10.50	China formally resolves to enter war
19.10.50	Chinese People's Volunteers commence to cross the Yalu River
25.10.50	Battle of Unsan
5.11.50	MacArthur orders destruction of 'every installation, factory, city and village' north of Chongchon River
6.11.50	Chinese forces withdraw temporarily
24.11.50	Commencement of MacArthur's 'end of war' offensive
25.11.50	Chinese counter-attack in west
27.11.50	Eighth Army 'bugs out'; Chinese counterattack in east— Chosin Reservoir
1.12.50	Task Force Faith annihilated
11.12.50	Evacuation from Hungman by Marine and army survivors
16.12.50	President Truman declares state of emergency

24.12.50	Hungman razed by US Navy and engineers
1.1.51	Chinese commence offensive south of 38th parallel
4.1.51	US-led forces abandon Seoul
1.2.51	UN General Assembly condemns China as 'aggressor'
7.3.51	Seoul re-taken by US-led forces
31.3.51	Battle line stabilises around 38th parallel
10.7.51	Armistice negotiations commence
27.7.53	Armistice treaty signed
21.6.57	US abrogates paragraph 13(d) of the Korean Armistice Agreement (nuclear weapons)

Documents

THE SECRETARY OF DEFENSE

WASHINGTON

27 SEP 1950

Dear Mr. President:

I am attaching, for your approval, a draft directive to the Commander of the United Nations' Forces in Korea implementing the primarily military aspects of NSC 81/1 which contains the agreed U.S. policy on future courses of action in Korea.

The Secretary of State and I have concurred in this directive, which was prepared by the Joint Chiefs of Staff except for the final paragraph proposed by the Department of State.

Your approval would permit the Commander of the United Nations' Forces in Korea to conduct the necessary military operations north of the 38° to destroy North Korean forces, subject to the conditions specified in paragraph 2 of the directive.

With great respect,

Faithfully yours,

G. C. MARSHALL

Enclosure

The President

The White House

"Approved - 9/27/50 - HARRY S. TRUMAN"

*The secret presidential approval to cross the
38th parallel: 27 September 1950*

DEPARTMENT OF THE ARMY
STAFF MESSAGE CENTER
OUTGOING CLASSIFIED MESSAGE

~~TOP SECRET~~
FLASH

PARAPHRASE NOT RE~~QUIRED~~
Joint Chiefs of Staff
M. M. Stephens Capt USN
Executive Secretary, JCS

TO: CINCFE (COMMAND) TOKYO JAPAN

NR: JCS 92985   29 SEP 50

From JCS to PERSONAL FOR Genl of the Army Douglas
MacArthur, SECDEF sends.

FOR HIS EYES ONLY.

Reference present report of supposed announcement
by Eighth Army that ROK Divisions would halt on 38th parallel
for regrouping: We want you to feel unhampered tactically and
strategically to proceed north of 38th parallel. Announcement
above referred to may precipitate embarrassment in UN where
evident desire is not to be confronted with necessity of a
vote on passage of 38th parallel, rather to find you have
found it militarily necessary to do so.

Signed G C Marshall

ORIGIN: JCS

DISTR: GEN VANDENBERG, GEN COLLINS, ADM SHERMAN, GEN MARSHALL

CM OUT 92985   (Sep 50)   DTG: 2920552   dmk
~~TOP SECRET~~

DECLASSIFIED
E.O. 11652, Sec. 3-402
DOD Directive 5200.30, June 13, 1979
By NLT-ALC NARS, Date 11-5-80

COPY NO. M-2

THE MAKING OF AN EXACT COPY OF THIS MESSAGE IS FORBIDDEN
16—53736-1   51 1454

1

*'For His Eyes Only' – MacArthur's instruction to 'feel
unhampered tactically and strategically': 29 September 1950*

THE WHITE HOUSE
WASHINGTON Dec. 6, 1950.

Mr. Hume:— I've just read your lousy review of Margaret's concert.

I've come to the conclusion that you are an "eight ulcer man on four ulcer pay."

It seems to me that you are a frustrated old man who wishes he could have been successful. When you write such poppycock as was in the back section of the paper you work for it shows conclusively that you're off the beam and at least four of your ulcers are at work.

Some day I hope to meet you. When that happens you'll need a new nose, a lot of beef steak for black eyes, and perhaps a supporter below!

Truman's pugnacious side (Letter to Paul Hume, music critic): 6 December 1950

THE WHITE HOUSE
WASHINGTON

Pegler, a gutter snipe is a gentle-
man along side you. I hope you'll
accept that statement as a more
insult than a reflection on your
ancestry.

H.S.T.

The situation with regard to the Far
Eastern General has become a political
one.

MacArthur has made himself a center
of controversy, publicly and privately. He has
always been a controversial figure.

He has had two wives - one a social light
he married at 47, the other a Tennessee girl
he married in his middle fifties after
No 1 had divorced him.

He was chief of staff in the Hoover regime,
made the front pages in the bonus affair.
He was advisor to the President of the Philippines
and Supreme Commander in the Pacific in
World War II

I made him Allied Commander in
Chief in Japan to sign the surrender documents for the United States.

Made Chief of the occupation forces
and Allied Commander for the United
Nations forces in Korea in June 1950.

Truman's petty side (MacArthur, the divorcee): 5 April 1951 have already been made.

This means all out war.
It means that Moscow, St.
Petersburg, Mukden, Vladivostock,
Pekin, Shanghai, Port Arthur,
Dairen, Odessa, Stalingrad and
every manufacturing plant in
China and the Soviet Union
will be eliminated.

This is the final chance
for the Soviet Government to
decide whether it desires to
survive or not.

*Truman's dangerous side (nuking Russia
and China): 27 January 1952*

J.C.S. 1837/26

25 February 1952

JOINT CHIEFS OF STAFF

DECISION ON J.C.S. 1837/26

A Memorandum by the Joint Advanced Study Committee

on

BIOLOGICAL WARFARE

Note by the Secretaries

1. At their meeting on 1 October 1951 the Joint Chiefs of Staff, having noted that they do not necessarily accept either the conclusions in the Enclosure or specific portions of the study in the Appendix, agreed to forward the Enclosure and Appendix to J.C.S. 1837/26 to the three Services, for comment as appropriate.

2. At their meeting on 25 February 1952, pursuant to approval of the recommendations in subparagraph 4 a of J.C.S. 1837/29, the Joint Chiefs of Staff amended the conclusions in the Enclosure, as incorporated in the revised page 282, and approved the conclusions in paragraphs 3 to 9, inclusive, as amended.

3. This decision now becomes a part of and shall be attached as the top sheet of J.C.S. 1837/26.

W. G. LALOR,

E. H. J. CARNS,

Joint Secretariat.

DISTRIBUTION

Gen. Bradley (C/JCS)   Gen. Smith (Dir. Plans, Air)

Biological warfare – the Joint Chiefs'
endorsement: 25 February 1952

E N C L O S U R E

STUDY BY THE JOINT ADVANCED STUDY COMMITTEE

on

BIOLOGICAL WARFARE

References: a. 1951 Tech. Est., RDB Cmte on BW*
b. Minutes of 28th Meeting, RDB Cmte on BW*
c. Comparative Evaluation of CW, BW, RW
(Noyes Rpt)*
d. Ad Hoc Cmte Rpt on BW (Haskins Rpt)*
e. Ad Hoc Cmte Rpt on CW, BW, RW
(Stevenson Rpt)*

GENERAL

1. The Joint Advanced Study Committee (JASC) has conducted a broad, general survey of the biological warfare (BW) field with the object of determining its military worth and its possible role in future warfare. The Committee has interviewed a wide cross-section of well qualified and key personnel in the BW field, both military and civilian, has studied pertinent documents in the files of the Department of Defense, and has weighed the conclusions reached by several committees appointed by the Secretary of Defense to study this subject. It is therefore believed that this study, with the discussion in the Appendix, reflects responsible current thinking on biological warfare.

2. For purposes of this study, BW has been considered to be an antipersonnel form of warfare, both when employed directly against man and when employed against animals and crops to reduce his food supply.

CONCLUSIONS

3. BW possesses great potential as a weapon of war.

4. National security demands that the United States acquire a strong offensive BW capability without delay. A sound military program requires the development of all effective means of waging war without regard for precedent as to their use.

* On file in J.C.S. Secretariat

5. A more vigorous test program including large-scale field tests should be conducted to determine the effectiveness of specific BW agents under operational conditions.

6. BW is distinctive as a weapon in that it does not destroy structures or property. The use of such a weapon would greatly simplify certain postwar economic rehabilitation problems.

7. If low production costs of BW agents can be realized, a partial solution may be offered to the acute need of maintaining a strong military posture for long periods without jeopardizing our economic structure. Further, the achievement of a BW capability may not compete with the procurement of our present weapons systems.

8. The small number of military personnel in the Services who are interested in, or accurately informed about, BW should be increased by establishing a BW indoctrination course.

9. The adoption of a positive military policy to the effect that the United States will be prepared to employ BW whenever it is military advantageous would serve to stimulate Service interest in the BW field and accelerate its development.

August 27, 1951

My dear Mr. Secretary:

I have received Mr. Lovett's letter of August 14, 1951, enclosing a memorandum by the Joint Chiefs of Staff regarding the policy on repatriation of Chinese and North Korean prisoners of war.

It is suggested that if and when the present armistice discussions reach the question of exchange of prisoners of war, the over-riding consideration should be the prompt return of all United Nations and Republic of Korea prisoners of war held by the Communists. With this consideration in mind, the Department of State is seriously concerned over the possibility that the proposed policy might jeopardize the prompt return of all United Nations and Republic of Korea prisoners of war following the conclusion of an armistice agreement. While the proposed policy is conditional upon "adequate safeguards for United Nations prisoners in Communist hands", it is not clear how such safeguards could effectively be established.

While the possible psychological warfare advantages of the proposed policy are recognized, it is difficult to see how such a policy could be carried out without conflict with the provisions of the 1949 Geneva Prisoner of War Convention which the United States as the Unified Command has expressed its intention of observing in the Korean conflict. The Geneva Prisoner of War Convention of 1949 requires, among other things, the prompt return of all prisoners of war upon the cessation of active hostilities. Although neither the North Koreans nor the Chinese Communists have observed the terms of that Convention, it appears to the Department of State that our best hope for alleviating the plight of United Nations and Republic of Korea personnel held as prisoners of war by the Communists and for obtaining their return lies in our continuing strictly to observe the terms of that Convention. In a broader sense, United States interests in this and future conflicts dictate, in my opinion, strict observance of the provisions of the Geneva Convention.

In

The Honorable
George C. Marshall,
Secretary of Defense.

1 2 3 4

Geneva Convention: Acheson's initial advice
for 'strict observance': 27 August 1951

In order to achieve in so far as possible the desired psychological warfare and humane objectives, the Department of State suggests that, prior to the reaching of an armistice agreement, individuals who have rendered outstanding assistance to the United Nations command or whose return to the Communists would, in all probability, result in their deaths, might be paroled as provided for in the Geneva Convention. Moreover, under no circumstances should Republic of Korea personnel who were forcibly impressed into the North Korean Army be returned to the Communists. This problem might be handled by taking steps prior to the conclusion of any armistice agreement to release such persons in consultation with the Government of the Republic of Korea. The foregoing suggestions are considered to be consistent with the principles of the 1949 Geneva Convention and thus do not afford a valid pretext for Communist failure to return United Nations and Republic of Korea prisoners of war.

The Department of State recognizes that this procedure presents certain complications, particularly as regards timing of release, safeguards, etc.

In view of the foregoing, and dependent upon the number of United Nations and Republic of Korea prisoners of war actually held by the Communists, it may be necessary to reexamine the present instructions to General Ridgway providing for an exchange on a man-for-man basis.

In addition to exchange of military personnel, the Department of State suggests that General Ridgway be instructed to make whatever arrangements he considers feasible, without becoming involved in the question of Korean civilian prisoners held by both the Republic of Korea and the North Korean regime, for the release of civilian internees such as the staffs of the British and French diplomatic missions in Seoul, the Apostolic Delegate, press correspondents, and other Americans and nationals of United Nations members, principally missionaries captured at the time of the invasion.

I would be very pleased to have representatives of the Department of State discuss the foregoing questions in greater detail with the Department of Defense in an effort to work out a practicable solution.

Sincerely yours,

/s/ DEAN ACHESON

FE:NA:UAJohnson:clh
G*FENolting:aja   8/23/51

1 2 3 4

Acknowledgements

The genesis of this book was my desire to understand the battle of Maryang San. In the end, I roamed far wider, but my first debt of gratitude must be to the old soldiers who inspired and taught me. The most important of these were the five young men from the graduating class of 1950 at the Royal Military College, Duntroon—Hughes, Falvey, Pears, Pembroke and Stewart. Each saw his first action at Maryang San; each distinguished himself; four were awarded Military Crosses; and the fifth was mentioned in despatches. Only Pembroke and Pears remain. Pears said recently—candidly and humorously—that the two of them were 'the best and the worst' of their class. However, as junior officers under Chinese fire, they were a band of brothers and the best among equals.

Beyond military matters, Leonid Petrov from the Australian National University provided me with my first reading list; Rudiger Frank from the University of Vienna led our small group through North Korea in 2016; Michael Kirby provided me with his own insights as Chairman of the United Nations Commission of Enquiry on Human Rights in North Korea; and Richard Broinowski, a former Australian ambassador in Seoul, was always encouraging.

Two venerable institutions provided me with incomparable opportunities for reflection, study and writing. The first was Wolfson College, Cambridge, where I commenced to write this book during the spring term of 2015. I am particularly indebted to then President, Sir Richard Evans, former Regius Professor of History, a world-renowned historian and prolific author, whose example and writings shaped my approach. The second was the Institute for Advanced Study at Princeton, former home of Albert Einstein and George Kennan, where I finished my toil during a mellow autumn in 2017. Both places were intellectually stimulating and physically beautiful.

As ever, I received invaluable assistance from libraries. Foremost among them was the Law Courts Library, where Ben Ross was exceptional in sourcing materials from other national and international libraries and institutions, including from the Library of Congress in Washington DC. The archives of the Truman Library were also indispensable and readily accessible. As was the official documentary historical record in the Foreign Relations of the United States (FRUS) series.

I could not, of course, have written this book without the scholarship of the writers and historians who have preceded me. In that sense, I have stood on the shoulders of giants. I need not mention them specifically, for they are all identified in the Notes on Sources. Nor is it feasible to mention every one of the many friends, colleagues and acquaintances who has answered individual queries or volunteered information. They know who they are. I remain ever grateful to each of them.

When the hard work was done and the book was in draft, I was fortunate to have distinguished and generous readers. Both Noam Chomsky and AC Grayling humbled me by their willingness to take valuable time out from their busy schedules to read the proof pages. As did other readers, including Geoffrey Robertson, who enthusiastically reviewed them, as he did with my last book. And Andrew Bacevich kindly read and approved the penultimate chapter 'New World Order'. I am grateful to all of them.

From day to day, the single most important person—with the exception of my wife—was my research assistant, Kim Khong. She will receive her reward in Heaven. Her tenacity, exactitude, research skills, good humour and sound advice knew no bounds. I was indeed fortunate. Special mention should also be given to my wonderful secretary of more than thirty years, Sue Page. Gone are the days when she would type the manuscript, but the three of us worked as a team and Sue's influence was seamless. Joanna Penglase again provided valuable additional external research assistance. And Captain John Sutton was a constant source of valuable information on infantry small arms tactics and weaponry.

Finally, I wish to thank my experienced publisher at Hardie Grant, Pam Brewster, who was so enthusiastic about producing this book. Our collaboration this time, as it was with my last book, has been personally satisfying and professionally rewarding. The team that Pam gathered around her for this project also deserves special mention, especially my sensitive editor, Bernadette Foley, and visionary book designer Nada Backovic.

Lastly, a writer's life is never easy but mine has always been blessed by a wife who is both a muse and a source of wisdom.

Index